LITERACY IN THE NEW MEDIA AGE

'In his new book, Gunther Kress shows us that as reading and writing move from page to screen, literacy is not just as a matter of language but a matter of motivated multimedia design.'

Jay L. Lemke, City University of New York

In this 'new media age' the screen has replaced the book as the dominant medium of communication. At the same time image is displacing writing and moving into the centre of communication.

In this ground-breaking new book, Gunther Kress considers the effects of a revolution that has radically altered the hitherto 'natural' relation between the mode of writing and the medium of the book and the page. Taking into account social, economic, communicational and technological factors, Kress provides a framework of principles for understanding these changes and their effects on the future of literacy.

Kress considers the likely larger-level social and cultural effects of that future, arguing that the effects of the move to the screen as the dominant medium of communication will produce far-reaching shifts in relations of power and not just in the sphere of communication. The democratic potentials and effects of the new information and communication technologies will, Kress contends, have the widest imaginable political, economic, social, cultural, conceptual/cognitive and epistemological consequences.

Literacy in the New Media Age is essential reading for anyone with an interest in literacy and its wider political and cultural implications.

Gunther Kress is Professor of English Education at the Institute of Education, University of London, UK. His publications include *Before Writing: Rethinking the Paths to Literacy* (Routledge, 1996), *Reading Images: A Grammar of Visual Design* (Routledge, 1996), and *Learning to Write*, 2nd edition (Routledge, 1994).

LITERACIES
Series Editor: David Barton
Lancaster University

Literacy practices are changing rapidly in contemporary society in response to broad social, economic and technological changes: in education, the workplace, the media and in everyday life. The *Literacies* series has been developed to reflect the burgeoning research and scholarship in the field of literacy studies and its increasingly interdisciplinary nature. The series aims to situate reading and writing within its broader institutional contexts where literacy is considered as a social practice. Work in this field has been developed and drawn together to provide books which are accessible, interdisciplinary and international in scope, covering a wide range of social and institutional contexts.

CITY LITERACIES
Learning to Read Across Generations and Cultures
Eve Gregory and Ann Williams

LITERACY AND DEVELOPMENT
Ethnographic Perspectives
Edited by Brian V. Street

SITUATED LITERACIES
Theorising Reading and Writing in Context
Edited by David Barton, Mary Hamilton and Roz Ivanic

MULTILITERACIES
Literacy Learning and the Design of Social Futures
Edited by Bill Cope and Mary Kalantzis

GLOBAL LITERACIES AND THE WORLD-WIDE WEB
Edited by Gail E. Hawisher and Cynthia L. Selfe

STUDENT WRITING
Access, Regulation, Desire
Theresa M. Lillis

LITERACY IN THE NEW MEDIA AGE

Gunther Kress

Routledge
Taylor & Francis Group

LONDON AND NEW YORK

First published 2003 by Routledge
2 Park Square, Milton Park, Abingdon, Oxon, OX14 4RN

Simultaneously published in the USA and Canada by Routledge
270 Madison Ave, New York, NY 10016

Reprinted 2004 Twice

Routledge is an imprint of the Taylor & Francis Group

© 2003 Gunther Kress

Typeset in Baskerville by The Running Head Limited, Cambridge
Printed and bound in Great Britain by The Cromwell Press, Trowbridge, Wiltshire

British Library Cataloguing in Publication Data
A catalogue record for this book is available from the British Library

Library of Congress Cataloging in Publication Data
A catalog record for this book has been requested

ISBN 0–415–25355–1 (hbk)
ISBN 0–415–25356–X (pbk)

FOR MICHAEL

CONTENTS

ix

CONTENTS

FIGURES

1

THE FUTURES OF LITERACY

Modes, logics and affordances

It is no longer possible to think about literacy in isolation from a vast array of social, technological and economic factors. Two distinct yet related factors deserve to be particularly highlighted. These are, on the one hand, the broad move from the now centuries-long dominance of writing to the new dominance of the image and, on the other hand, the move from the dominance of the medium of the book to the dominance of the medium of the screen. These two together are producing a revolution in the uses and effects of literacy and of associated means for representing and communicating at every level and in every domain. Together they raise two questions: what is the likely future of literacy, and what are the likely larger-level social and cultural effects of that change?

One might say the following with some confidence. Language-as-speech will remain the major mode of communication; language-as-writing will increasingly be displaced by image in many domains of public communication, though writing will remain the preferred mode of the political and cultural elites. The combined effects on writing of the dominance of the mode of image and of the medium of the screen will produce deep changes in the forms and functions of writing. This in turn will have profound effects on human, cognitive/affective, cultural and bodily engagement with the world, and on the forms and shapes of knowledge. *The world told* is a different world to *the world shown*. The effects of the move to the screen as the major medium of communication will produce far-reaching shifts in relations of power, and not just in the sphere of communication. Where significant changes to distribution of power threaten, there will be fierce resistance by those who presently hold power, so that predictions about the democratic potentials and effects of the new information and communication technologies have to be seen in the light of inevitable struggles over power yet to come. It is already clear that the effects of the two changes taken together will have the widest imaginable political, economic, social, cultural, conceptual/cognitive and epistemological consequences.

The two modes of writing and of image are each governed by distinct logics, and have distinctly different affordances. The organisation of writing – still leaning on the logics of speech – is governed by the logic of time, and by the

1

logic of sequence of its elements in time, in temporally governed arrangements. The organisation of the image, by contrast, is governed by the logic of space, and by the logic of simultaneity of its visual/depicted elements in spatially organised arrangements. To say this simply: in speaking I have to say one thing after another, one sound after another, one word after another, one clause after another, so that inevitably one thing is first, and another thing is second, and one thing will have to be last. Meaning can then be – and is – attached to 'being first' and to 'being last', and maybe to being third and so on. If I say 'Bill and Mary married' it means something different to 'Mary and Bill married' – the meaning difference perhaps referring to which of the two is closer to me. In a visual representation the placement of elements in the space of representation – the page, the canvas, the screen, the wall – will similarly have meaning. Placing something centrally means that other things will be marginal, at least relatively speaking. Placing something at the top of the space means that something else will likely be below. Both these places can be used to make meaning: being *central* can mean being the 'centre', in whatever way; being *above* can mean being 'superior', and being below can mean 'inferior'.

The point is that whether I want to or not I have to use the possibilities given to me by a mode of representation to make my meaning. Whatever is represented in speech (or to some lesser extent in writing) inevitably has to bow to the logic of time and of sequence in time. The world represented in speech or in writing is therefore (re)cast in an actual or quasi-temporal manner. The genre of the *narrative* is the culturally most potent formal expression of this. Human engagement with the world through speech or writing cannot escape that logic; it orders and shapes that human engagement with the world. Whatever is represented in image has to bow, equally, to the logic of space, and to the simultaneity of elements in spatial arrangements. The world represented in image is therefore (re)cast in an actual or quasi-spatial manner. Whatever relations are to be represented about the world have inevitably to be presented as spatial relations between the depicted elements of an image. Human engagement with the world through image cannot escape that logic; it orders and shapes how we represent the world, which in turn shapes how we see and interact with the world. The genre of the *display* is the culturally most potent formal expression of this. 'The world narrated' is a different world to 'the world depicted and displayed'.

To get closer to the core of that difference we need to ask more specifically about the affordances of each of the two modes. Is the world represented through words in sequence – to simplify massively – really different to the world represented through depictions of elements related in spatial configurations? Let me start with a very simple fact about languages such as English (not all languages of the world are like English in this respect, though many are). In English if I want to say or write a clause or a sentence about anything, I have to use a verb. Verbs are, by and large, words that represent actions, even if the actions are pseudo-actions, such as *seem, resemble, have, weigh* and so on. There is one verb which is not really about action, the verb *be*, which names relations between entities – 'John is my uncle', or states of affairs – 'the day is hot'. But whichever I choose, and normally it is an actional verb, I cannot get around the fact that I have to name the relation, and refer to either a state or an action, even if I do not want to do so at all. 'I have a holiday coming up' is not really about ownership stated by *have*; nor is 'I think that's fine' really about what I think – it is saying that I feel fine in relation to whatever 'that' is. Yet both speech and writing absolutely insist that I choose a name/word for an action, even though I do not wish to do so.

To take another example, if I am in a science lesson and I am talking about cells, and the structure of cells, I might want to say 'every cell has a nucleus'. As in my example above, I have to use a word to name a relation between two entities – cell and nucleus – which invokes a relation of possession, *have*. I actually do not think of it as being about possession, but it is a *commitment* which language forces me to make. If I ask the class to draw a cell, there is no such commitment. Now, however, every student who draws the cell, has to place the nucleus somewhere in the cell, in a particular spot. There is no way around that, whether the nucleus actually has this or that specific place in the cell or not. There is a demand for an epistemological commitment, but it is a totally different one in the case of the two modes: commitment to naming of a relation in one case – 'the cell owns a nucleus', and commitment to a location in space in another – 'this is where it goes'.

Let me make another comparison of affordances, to draw out the impact of the shift. In writing, I can use 'every cell has a nucleus' without having any idea what a nucleus actually is, does, looks like and so on. The same applies to *cell*; nor do I know what *have* actually means in that structure – other than a kind of 'there is'. The reason for that is that words are, relatively speaking, empty of meaning, or perhaps better, the word as sound-shape or as letter-shape gives no indication of its meaning, it is there to be filled with meaning. It is that 'filling with meaning' which constitutes the work of imagination that we do with language. In what may seem a paradox given common-sense views about language, I want to say that words are empty of meaning, relatively. If someone says to me 'I have a new car', I know very little indeed about that person's vehicle. It is this characteristic of words which leads to the well-known experience of having read a novel and really enjoyed it – filling it with our meaning – only to be utterly disappointed or worse when we see it as a film, where some others have filled the words with their very different meanings.

At the same time, these relatively empty things occur in a strict ordering, which forces me to follow, in reading, precisely the order in which they appear. There is a 'reading path' set by the order of the words which I must follow. In a written text there is a path which I cannot go against if I wish to make sense of the meaning of that text. The order of words in a clause compels me to follow, and it is meaningful. 'Bill and Mary married' has a point of view coded in the reading path which makes it different from 'Mary and Bill married'. If I have

3

two clauses – 'The sun rose, the mists dissolved' – then the order in which I have put them structures the path that my reader must follow. 'The mists dissolved and the sun rose' has a quite different meaning, a near mystical force compared to the mundane 'the sun rose and the mists dissolved'. But the affordance which is at issue here is that of temporal sequence, and its effects are to orient us towards causality, whether in a simple clause ('the sun dissolved the mists'), where an agent acts and causes an effect, or in the conjoined clauses just above. The simple yet profound fact of sequence in time orients us towards a world of causality.

Reading paths may exist in images, either because the maker of the image structured that into the image – and it is read as it is or it is transformed by the reader, or they may exist because they are constructed by the reader without prior construction by the maker of the image. The means for doing this rest, as with writing, with the affordances of the mode. The logic of space and of spatial display provides the means; making an element central and other elements marginal will encourage the reader to move from the centre to the margin. Making some elements salient through some means – size, colour, shape, for instance – and others less salient again encourages a reading path. However, I say 'encourages' rather than 'compels' as I did with writing. Reading the elements of an image 'out of order' is easy or at least possible; it is truly difficult in writing.

However, while the reading path in the image is (relatively) open, the image itself and its elements are filled with meaning. There is no vagueness, no emptiness here. That which is meant to be represented is represented. Images are plain full with meaning, whereas words wait to be filled. Reading paths in writing (as in speech) are set with very little or no leeway; in the image they are open. That is the contrast in affordance of the two modes: in writing, relatively vacuous elements in strict order (in speech also, to a somewhat lesser extent); and full elements in a (relatively) open order in image. The imaginative work in writing focuses on filling words with meaning – and then reading the filled elements together, in the given syntactic structure. In image, imagination focuses on creating the order of the arrangement of elements which are already filled with meaning.

This is one answer to the cultural pessimists: focus on what each mode makes available, and use that as the starting point for a debate. There is then the further question of whether in the move from the dominance of one mode to the other there are losses – actually and potentially – which we would wish to avoid. On the one hand, the work of imagination called forth by writing – even in the limited way I have discussed it here (and the kinds of imaginative work and the potential epistemological losses I have suggested – the loss of an underlying orientation towards cause as one instance) may make us try to preserve features of writing which might otherwise disappear. On the other hand, I may actually not want to live in a semiotic/cultural world where everything is constructed in causal ways, whether I want it or no t– as just one example. I will

4

return to the question both of affordances and of gains and losses in other places in the book.

Affordances of mode and facilities of media

The shift in mode would, even by itself, produce the changes that I have mentioned. The change in media, largely from book and page to screen, the change from the traditional print-based media to the new information and communication technologies, will intensify these effects. However, the new media have three further effects. They make it easy to use a multiplicity of modes, and in particular the mode of image – still or moving – as well as other modes, such as music and sound effect for instance. They change, through their affordances, the potentials for representational and communicational action by their users; this is the notion of 'interactivity' which figures so prominently in discussions of the new media. Interactivity has at least two aspects: one is broadly interpersonal, for instance, in that the user can 'write back' to the producer of a text with no difficulty – a potential achievable only with very great effort or not at all with the older media, and it permits the user to enter into an entirely new relation with all other texts – the notion of hypertextuality. The one has an effect on social power directly, the other has an effect on semiotic power, and through that on social power less immediately.

The technology of the new information and communication media rests among other factors on the use of a single code for the representation of all information, irrespective of its initial modal realisation. Music is analysed into this digital code just as much as image is, or graphic word, or other modes. That offers the potential to realise meaning in any mode. This is usually talked about as the multimedia aspect of this technology, because with the older media there existed a near automatic association and identification of mode (say, writing) with medium (say, book).

With print-based technology – technologically oriented and aligned with word – the production of written text was made easy, whereas the production of image was difficult; the difficulty expresses itself still in monetary cost. Hence image was (relatively) rare, and printed word was ubiquitous in the book and on the page. With the new media there is little or no cost to the user in choosing a path of realisation towards image rather than towards word. Given that the communicational world around us is moving to a preference for image in many domains, the new technology facilitates, supports and intensifies that preference. What is true of word and image is also increasingly true of other modes. The ease in the use of different modes, a significant aspect of the affordances of the new technologies of information and communication, makes the use of a multiplicity of modes usual and unremarkable. That mode which is judged best by the designer of the message for specific aspects of the message and for a particular audience can be chosen with no difference in 'cost'. Multimodality is made easy, usual, 'natural' by these technologies. And such naturalised uses of modes will lead to greater specialisation of modes: affordances of modes will become aligned with representational and communicative need.

The new technologies allow me to 'write back'. In the era of the book, which partly overlapped with the era of mass communication, the flow of communication was largely in one direction. The new technologies have changed unidirectionality into bidirectionality. E-mail provides a simple example: not only can I write back, but the moment I hit the reply or forward button, I can change the text that I have just received in many ways. If an attachment has come with the e-mail I can in any case rewrite it and send it anywhere I wish. In that process the power of the author, which has been such a concern in the era of the dominance of the old technologies and of the mode of writing, is lessened and diffused. Authorship is no longer rare. Of course the change to the power of the author brings with it a consequent lessening in the author's or the text's authority. The processes of selection which accompanied the bestowal of the role of author brought authority. When that selection is no longer there, authority is lost as well. The promise of greater democracy is accompanied by a levelling of power; that which may have been desired by many may turn out to be worth less than it seemed when it was unavailable.

Ready access to all texts constitutes another challenge to the former power of texts. There was a certain fictionality in any case to the notion of the author as the source of the text. Just as no one in a speech community has 'their own words' – the frequent request in schools for putting something in 'your own words' notwithstanding – so no one really ever originated their own texts. The metaphor of text-as-texture was in that respect always accurate: our experience of language cannot be, is never, other than the experience of texts. Our use of language in the making of texts cannot be other than the quotation of fragments of texts, previously encountered, in the making of new texts. The ease with which texts can be brought into conjunction, and elements of texts reconstituted as new texts, changes the notion of authorship. If it was a myth to see the author as originator, it is now a myth that cannot any longer be sustained in this new environment. Writing is becoming 'assembling according to designs' in ways which are overt, and much more far-reaching, than they were previously. The notion of writing as 'productive' or 'creative' is also changing. Fitness for present purpose is replacing previous conceptions, such as text as the projection of a world, the creation of a fictional world, a world of the imagination.

The dominance of the screen as the currently most potent medium – even if at the moment that potency may still be more mythical than real – means that it is these practices and these conceptions which hold sway, and not only on the screen but also in all domains of communication. The affordances and the organisations of the screen are coming to (re)shape the organisation of the page. Contemporary pages are beginning to resemble, more and more, both the look and the deeper sense of contemporary screens. Writing on the page is not immune in any way from this move, even though the writing of the elite using the older media will be more resistant to the move than writing elsewhere. It is possible to see writing once again moving back in the direction of visuality, whether as letter, or as 'graphic block' of writing, as an element of what are and will be fundamentally visual entities, organised and structured through the logics of the visual. It is possible to see writing becoming subordinated to the logic of the visual in many or all of its uses.

Right now, an objection

It may be as well to try and answer here and now three objections that will be made. One is that more books are published now than ever before; the second is, that there is more writing than ever before, including writing on the screen. The third, the most serious, takes the form of a question: what do we lose if many of the forms of writing that we know disappear?

To the first objection I say: the books that are published now are in very many cases books which are already influenced by the new logic of the screen, and in many cases they are not 'books' as that word would have been understood thirty or forty years ago. I am thinking here particularly of textbooks, which then were expositions of coherent 'bodies of knowledge' presented in the mode of writing. The move from chapter to chapter was a stately and orderly progression through the unfolding matter of the book. The contemporary textbook – since the late 1970s for lower years of secondary school and by now for all the years of secondary school – is often a collection of 'worksheets', organised around the issues of the curriculum, and put between more or less solid covers. This is still called a book. But there are no chapters, there is none of that sense of a reader engaging with and absorbing a coherent exposition of a body of knowledge, authoritatively presented. Instead there is a sense that the issue now is to involve students in action around topics, of learning by doing. Above all, the matter is presented through image more than through writing – and writing and image are given different representational and communicational functions.

These are still called 'book', though I think we need to be wary of being fooled by the seeming stability of the word. These are not books that can be 'read', for instance, in anything like that older sense of the word 'read'. These are books for working with, for acting on. So yes, there are more 'books' published now than ever before, but in many cases the 'books' of now are not the 'books' of then. And I am not just thinking of factual, information books but of books of all kinds.

And yes, there is more writing than ever before. Let me make two points. The first is, who is writing more? Who is filling the pages of websites with writing? Is it the young? Or is it those who grew up in the era when writing was clearly the dominant mode? The second point goes to the question of the future of writing. Image has coexisted with writing, as of course has speech. In the era of the dominance of writing, when the logic of writing organised the page, image appeared on the page subject to the logic of writing. In simple terms, it fitted in how, where and when the logic of the written text and of the page suggested. In the era of the dominance of the screen, writing appears on the screen subject to the logic of the image. Writing fits in how, where and when the logic of the image-space suggests. The effects on writing, as is already 'visible' in any number of ways, tiny at times, larger at others, will be inescapable.

That leaves the third objection. It cannot be dealt with quickly. It requires a large project, much debate, and an uncommon generosity of view. On one level the issue is one of gains and losses; on another level it will require from us a different kind of reflection on what writing is, what forms of imagination it fosters. It asks questions of a profounder kind, about human potentials, wishes, desires – questions which go beyond immediate issues of utility for social or economic needs. I attempt some answers at different points in the book.

What do I hope to achieve with this book? There is a clear difference between this book and others dealing with the issues of literacy and new media. The current fascination with the dazzle of the new media is conspicuous here by its absence. I focus on just a few instances and descriptions of hypertextual arrangements, internet texts, or the structure of websites. I am as interested in understanding how the *sentence* developed in the social and technological environments of England in the seventeenth century, as I am in seeing what sentences are like now. The former like the latter – in showing principles of human meaning-making – can give us ways of thinking about the likely development of the sentence in the social and technological environments of our present and of the immediate future. In that sense the book is out of the present mould; in part it looks to the past as much as to the present to understand the future. It is a book about literacy now, everywhere, in all its sites of appearances, in the old and the new media – it is about literacy anywhere in this *new media age*.

So what can readers hope to get from the book? My sense is that what is needed above all is some stocktaking, some reflection, a drawing of breath, and the search for the beginnings of answers to questions such as: Where are we? What have we got here? What remains of the old? What is common about the making of representations and messages between then and now, and in the likely tomorrow? I think that what we need are new tools for thinking with, new frames in which to place things, in which to see the old and the new, and see them both newly. That is what I hope the book will offer its readers: a conceptual framework and tools for thinking about a field that is in a profound state of transition.

2

PREFACE

This book is about alphabetic writing. It appears, however, at a moment in the long history of writing when four momentous changes are taking place simultaneously: social, economic, communicational and technological change. The combined effects of these are so profound that it is justifiable to speak of a revolution in the landscape of communication; this revolution is producing far-reaching effects in the uses, functions, forms and valuations of alphabetic writing. Social changes are unmaking the structures and frames which had given a relative stability to forms of writing over the last two hundred years or so. Economic changes are altering the uses and purposes of the technology of writing. Communicational change is altering the relations of the means by which we represent our meanings, bringing image into the centre of communication more insistently than it has been for several hundred years, and thereby challenging the dominance of writing. Lastly, technological change is altering the role and significance of the major media of dissemination. The screen is beginning to take the place of the book, and this is unmaking the hitherto 'natural' relation between the mode of writing and the medium of the book and the page.

After a long period of the dominance of the book as the central medium of communication, the screen has now taken that place. This is leading to more than a mere displacement of writing. It is leading to an inversion in semiotic power. The book and the page were the site of writing. The screen is the site of the image – it is the contemporary canvas. The book and the page were ordered by the logic of writing; the screen is ordered by the logic of image. A new constellation of communicational resources (from now on I shall speak of them as *semiotic resources*, that is, resources of and for making meaning) is taking shape. The former constellation of *medium of book* and *mode of writing* is giving way, and in many domains has already given way, to the new constellation of *medium of screen* and *mode of image*. The logic of image now dominates the sites and the conditions of appearance of all 'displayed' communication, that is, of all graphic communication that takes place via spatial display and through the sense of sight. That now includes writing, which is becoming display-oriented. When in the past image appeared on the page it did so subject to the logic of writing, the relation of image to writing which we still know as 'illustration'.

When writing now appears on the screen, it does so subject to the logic of the image.

The chain of this effect runs further. The screen and its logic more and more now provide the logic for the page also. As one element in the communicational landscape which is dominated by the logic of the organisation of the visual modes, writing is coming to experience the effects of visualisation once again. The effect is that alphabetic writing is undergoing changes in its uses and in its forms as significant as any that it has experienced in the three or four thousand years of its history. All this is taking place in a larger environment in which the social and political frames which up to now had supported writing as the dominant mode of representation – and the book as its natural and dominant medium – are weakening or have already disappeared.

This does not 'spell' the end of alphabetic writing. Writing is too useful and valuable a mode of representation and communication – never mind the enormous weight of cultural investment in this technology. But it is now impossible to discuss alphabetic writing with any seriousness without full recognition of this changed frame. My use of 'alphabetic' in front of 'writing' is one consequence of this shift. The pressing use of image is forcing a reassessment of what writing is, what it does and does not do, and what it can and cannot do; it forces an insistence on its very materiality – the physicality, the materiality of the *stuff* that is involved. This in turn forces us to attend to the sensory channels that are drawn in. Once we attend to this, it becomes clear that there is a deep difference in the potentials of image and writing, with the latter – as alphabetic writing – still retaining its strong relation to sound and its potentials, and the former with its use of light, space and vision and their potentials. In this context 'writing' becomes newly problematic. Writing which is tied still to sound via the alphabet is different to writing which is not linked to sound, as in those writing systems which use 'characters' and are oriented much more to representing concepts through conventionalised images, rather than through sounds transcribed imperfectly in letters.

All this has led me to adopt a somewhat unusual approach for this book on 'literacy'. I try to take account of four factors: the social – in the weakening or disappearance of relevant social 'framings'; the economic – in the changing communicational demands of the economies of knowledge and information; the communicational – in the new uses and arrangements of modes of representation; and the technological – in the shape of the facilities of the new media. Just to hint at examples, for the first I would point to changes in relations of (social) power which are changing levels of 'formality' in all aspects of writing. In relation to the second, there are above all the profound questions about the adequacy of writing to an information-based economy, and then the greater specialisations in the tasks of writing that flow from this. The third is demonstrated by the increasing use of image as a means of communication; while the fourth is best illustrated by the changing relations of the media of the page – the 'print-media', book, magazine, newspaper – and the screen.

We cannot now hope to understand written texts by looking at the resources of writing alone. They must be looked at in the context of the choice of modes made, the modes which appear with writing, and even the context of which modes were not chosen. In the context of a book on literacy (still) the mode that occurs most frequently with the mode of writing is the image, whether in the print-media, or on the screen. We need to be aware however, that on the screen writing may appear with the modes of music, of colour, of (moving) image, of speech, of soundtrack. All these bear meaning, and are part of one message. The mode of writing is one part of that message, and so writing is *partial* in relation to the message overall.

In all this, one of our major problems is not just change itself, but the fact that we are forced to confront this world of change with theories which were shaped to account for a world of stability. There is an urgent need for theoretical accounts that tell us how to understand communication in periods of instability.

That is the present reality. The processes which are at work have not yet run their course. Just as one example, in the area of technology, the prospect of relatively reliable speech-recognition is already on the horizon; it is one further factor which will have profound if not precisely predictable consequences. Writing will be moved more in the direction of becoming – once again – the transcription of speech, just at the very time when the screen is pushing writing in the direction of visuality. I have attempted to capture some of the more obvious and I hope also more significant features of this moment, and have tried to focus on change not nostalgically but realistically. Change is always with us, for the simple reason that humans act, and act with intent. They work, and work produces change. Change is not neutral, nor is it the same at all times in history: it is always change of a particular kind, moving in particular directions, favouring one group rather than another. The real difference between times of seeming stability and times such as this is that now, we – unless *we* are politicians – can neither pretend that there is stability nor demand it, other than as an ideological act.

Where possible I want to indicate what the relations between the wider social and economic environment and the forms and means of communication might be like. To communicate is to work in making meaning. To work is to change things. That is the reason I like the metaphor of the 'communicational landscape'. The 'scape' in 'landscape' is related to the English word 'shape', and it is also related to the German word 'schaffen' – meaning both 'to work' and 'to create'.

Any landscape, the communicational included, is the result of human work. 'Human' and therefore full of affect and desire; 'human' and therefore always social and cultural. To make meaning is to change the resources we have for making meaning, to change ourselves, and to change our cultures. Many of the issues that I focus on here have been much discussed already, in many ways they have become clichés already. Maybe by putting the clichés into this

11

framework I can show their significance anew. If there is change, there is also much that persists. There are, I am certain, stable truths about representation and communication as persistent human and social processes. I try to focus on that which is stable while insisting that the meanings and the potentials of that which persists are nevertheless constantly altered by human semiotic work in changing social and economic environments.

Some large questions are posed for considerations of literacy by all this. Such as, what are the potentials of image as a resource for making meaning? Can image do what writing does? Is it simply an alternative, perhaps a parallel mode? Can image do things that writing cannot do? Or what is it that writing can do that image cannot? If modes have distinct affordances then their potentials for representing are partial. When we think of the affordances of modes in communication, we can no longer think of writing, or indeed of 'language', either as grand abstractions or as sufficient to all demands of representation and communication. That is a revolutionary position. It forces us to think of (alphabetic) writing in a deeply challenging way. And so the really large question is, what is it that is distinctive about the resource of writing?

Always present is the issue of the media for the dissemination of meanings as messages. The *book* has now been superseded by the *screen* in the role of dominant medium of communication – using screen as a shorthand term for the new communication and information technologies. At one level, the screen is simply a surface, the site of the appearance of textual ensembles, the visible display of the actions and effects wrought with the technology. The actual power of the technologies lies in the fact that at one level all information is held in the one code of binary numbers, and from that code information can be re-presented in any mode, whether as music, colour, speech, writing or image. Hence the realisation of meaning in the mode of writing is now just one possibility among others: when meaning can as easily emerge in music as in writing, then the latter has lost its privileged position. Writing becomes equal to all other modes in a profound sense: the question then is the mundane and fundamental one about the 'potentials' of each mode in relation to specific tasks.

The vast social changes of the present, which move – in their different ways and at differing pace – in the direction of abolishing, ameliorating and remaking social hierarchies, are profoundly implicated in all this. The new technologies have a vast role, but they do not determine social change. The often remarked changes to the forms of writing in e-mail are a consequence of the unmaking of the social frames of power at least as much as of technology. To use speech-like forms in writing is a sign of 'informality', itself the sign of a lessening in social 'distance', a sign of the reduction in social power difference. It is a feature of the technology of e-mail that it puts people in each other's presence – not geographical but temporal co-presence. 'Presence', seen semiotically, is just that: not absence, and not distance. It is the social meaning of 'not distant' which gives rise to 'informality', just as 'being distant', semiotically, gives rise to formality. It is an affordance of the technology that gives rise to and can be used for the expression of social factors, and so changes the form of signs in writing. But it is the social conditions which enable that use in the first instance. Nevertheless, we also have to remain aware that technology as tool has its shaping effect. The possibilities of technical production effect the facility with which we may use the various modes. Colour printing is still expensive; working with images, even with the new technologies, has greater costs, both in terms of computer storage and in terms of the user's technical competence.

I think that at this time it is essential to look at quite basic, deep and also extremely simple things. The book will have something to say about the *stuff* of writing, its materiality, and its relation to the *stuff* of speech. This is a necessary step at a time when there threatens a new separation of the human body and technology. It will say something about image, and its relation to writing. It will say something about *work*, because it is human work that shapes all that we recognise as cultural, and which makes us human. The book will focus on how we use these resources in our everyday making of meaning as messages. It will pay attention to the context of the social, economic and political changes of the present period and those of the near future. But it cannot do all these equally. So the focus will, after all, be on writing in the present, with speculation just here and there about its future.

I know that despite the grand canvas here, my interests are partial. They lie in the materiality of the resources, and in how humans work with them in the demands of their lives. I am interested in this matter of material, of stuff, and how humans have worked with it and have worked it. I am aware that this partial focus needs to be complemented – matched – with the interests and the work of those who look much more and in great detail at *practices*. And the by now very extensive work in the area of literacy practices (and literacy events) needs to be complemented by work on the affordances and potentials of the stuff, the material which is involved in the practices. In my view, practices can only be understood when the potentials and limitations of the tools with which one practises are understood. And the stuff is culturally remade precisely in those practices. Theories are designed – like all tools – to do specific things. Extending one theory too far, into a domain for which it was never meant, does no one a service; I hope that I have observed well the limits of a semiotic, multimodal approach to these questions.

This may sound as though my academic interests are as they are for reasons of some objective notion of greater insight or better theory. So maybe I should say that I think that 'academic interests' are never just that, blandly and abstractly. Work is always meaningful, it is a 'sign' of who the person working is; and if it is *chosen work* then even more so. My interest, and the form of my interest, in speech and writing and the connections of these with culture and with power, is such a sign. I came to a new culture and its forms of communication – not just of 'language', but of clothing, food, styles of housing, forms of leisure, gendered being and gendered relations, all the vast and subtle meanings, the value system to which we give the name 'culture' – at the age of sixteen, when I had already learned them in another culture, with its 'language'. Coming to that new society and its cultures in a particular way – mid-teenage, immigrant, 'German' with all its meanings in an only just post-war Australia – gave me a felt sense of what that difference is about. That is the source of my interests and of the line that I have followed in my academic work. The question I have asked for myself is, 'what knowledge do we need to produce and what resources do we need to make available, openly and explicitly, so that such issues can be handled productively by all?' In time, there was for me the sharper version of that question: how could transparency lead to wider social change? Knowing, as experience, the effects of culture – feeling it in my body even now in the move, say, from one language to another, from one style of writing to another – has given my academic work its shape and purpose: trying to understand how we as humans come to be who we are in our cultural and social environments. Of course, all the modes of communication are implicated in this, not only those which our cultures treat as the major modes.

My emphasis on *work*, throughout the book, is meant as more than a rhetorical flourish. Intellectual endeavour is work, and work always in the company – at times close, at times too distant – of others. Much of what is in this book continues work in the past with David Aers, Bob Hodge and Tony Trew. I am sometimes told that I have moved from the interest of that earlier work, with its political edge and with its eye on social change. That is not how I see it. I also see the book in one line with my earlier writing on questions of 'literacy' – though I thought of it then as 'writing'. But I have learned some things along the way. Over recent years that learning has been first and foremost in constantly pleasurable work and conversation with Carey Jewitt. Theo Van Leeuwen and I have talked and worked for many years now on such things. Both will no doubt recognise much here as theirs; all I can say is 'thank you'. The term 'affordances' – as well as much else – I took from Jon Ogborn; it has become central in how I think about representation. I owe much to Mary Scott's subtly theorised writing in academic literacy. In my work environment I have been fortunate in colleagues and fellow researchers – Bob Cowen, Anton Franks, Lesley Lancaster, Di Mavers, Charmian Kenner, Paul Mercer, Kate Pahl, Euan Reid. I owe to them more than just the pleasure of collegial challenge. More distantly now but always present, and over a long period, I have benefited from the friendship and the ideas of Bill Cope and of Mary Kalantzis. Much that is now part of 'my' thinking about economic environments and their effects I learned from Jim Gee. Jim Martin's friendship and generous intellectual support for what at times seemed, even to me, wilder thoughts, often proved an essential prop. In 1990 I attended a lecture given by David Barton at the University of Lancaster, in which he outlined his ideas and those of others working 'in' literacy at Lancaster – Romy Clark, Mary Hamilton, Roz Ivanic – in which literacy practices, a term not then in my repertoire, are tracked in the micro-histories of everyday lives. Strangely, given that 'the social' had been an overt concern in the work I had done before, it proved a most fruitful moment for me. I saw differently from then on. Now, by what is for me a delightful coincidence, I am able to contribute to the series of which he is the editor. And over recent years I have been fortunate in having many enjoyable interactions with Brian Street, here in London, where we have put our ideas next to each other, certainly with great benefit to me.

And then there are those whose work is essential for there to be books at all. Louisa Semlyen provided me with the constant encouragement of just the right mixture of juicy carrot and barely wielded stick through the longish period of gestation of this book. I give her my sincerest thanks for her support. Academic work goes side by side with the work of life, and life is lived with many others. Of those others Jill Brewster's never-failing support has made possible what I have achieved.

3

GOING INTO A
DIFFERENT WORLD

Into new contexts for writing

The world of communication is not standing still. The communicational world of children now in school is both utterly unremarkable to them and yet it looks entirely different to that which the school still imagines and for which it still, hesitantly and ever more insecurely, attempts to prepare them. All of us already inhabit that new world. Some of us still use the older forms of communication and at the same time have become comfortable enough with many of the possibilities of the newer forms of communicating on paper or on the screen – not fully realising and yet at the same time uncomfortably aware of the profound changes that are taking place around us. We no longer regard it as unusual that we can change fonts in mid-text, that we can **embolden** the typeface or *italicise* it, and all with next to no effort.

Of course such changes make only a small difference to the meaning of our 'written' texts. Layout, on the other hand, also very readily manipulated now, does change the deeper meanings of the text. It matters whether I put my ideas smoothly flowing along the lines of the page, or whether I present them to you as bullet-points:

- The 'force' and
- the 'feel' of the text have changed. It has become
- more insistent,
- more urgent,
- more official. It is now about
- presenting information.

Layout is beginning to change textual structures; that much is clear. With such changes – which may seem superficial – come others, which change not only the deeper meanings of textual forms but also the structures of ideas, of conceptual arrangements, and of the structures of our knowledge. Such seemingly superficial changes are altering the very channels in which we think. Bullet points are, as their name suggests, bullets of information. They are 'fired' at us,

16

abrupt and challenging, not meant to be continuous and coherent, not inviting reflection and consideration, not insinuating themselves into our thinking. They are hard and direct, and not to be argued with.

The more profound changes have come, over the last two decades or so, from a number of distinct yet connected factors. Even though they involve the new information and communication technologies, they constitute a revolution of a social and not just a technological kind. These changes are unmaking the era of mass communication and its social structures, through a new distribution of the means of access to the production and reception of messages in the public domain. This constitutes a restructuring of power in the field of representation and communication, in which the technology of writing is deeply implicated. Before, the power to produce messages for dissemination in the public domain lay with the few who had access to and control of the media for disseminating messages.

At different points in history, that access has been – and still often is – tightly regulated by authorities of the state, the church or the 'party', of 'capital', or of others. The relation of those who produced messages and could disseminate them to those who received them was that of *few* to *many*. These were the conditions of the era of mass communication. The new information and communication technologies have produced the technological condition where all can publish to all, and by means of that enormous change they have abolished the era of mass communication. But this is a technological condition, and exists 'in principle' only, for if, in the past, power attached to the control of the means for dissemination of information, it does so still, and it is not likely that that power will be ceded easily and without contest by those who have it now to those who do not have that power. In other words, the potentials of these technologies imply a radical social change, a redistribution of semiotic power, the power to make and disseminate meanings. This change becomes even more potent now, when the new economies are increasingly economies in which information is both the major resource in production and the main commodity for consumption.

The change to existing distributions of power could only come about with such relative ease – so far at least – because the previous structures of control of that power had become radically unsettled, through the effects of globalisation. However clichéd and contested the concept may be, globalisation of both finance capital and popular culture – all cultural production is 'popular' the moment it becomes a commodity – is a fact. Its effects at the level of the 'Western' nation state have been to dissolve both the frames which had held structures of power in place and the connections that obtained between them.

First and foremost of these were the previously tight relations of nation state and national economy on the one hand, and of nation state, national economy and the meanings and values of 'citizenship' on the other. Other institutions, such as the church or 'the party', have played significant roles, semi-independently of state and economy. But from these connections all power

17

flowed, and all relevant value systems, public and private, were derived. It was these connections which produced and sustained the structures of the mass society, the economies of mass-production, 'mass' institutions such as hospitals, police forces, the mass (conscription-based) army, schools, railways and, of course, the institutions of mass communication, the publishing industry in general, books, newspapers and, later, radio and terrestrial television. All these together produced a tightly organised value system to give meaning to all aspects of lives lived in that structure of frames.

The uses and the forms of literacy have been tied into these structures, and still remain tied into their new configurations. Individual users of the technology of 'literacy' are integrated into such webs of structures. In making their meanings as messages in these webbed domains, individuals constantly sustain, produce and transform the resources of the technology of literacy, in line with the needs, demands, meanings and desires which they live and experience in these environments. In this way the shape of the resources becomes, and then *is*, an expression and reflection of the meanings that individuals make. To use a small example, we know that levels of formality, as one index of social power relations, have changed; this is reflected in the resources of language and hence of literacy through their use in the contexts of the new social arrangements. If the boundaries of (the always socially produced notions of) the public and the private have changed, or have become seemingly more blurred, or have in some cases disappeared, then the markers of those boundaries will also change in the resources of literacy. One such set of markers of the distinction between the public and the private concerned a more or less strongly maintained difference in use of (informal) speech, that is, speech relatively unmarked for power-difference, and (formal) writing, that is, writing marked by power-difference. In that situation it was regarded as 'inappropriate', inadmissible even, to use speech-like forms in writing. Academic writing, professional writing of various kinds, official writing, all were marked by a strict observation of this difference. The use of the agentless passive – 'it has been claimed that . . .' – was one such marker in academic writing; another was the use of highly complex sentence syntax. All these are now beginning to disappear, at different pace in different domains. So, for example, in some disciplines, and in some universities in the English-speaking world, it is no longer required to write theses or academic articles using such forms.

Of course, these changes have been spurred along by the rapid development of the 'new media'. But to look for the explanation for such changes in the new technologies, in communication more widely, or in the resource of literacy more narrowly, is to mistake the effect for the cause. Technologies become significant when social and cultural conditions allow them to become significant. The new information and communication technologies have both made possible and been a part of the more profound force of (economic and cultural) globalisation. The unfettered movement of finance capital is made *technologically* possible by electronic communication, though it is made *politically* possible by the global power of transnational finance capital; it has provided the conditions of that freedom. The same applies to the free movement around the globe of cultural commodities – whether the products of Holly- or Bollywood. The free movement of cultural commodities has been as significant in unmaking the formerly relative stabilities and distinctiveness of cultural forms and values as have the effects of economic globalisation, even if differently so. Cultural globalisation has been the servant of economic globalisation in two ways. It has provided the conditions of the appearance of 'naturalness' to the globalisation of capital. After all, if it has become commonplace that I have access to the cultural products of anywhere, here, in my locality, it will seem perverse that other commodities should not be equally available. Cultural globalisation has prepared the ground for a global market for commodities which are in any case now more and more 'cultural'.

The new environment of writing

It is there that we need to look to understand the changes in communicational practices, those of literacy included, which are remaking the world around us. However, from the point of view of this book, a book focused on literacy in the new media age, there are two issues of absolute significance which bear more directly on communication through writing. The first relates to the media of communication: the effects of the ubiquity and dominance of the 'screen', and its effect on writing. The second concerns not the media but the modes of communication: the ever-increasing presence of image – in all forms – in contemporary messages.

To make a comment briefly on both of these, until relatively recently – say the last three or four decades – the medium for the dissemination of writing was the book and the page. An entirely reciprocal relation existed between the medium (the book or page) and the mode (writing). The forms of writing structured the appearance of the page, as much as the organisation of the book. Conversely, the book and the page gave shape to far-reaching aspects of the grammatical and textual forms of writing. This extended from sentence to paragraph to chapter – to all aspects of the conceptual shaping of ideas in writing, to the sentence as a complex idea, to the chapter as a coherent exposition of an internally cohesive 'body' of knowledge – and to the aesthetics, the 'look', of writing. This could be the shape and look of writing on the page, or the size of chapters and of sections of the book. The logic of the mode of writing shaped and organised the book and its pages. The potentials of the medium of the book and the page gave rise both to the shaping of knowledge and ideas and to the distributions of power between those who could produce the written text and distribute the book and those who received the book and its text as authoritative objects.

If the book was organised and dominated by the logic of writing, the screen is organised and dominated by the image and its logic. The logic of (alphabetic) writing, to say this briefly at this stage, is the logic of sequence in time, leaning heavily still on the temporal logic of speech, though shaped also by centuries of the practices of writing (in English, say). The logic of writing is temporal/sequential; the elements of speech certainly, and those of writing in a quasi-fashion, unfold in time and in sequence. In speech that sequence is temporal, in writing it is linear/spatial, with a quasi-temporality as I read along the line, in time. The logic of image on the other hand is spatial/simultaneous. All the elements of the image are related in spatial arrangements, and they are simultaneously present. Writing is the ordering of elements (syntactic/grammatical and lexical) in the conventionalised sequences of syntax; image is the ordering of elements ('depictions') in a more or less conventionalised and spatially simultaneous 'display'. This latter form of relations between elements, this logic, dominates the screen. In writing, much of the meaning of the text and of its parts derives from the arrangements of syntax; in the image, much of the meaning of the image derives from the spatial relations of the depicted elements. When writing appears on the screen, as it does now and will continue to do, it will increasingly – as is indeed the case now – be reshaped by this logic. Writing will more and more become organised and shaped by the logic of the image-space of the screen. This is one inescapable effect of the potentials of the screen, and the technology of the new media.

Just as the medium of the book, in its reciprocal relations with writing, shaped that mode and what that mode could do, so the new relations of the medium of screen with the mode of writing will shape all aspects of the form of writing. This is beginning to happen already, and it will reshape the possibilities of the arrangements of knowledge, information and ideas. The screen offers entirely different possibilities of arrangements, formal and therefore conceptual, to those of the page.

The second issue mentioned above, is that of the (re)new(ed) emergence of the mode of image into the domain of public communication. Of course, image has always 'been there', even in the book, as illustration. Certainly it has been on the walls of churches, and there often accompanied by the explanatory speech of the priest, 'this is the life of our lord', and there often as a full means of communication. At the moment image is coming ever more insistently into the domain of everyday communication, as a full means of representing ideas, information and knowledge. Coupled as it is with the simultaneous switch from the dominance of the book to that of the screen, that is, a switch from the medium that privileged writing to the medium that privileges image, it is clear that the increasing prevalence of image will have profound effects on writing. The major one among these derives from what I will call the 'functional specialisation' of modes.

If two modes – say, image and writing – are available and are being used for representing and communicating, it is most likely that they will be used for distinct purposes: each will be used for that which it does best and is therefore best used for. Two consequences arise: one, each mode carries only a part of the informational 'load'; no mode fully carries all the meaning. Two, each of the two modes will be used for specialised tasks, the tasks which are best done with that mode. As a consequence writing is no longer a full carrier either of all the meaning, or of all types of meaning. Other, more directly social, reasons also have their effects, for instance general changes in the 'audiences' of the various media, which pose questions such as 'who reads books?', 'for what reasons?', 'for what purposes?', and similarly for all other media as well, of course.

The combined effects of the changes in the media and in the uses of modes reach further still; they are not confined to the screen, but affect all media and all modes. The modes which dominate the dominant medium, the screen – spatially organised arrangements of image and writing in specific layouts – have come to dominate pages of all kinds, and the book as well. It has frequently been commented on that the pages of newspapers and magazines are more and more like the screens of certain television programmes. This is true of many segments of the print-media, of publicity materials and of textbooks, and increasingly of 'literary' forms such as the travelogue, the biography and even the novel. But these new generic forms are not amenable to the same conceptual structures, the same structures of ideas, information and knowledge as were the other, the older forms. New textbooks are not 'books' in the older sense: carefully structured, coherent expositions of knowledge, knowledge to engage with reflectively and to 'absorb'. The new 'books' are often collections of worksheets; no careful development of complex coherent structures here, and no deliberate carefully reflective engagement with these pages. These are books to work with, to do things with, to act with and often to act on.

In this process, writing is undergoing changes of a profound kind: in grammar and syntax, particularly at the level of the sentence, and at the level of the text/message. Writing now plays one part in communicational ensembles, and no longer *the* part. Where before all information was conveyed in writing, now there is a decision to be made: which information, for this audience, is best conveyed in image and which in writing? In this form, that is a very new role for writing to have. For those who use writing, it requires new thinking, and different dispositions towards communication.

Writing and literacy

Clearly, then, 'literacy' is by no means all there is to contemporary communication. Other resources, images above all, are used, sometimes more insistently than those of 'literacy' or alphabetically written 'words' in meaningful arrangements. Given that in the world of the new media there are numerous modal resources involved in the making of 'messages' – word, spoken or written; image, still and moving; music; objects as 3D models; soundtrack; action – it has in any case become essential to ask what we mean by 'literacy'. Of course, that is the issue which will be explored (in theory and in examples) throughout this book. But it may be best to have some clarification right here and now.

21

In English-speaking contexts, we have this word 'literacy'. As it is being used in ever-extended meanings, we might decide to stretch its use still further to cover any resource involved in the making of any 'message', whether through word or image or otherwise.

For me, two reasons speak against that. One is that we need to be aware that other languages do not have such a word. They name the field differently: *alphabetismus* in German; *alphabetisme*, in French as in other romance languages. In languages which do not use a version of the alphabet, Chinese or Japanese for instance, quite different wordings exist: in Japanese, for instance 'the recognition of letters' (mon-mou); in Chinese there are a range of phrases, for instance 'know-character-ability', 'normal raise/bring-up', 'to have received education'.

Of course, we could attempt to insist that as the English language already rules the world, the English word *literacy* should do also, or that other languages should at least produce translations of this word, as in *lettramento* in (Brazilian) Portuguese, or *Literalitäet* in German-speaking contexts. Of course, we might reflect on what the differences in naming actually mean, and whether the extension of the English word *literacy* to all contexts of communication, or to other cultures, to their languages and to their ways of representing, is really the best way to go. A vast range of meanings is gathered up in the word; in anglophone contexts it can be anything from 'making reliable links between the letters of a written text and the sounds of speech' to 'being able to make readings of texts of the elite, which conform to the readings of the elite culture'. The more that is gathered up in the meaning of the term, the less meaning it has. Something that has come to mean everything, is likely not to mean very much at all.

The time is right to reflect, and to rethink radically. In any case, there are strong reasons against imperialisms in naming, whether in a culture or across cultures. There is also the overwhelming reason that the conditions of our present and of the near future – economic, social, technological – are ushering in a distinctively different era of communication. In the process some of our culture's most profound notions are coming under challenge: what reading is; what the functions of writing are; what the relations of language to thinking, to imagination, to creativity might be. Is the imagination that rests on word different to the imagination that rests on image? A vast change is under way, with as yet unknowable consequences. It involves the remaking of relations between what a culture makes available as means for making meaning (what I shall call, throughout the book, representational modes – speech, writing, image, gesture, music and others) and what the culture makes available as means for distributing these meanings as messages (the media of dissemination – book, computer-screen, magazine, video, film, radio, chat and so on). 'Literacy', in whatever sense, is entirely involved in that.

This *is* the moment for taking stock. If we do not reflect, we are likely to carry all sorts of baggage along with us, willy-nilly and unexamined, from the former period into the new, where it will prove more problematic than it had ever been before. In the book I will attempt to unsettle some accepted notions, and to ask questions in areas which might seem too obvious to need questioning even now. I hope that the result will be worthwhile.

Literacy

To put it baldly at this point, and before I have presented any of the arguments, for me *literacy* is the term to use when we make messages using letters as the means of recording that message. When we communicate through numbers, we use the term 'numeracy', and for very good reasons: the meaning-potential and the meanings made with numbers are very different from those made with letters. This is so even though we can retranscribe numbers into letters and words, as when the stall-holder says 'that'll be five euros seventy-five cents'. My approach leaves us with the problem of finding new terms for the uses of the different resources: not therefore 'visual *literacy*' for the use of image; not 'gestural *literacy*' for the use of gesture; and also not 'musical *literacy*' or 'soundtrack *literacy*' for the use of sound other than in speech; and so on.

It may be that when we speak in popular, everyday contexts, these metaphoric uses, extending infinitely – visual literacy, gestural literacy, musical literacy, media literacy, computer-, cultural-, emotional-, sexual-, internet- and so on and so on – are fine, though I have my doubts even then. I would want to exclude another currently fashionable use of the term, which is to indicate certain kinds of production-skills associated more or less closely with aspects of communication, as in computer literacy, or (aspects of) media literacy. Instead I want to make a threefold distinction in our naming-practices:

1   words that name the resources for representing and their potential – speech, writing, image, gesture;
2   words that name the use of the resources in the production of the message – literacy, oracy, signing, numeracy, (aspects of) 'computer literacy' and of 'media literacy', 'internet-literacy'; and
3   words that name the involvement of the resources for the dissemination of meanings as message – internet publishing, as one instance.

The new technologies of information and communication complicate this picture seriously, in that they bring together the resources for representation and their potential with the resources of production and the resources of dissemination. It is this conflation which has led to some of the too ready extension of the term 'literacy': using the computer has aspects of all three. It is difficult to deal with this neatly. On the one hand the computer brings all three together. On the other hand, to use writing, whether on the screen or on the page, is to be involved specifically with that resource – writing – and its potentials; to use images whether on the screen or on the page, similarly. These are distinct resources and require distinct competencies in their use and their design, no matter whether on the page or on the screen. To use both modes, image and writing, together, as is ever more frequently the case with the new technologies, is to be involved in the *use* of the resources of visual composition (layout), in the *use of the visual mode of image*, in the *use of the mode of writing*, and all in ways which both draw on the existing knowledges and resources and yet are also quite new.

When we see the finished message, it seems as though the maker of the message has simply made use of everything that was there to use, that she or he has drawn on whatever resources were available and serviceable, without distinguishing between resources. Yet even now, in this situation of change and flux, we can tell differences: between the use of the mode of writing and that of image, between the page that works, the screen that looks good, and those which do not. If we have the means, the knowledge, however implicit, for making discriminations, then clearly we have the means for making the complex design decisions also, in the first place.

Given this situation, I think it is more important than ever to understand the meaning-potentials of the resources as precisely and as explicitly as we can, to keep things clear and distinct where we can, at one level. The sculptor must know the potentials of this kind of wood, of that kind of stone, of these metals, of silicone and of fibreglass. The designer must know what resources will best meet the demands of a specific design for a specific audience. Both of them would be puzzled and fail to understand an approach that did not start from such knowledge, from knowing what the different modes are and what they can best do.

So to return to the issue: we can have *writing* or *speech* as the names of two resources for making meaning. Using pencil, pen, (computer) keyboard or whatever else are then separate and different matters, involving the *skills* of both production and dissemination, which may be more or less closely integrated with the potentials of the resource. *Literacy* remains the term which refers to (the knowledge of) the use of the resource of writing. The combination of knowledge of the resource with knowledge of production and perhaps with that of dissemination would have a different name. That separates, what to me is essential, the *sense of what the resource is* and what its potentials are, from associated questions such as those of its *uses*, and the issue of whatever skills are involved in using a resource in wider communicational frames.

It also separates the issue entirely from that further set of metaphoric extensions, as in *cultural, emotional, sexual, social literacy*, and many more. Literacy, in all its aspects, is entirely social, cultural and personal. And so, of course, all matters social and cultural, economic and political, as much as those which are affective or emotional, have their impact. But that is not, for me, a good enough reason to bring all these into discussions of literacy in an undifferentiated way. I have no objections if such terms are used in popular settings, or if such usages exist. There is in any case an absolute need to keep popular and academic modes of working and naming quite separate. The danger of extending the term too far is that of dragging things which are and should remain entirely outside the social regulations that literacy is subject to into that domain, to push social regulation into domains where there is no need for it to exist. I would want to know what it means for someone to use terms such as *cultural literacy* or *sexual literacy*, what judgements are made, implicitly or explicitly, on whom, and what the effects are of such judgements on those who are being judged, on this as on other occasions. But those are general intellectual, social, political concerns of mine, as a member of my social group.

A next step: the alphabet

This begins to answer questions such as 'what do we mean by literacy?' and 'how can we begin to define the term?' We can speak about the resource and the use of the resource as distinct issues, aware that in practice the two are never separable. As I mentioned, the word does not exist in other languages. Other languages have words, as English does, for things like fruit, water, stones, food, earth – concrete things, which are 'there', so to speak. 'Literacy', like 'liberty', seems to be something that exists because a social group has decided that it does, and has given it a name whose grammatical status as noun suggests that it has a real existence. Other social groups seem not to see it in that way at all. It is worth asking 'why not?' and to ask what it is that *they* see. The cultures that make mention of the alphabet in some way clearly recognise its effects, but do not, seemingly, go beyond that in their initial naming.

The alphabet does two things: it tends to act as a means for representing the sounds of speech, in some more or less direct way; it is also now a means, directly, without going via speech, for using graphic elements on a page or on a screen. This dual function is worth following further, if only because the second aspect is frequently lost sight of. It is not necessary to be able to connect the sounds of speech with the letters of an alphabet in order to be able to read or to write. 'Sight recognition' of words works perfectly well for many people. Nor do those who are speech- and hearing-impaired, for instance, need to hear a word 'in their heads' or in their ears in order to read it. This is much the same as when I am in Italy or France, where I do not need to understand the shopkeeper's (spoken) mention of the price of my purchase, just so long as I can see the figure on the electronic display at the till, or she is prepared to write out the numbers on a bit of paper for me, in the market, say.

The alphabet can be a bridge between the spoken version of a 'language' and its written form, and like any well-used bridge it keeps the two sides in touch with what is on the other side. The written form is tied, relatively, to spoken versions, as is obvious in the case of the 'assimilation' of loan-words. There it tends to be the spoken version that influences the written. But the fact that writing has a power of its own becomes obvious in cases when there is an attempt at 'spelling-reform', when reformers meet a reluctance to let the archaic written form be brought into line with current pronunciations – say, the case of 'knight' versus 'nite'. The written version cannot move too far from the spoken, lest it become 'unreadable'. But at the same time, in a literate society, the written form exercises a constant pressure on the spoken form, slowing the speed of change that spoken language might otherwise be subject to. Perhaps most importantly, the inevitable authority of the written form has a levelling and homogenising effect, as there is a tendency for speakers of different dialects to attempt to approximate their pronunciations to the orthography of writing in their reading of written texts.

In alphabetic cultures this relation is subject to greater or lesser regulation at different times and in different societies. It is, among other things, one means of exerting and exercising 'authority', and a means for trying to bring about conformity and stability. 'Spelling' was used in that way in the attempts by the Tudor state to spread and entrench its authority. Alphabetic writing is a readily available metaphor for the expression of all kinds of social factors. At the moment – the year 2002 at the time of writing – there is a heavy emphasis, in the school systems of anglophone societies, on correctness of spelling, and an insistence on the rules for the transliteration of letters (in words) into sounds (in words), as in the practice of 'phonics', so called. This is more than mildly paradoxical at a time when English, as a language, is escaping the control of those who previously had been able to (deceive themselves that they could) legislate in this way. English is now the language – both as a first language or as an other language – of very many different communities around the world, all of whom pronounce English in increasingly distinct and different fashion.

Of course, it might be said that this is precisely a ground for insisting on maintaining a close relation between sound and letter, for reasons of continued communicability and comprehension. But there are too many real problems: for one thing, the changing Englishes around the world are subject to quite other forces – for instance the influence of the sound-systems of the other languages spoken in a particular locality together with English. Indian English sounds as it does because of the sound-systems of Hindi, Urdu, Bengali and many others; as does Welsh English, which reflects the sound-system of Welsh. For another reason, it is quite simply an impossible undertaking to settle on one of these forms of English as the standard by which all others would have to arrange themselves. That had never been a possibility, and it certainly is not now.

Of course, this enterprise of insisting on conformity between letter and sound is also paradoxical given the fragmentary and centripetal forces of globalisation. What might be possible is a *relatively* unified form of spelling. Not only is it likely to be sustainable, it is desirable and even necessary for English to function as a global language. The effects and uses of the new media are likely to support this. But the insistence on the close and 'logical' link between sound and letter is a forlorn enterprise. English the language is, in that respect, heading in a similar direction to the different forms (languages or dialects) of Chinese and their writing system: relatively unified, mutually and widely comprehensible writing system, only loosely linked to the sound-systems of the different 'dialects' or languages of Chinese.

But perhaps the most significant effect of the alphabet is its effect on the views of language by those who use it. The alphabet focuses its users on *language as sound*: in one of its guises (and probably, historically, its early use) the alphabet represents sounds. Users of the alphabet therefore tend to think of language first and foremost as a system of sounds. Sounds occur in two kinds of combinations, once as *larger sound-units*, 'syllables', and once as *meaning-units*, 'words'. There is a complex relation between syllable and morpheme – the unit of sound-form and the unit of meaning-form. Ideas are expressed as morphemes – in *oxen* there are two morphemes: the lexical, meaning-bearing morpheme *ox*, and the grammatical meaning-bearing unit *–en*, the plural affix. But this expression of meaning is not there at the first step. By complete contrast, the situation with a character-based writing system is that characters represent ideas, or maybe – there is no real agreement on this among those who understand this system – words. So for users of character-based writing systems, the focus is on meaning, as a first step. At a second step, there are then indications, either in the character itself or in rules and conventions for sounding characters in a particular dialect, as to how that character can be sounded. The character-based writing system records ideas, and sounds can be attached to the characters. Language appears, at a first step, as a system of ideas, which can be 'sounded'. The alphabet/letter-based writing system records sounds, and ideas can be attached to strings of letters. For the user of the letter-based system, the focus is on sound, as a first step. At a second step, ideas can be attached to these.

Setting the difference between the systems out in this fashion brings us to the second issue: do we include a character-based writing system in our definition of literacy? If so, we have taken a giant step: literacy is now not defined as the technology for transcribing sounds as letters, or as the technology for making graphic marks called letters combine into units called 'words'. Literacy can now be any system of transcription or recording, whether of sounds or of ideas. If it can be both the technology for transcribing sounds or for transcribing ideas, or mixtures of the two, then 'literacy' has come to mean 'transcription system' simply, and the decision for us to settle is then what it is we wish to transcribe and how, and with what resources, we wish to transcribe or record it . That system is then not (just) tied to language, but can extend to music, to numbers and to many other forms of 'expression'. But it has then become so broad, in its aim of inclusiveness, that it has lost any real 'bite', or any usefulness as a technical term.

Two further questions open up here, most immediately the question 'what is language?' (as against the question 'what is music?' or 'what is the system of numbers?'), with the implication that we call everything 'language' or that we wish to reserve 'language' for a specific system of making meaning. The second question, already half stated, is, 'what is it that we are transcribing?' Are we always transcribing some meaning system into some visible or audible form, or are we simply translating from one transcription system to another? A case of the latter might be the system of Morse code. Here we have one transcription system, namely the alphabet, and a second system into which it is transcribed.

The operators of Morse code are not concerned with meaning. They do not bother, like the translator of a short story or poem or report from one language into another, with possibilities of equivalence – is there a word for '*Weltschmerz*' in English, or how do you translate the *genre* of the Elizabethan sonnet into Chinese? The operator of Morse code is concerned with accuracy and precision in the application of the code, that is all.

Transcription systems

To begin with the second question first, a transcription system is always partial. Take the alphabet again, as an example. I said that one thing that it does is to offer a means for transcribing sounds into letters. But we all know that that is only partially so. The alphabet was not designed for one particular language; it evolved in its use by many cultures and many, very different, languages. Each culture bent and twisted and shaped a system that did not fit its own language well. All cultures that use it make the best possible use of a system which was never meant for their specific language in the first place. That leads to the well-understood problem of a 'lack of fit'. In most or all languages which use the alphabet, from north-western Europe through the Middle East to the Indian subcontinent, the sound-systems of the languages are quite out of kilter with the letter-system, so that the transcription can only ever and at best be an approximation of the one to the other.

But the more important partiality is a different one: the alphabet selects only a small range of the sound features of a language – broadly speaking, vowels and consonants and variants of these. It does not attend, for instance, to intonational features, the up and down of the voice, or to rhythmic features, or to length, loudness or general pitch-level (is the voice-level high or low?). These decisions are not made on the basis of meaning, or rather they are made on the basis of a selection of one kind of (potential for) meaning over others. What is recorded are the sounds which form words – or rather, conventionalised understandings of sounds that form words. Anyone who has looked at the early, or not so early, spelling of children will know what this is about. Early spellings by children attempt to record anything and everything that seems meaningful in the sounds of language. They are attempts by young humans who, on the one hand, have the most acute hearing and an absolute obsession with precision in transcription and, on the other, have as yet no or little knowledge of the conventions which govern the transcription of speech, whether as consonant and vowel sounds or as something else, and whose hearing has not therefore become structured by those conventions. So what they record is what they hear and, in that, what seems to them most significant at this moment. That is what is recorded and transcribed by them and often what they record goes well beyond sounds that form spoken words transcribed as letters which form written words.

Not recorded and not transcribed in conventional spelling are a whole range of other meanings. Because they are not included in the conventions of transcription, they become overlooked and then become unofficial meanings; they are or have become ruled out from the range of officially recognised meanings. They are regarded as expressions of emotion, of attitude, of emphasis, of individual whim, often of mere dysfunction, of 'noise'. Yet at the same time we are aware that some of these have meanings after all. In some forms of English, as in many other languages, a 'rising intonation' has grammatical meaning, so called. 'You went there on Saturday' said with a continuously rising intonation is taken as a question, despite the fact that its syntactic form indicates a 'declarative'. But intonation is much more flexibly used than just that. If I say to my guests, in my house, 'it's cold in here', with a rising intonation they will understand that (syntactic declarative) as a question of a particular kind, indicating my surprise, and inviting a certain kind of response: 'yes, I wouldn't mind if you closed the window'; while the response to 'is it cold in here?' said with high pitch on 'cold' and a falling intonation from there on, might produce the sarcastic response 'no, I always wear my overcoat for dinner'.

The 'question mark' has been invented to capture some of these kinds of meaning, meanings which are assumed to be 'grammatical' because they apparently change a statement (in the form of a declarative, syntactically speaking) to a question (an interrogative, syntactically speaking). In fact, nothing has been changed; the utterance with that intonation was always a question. The problem is that we focus so much on written words and their order that we come to believe that in order to speak we first produce a written syntactic form with one kind of semantic intent in mind, and then superimpose an intonation on that, in our speaking out of the written form, which then, to our surprise, turns 'it' all into something else. It is our focus on the written word and on the arrangement of words in the syntax of writing which leads us to regard the written version as basic, for speech as for writing. That basic form is then changed by intonation or other things. As a notion of how language works it could hardly be more mistaken.

In Spanish writing the question mark is placed at the beginning of the relevant unit, to signal the intonational implementation from the beginning. Exclamation marks also belong in this group of devices. Other features of speech, which are not captured by the transcription as letters, are at times 'lexicalised' – they are put into words. In the conventions of the novel, for instance, the directly transcribed words of a character are followed by 'she said *laughingly*', 'he said *breathlessly*', 'they *paused*, lost in the wonderment of their feelings'. In actual speech such lexical commentary is not necessary – the spoken elements are there in the speech, for all to hear. But they are never transcribed. Different cultures within the broad range of alphabetic writing cultures – ranging from the scripts of the Indian subcontinent, via those of the Middle East to those of Europe, the Americas and Africa – have different conventions around the question of transcription, and have made different provision for recording some of these unofficial meanings. The alphabet itself – and with it this resource in literacy – is, however, severely limited in that regard.

It is important to insist that while these are 'unofficial meanings' they are never meanings that are not meant, even though we have decided to rule them out as 'unofficial', as meanings that do not belong into that which we have defined as language. It becomes clear that definitions and conventions of transcription have fundamental consequences for how we see language and for what we regard as language, for what is included and for what is excluded, as much as for basic conceptions of what the resource of language is. One further example, to make the point. In linguistics, a distinction is made between 'tonal languages' and those which are not. Chinese, Thai and some West African languages such as Igbo and others belong to the former group. Tonal languages are defined by the characteristic that intonation has lexical effect: the same group of sounds said with different tones produces different meanings or words. In English, by contrast, it is assumed that tone does not have lexical effect, but has grammatical effect only, as in the example mentioned earlier. In fact, that is not the full story even for English: if I say the word 'yes' with differing intonations – say a clearly falling intonation compared to a rising or a 'wavering' one, I do in fact produce very different meanings, and hardly the same word. They are very different 'yeses', and the last two do not in fact mean 'yes' (as clear affirmation) at all, in fact they mean kinds of 'no'. They are in fact different words. English, it seems, has some features that resemble a tonal language.

So what we might say is this: the alphabet, as a transcription system, is a mnemonic for certain aspects of sound, largely those that form words, not precisely so, but nearly enough. It is not a system for transcribing all important and meaningful sound; it is hugely partial. Unlike character-based systems, it is not focused on meaning, and therefore treats language as being primarily about sound. The letters of the alphabet are also a means for the visible representation of written words without 'passing through' speech first.

In the 'West' we are used to what is, from the perspective of many cultures, truly odd, in having a single transcription or writing system for a language. In many parts of the world the situation is that one language can be recorded by many transcriptional systems. In such cultures any one writer might use one or two or three different transcription systems to write the one language, so much so that even a single word might be represented using two or three transcription systems, each bringing with it clear meanings of a cultural/social kind. That is a useful reminder that transcription systems are not meaning-neutral: social meanings attach to them. One such important meaning, in the 'West', is the assumption that the alphabet represents the 'finest achievement' of human culture, and that the highest forms of rationality – certain forms of abstraction – are embedded in it. This may explain one part of the objection to image-based transcription systems, and to images themselves as a representational resource, namely what is seen as their lack of producing abstraction. Such an approach rests on an entire misunderstanding of how different transcription systems produce abstractness.

The implications of all this – what is recorded, what is not, what views of language open up, what is closed off to thought and so on – have not been widely explored in the 'West'. Writing has been so much in the centre that it has simply not been possible to pose such questions. The writing, thinking and research that there is has never formed a part of the mainstream of linguistic work. Given that language, and the transcription systems that cultures have developed over the millennia, are among the most potent social icons and metaphors, this has been a huge limitation on thinking.

Language, speech, writing

My lengthy account of the transcription system of the alphabet has had several aims. One is to show that it truly matters what we decide to include as being a part of language. It also shows that what we include is always a convention, established and maintained for social reasons. What has been established for social reasons can be undone for social reasons. Academic disciplines have their reasons for including and excluding elements from the domain that they have made their own. In the case of linguistics, the wish to emulate the natural sciences explains many of the exclusions which it has erected around its conception of language. One of my aims has been to show that the relation between language as spoken and language as written is far from straightforward, even if we remain at the level of sound and letter alone – which of course we cannot do in any fuller discussion of either language or of literacy. But above all I want to demonstrate that it is impossible to remain abstract about 'language' or 'literacy', and yet at the same time retain a real interest in understanding what they are like. Speech and writing are deeply different. That they were treated as 'the same' in most of the mainstream theories of language (which simply talked about language-as-such) under the broad abstraction of 'language' for nearly all of the last century, has much to do with the fact that theoretical abstraction had ruled, in the service of establishing regularities or rules that might emulate those produced in the natural sciences. Indeed, speech and writing are still seen as 'much the same' in much writing in linguistics, sociolinguistics and the ethnographic approaches to literacy. There the two are seen as existing on a continuum, not really distinguishable in terms of their affordances, shall we say. The point of view which I advocate here, namely that the two are distinct modes, is not the mainstream view.

Establishing that language has 'rules' made it seem a subject fit for 'scientific enquiry', and made linguistics fit to take its place among the 'sciences'. Anything that proved troublesome to that goal was excluded. Yet lives are messy, and, within the broader frames set in cultures and in society, they are endlessly variable. Any meaning-making system that has to cope with that messiness and its ceaselessly nuanced, subtle variability is not likely to be readily reducible to rules. In some important areas of grammar and syntax there are of course strong, rule-like regularities, such as the agreement in number of subject and verb in English, even though in the Norfolk dialect of English, for instance, that

31

is not a rule. But across language as a whole, variability, dynamism, change, flux are the order, rather than the rigidity of unchangeable rules.

For me it is now a real question whether we can talk about some phenomenon called 'language' in any serious sense at all, and if we do so, what it is that we are actually talking about. I wonder whether the concept of 'language' is a fiction that gets in the way of thinking clearly. Maybe it is essential to talk of speech and its regularities as one mode, and writing and its regularities as another. And yet there are points where, in alphabetically transcribed languages, speech and writing are closely enough connected that the term 'language' does have its uses.

These may seem remote arguments, though they do have real effects in everyday lives, such as in school curricula for instance, or in attitudes to correctness, to social order and to the role of authority whether in language or much more widely in social lives.

Staying with abstract notions of language may have its uses, though understanding the potentials of the resources of speech or of writing in making meaning is not one of them. For that we need to focus on the very materiality of these resources to understand their potentials in their actual use. How does the fact that speech necessarily happens in time affect the meanings that we make with it? How does the fact that – in cultures with a longer history of writing – it has freed itself from temporality in some ways, but has been subject, in its graphic display, to some of the effects of space, affect the meanings that we can make in that mode? Further, we need to understand the histories of the shaping of both in their social use. We need a quite new way of thinking about resources, their use and the users; we need a new theory of meaning and meaning-making, a new theory of semiosis. For that, both speech and writing need to be discussed in terms of their materiality as much as in terms of their cultural shaping, in very concrete, quite non-abstract ways. To understand the potentials of the resource of writing we need to understand the potentials of the resource of speech – as of other resources – in their differences and in their similarities. Only at that stage might it again be useful and possible to reintroduce the notion of 'language'.

Much of the book will be concerned with showing that we need to attend to the *materiality* of the resources, the material *stuff* that we use for making meaning. The sculptor who does not understand the potentials of the material with which he or she works is at an entire disadvantage in their work. Of course he or she will also need to know the traditions of sculpture, in their own or in other cultures – not only what can be done with fibreglass but also what has been done with that material. After all, what they make now derives part of its meaning from its contrast with what has been made before.

At the level of stuff, speech and writing are obviously different. One exists as the materiality of sound in time, and the other as the materiality of graphic marks in two-dimensional space. A question that is pressing is, is it possible to make the same meanings with sounds in time (and all the cultural elaborations of that) as with light in space (and the elaborations of that)? This becomes urgent now that the new technologies permit a ready and easy choice: shall I represent this as written text or as image? The increasing use of images on screens as elsewhere demands an answer to that question. Is that which I wish to 'say' a different thing when it is said in the mode of speech or in the mode of writing or in the mode of image? While we use the abstraction 'language', this cannot be posed as a question. But if 'literacy' is both a resource and a skill in the use of the resource, a technology for 'handling' meaning, then I need to know at least as much about the materials I wish to use as the sculptor needs to know about the materials for sculpting. What meanings depend on the use and the potentials of the resource of writing, or on that of speech, or on both, or on the resources of 'language-as-such' contrasted, say, with 'image'? If speech and writing are distinct in important ways, then what remains as the unifying factor for the term 'language'?

My approach is that the potentials of the resources of speech and of writing are distinct, at many levels and in many ways. Their difference as material stuff determines that that is so. At the same time, cultures do very different things with the materials on which they work. Writing cultures have shaped the resources of writing in many different ways, which means that we need to know the social meanings that inhere in the resource as we have it available to us now. Societies attribute different values to the resources of speech and of writing, and regulate the relation between them in different ways. Hence we need to understand what social regulations govern their relation now, for whom, in what environments. Depending on the strength of such regulations, any individual's sense of the relation of speech and writing will differ, and for a variety of reasons. For some members of a writing culture, writing will be the transcription of speech; for others, the two will be quite distinct. Others will have a clear sense of the variability of that relation, either in general or in specific circumstances. When I came to understand for myself, some twenty-five years ago, that this relation and its formal expression had much to do with social power and the maintenance of social groups, I made a decision to make my own writing closer to the 'rhythms' of informal speech than to those of formal academic writing. I wanted to make my writing indicate solidarity with a wider group of readers with a more general professional interest rather than solidarity with a small and elite group of my academic peers.

Throughout the book I will come to detailed discussion of how writing and speech 'work', as resources for making meaning. Here I will simply say again that the two fundamental differences are on the one hand the 'logics' of time and space, and on the other hand the material stuff of sound and of graphic marks, of light. The logic of time has consequences for planning speech and for its reception, and hence consequences for the structures of speech at any level – textual and sub-textual units, sentences, clauses, words, sounds. The potentials of sequence in time are many, from the meanings of temporal ordering – what is mentioned first or last, the difference in meaning between 'Bill married Mary' and 'Mary married Bill' for instance; to the meanings of causality, the meaning of 'Mary came into the room, and Bill left' or 'Bill came into the room, and Mary left'. These potentials shape the forms and meanings of speech, and as echoes, shape the forms and meanings of writing, in all respects. The logic of space (and the absence of the demands of the logics of time) equally has consequences for planning and reception, and therefore for structures at any level – graphic marks, sentences, sub-textual and textual units. It also holds potentials, largely those of display in space. The material of sound has potentials which the material of the graphic does not, and vice versa. Each offers complementary potentials to other resources: display in space offers the complementary meanings of image and writing; sequence in time offers the complementary possibilities of gesture and speech. And similarly with all other materials, whether of sound, of graphic marks, of gesture, of action or of 3D construction.

These differences in potential can be worked and have been, in different cultures and in different historical periods, into the distinctive potentials of different modes. At times similarities have been foregrounded. The points at which there are contacts of particular strengths between speech and writing are between letter and sound; between spoken word and written word; and, a major point of contact, at the level of the unit of the clause. It could be said that 'language' is the modal resource which is distinctive and unified by having *names in arrangements*; and which differs from the mode of the visual, for instance, in the logics and the materialities of that realisation. Perhaps the connections at these points are strong enough to retain the notion of 'language' as an important one.

At the present moment we are once again at a point where the relation of speech and writing, and the questions around 'language', are being remade. The new technologies of information and communication are playing a significant role in that, and one part of my aim in this book is to describe and to speculate about that new set of relations, and the consequent changes to speech, to writing, and above all, of course, to the notion of 'literacy'.

34

4

LITERACY AND MULTIMODALITY

A theoretical framework

A need for new thinking

The changes in the conditions surrounding literacy are such that we need to reconsider the theory which has, explicitly or implicitly, underpinned conceptions of writing over the last five or six decades. I have already said, insistently, that the major change is that we can no longer treat literacy (or 'language') as the sole, the main, let alone the major means for representation and communication. Other modes are there as well, and in many environments where writing occurs these other modes may be more prominent and more significant. As a consequence, a linguistic theory cannot provide a full account of what literacy does or is; language alone cannot give us access to the meaning of the multimodally constituted message; language and literacy now have to be seen as partial bearers of meaning only. The co-presence of other modes raises the question of their function: are they merely replicating what language does, are they ancillary, marginal, or do they play a full role, and if they do, is it the same role as that of writing or a different role? And if they play a different role, is that because of their constitution, their make-up, because of their affordances? But if that were the case, we would need to ask whether language – as speech or as writing – has its special potentials and its limitations, its own affordances. That is a new question to ask of language and of literacy.

There is a consequence for notions of meaning: if the meaning of a message is realised, 'spread across', several modes, we need to know on what basis this spreading happens, what principles are at work. Equally, in reading, we need now to gather meaning from all the modes which are co-present in a text, and new principles of reading will be at work. Making meaning in writing and making meaning in reading both have to be newly thought about.

Here I will outline some elements of such a theory of literacy; it cannot be complete, but it may provide some useful tools. This theory, as I said, cannot be a linguistic theory. The modes which occur, together with the language-modes of speech and writing, on pages or screens, are constituted on different principles to those of language; their materiality is different; and the work that cultures have done with them has differed also. The theoretical change is from linguistics to semiotics – from a theory that accounted for language alone to a theory that can account equally well for gesture, speech, image, writing, 3D objects, colour, music and no doubt others. Within that theory, the language-modes – speech and writing – will also have to be dealt with semiotically; they are now a part of the whole landscape of the many modes available for representation – though of course special still in that they have a highly valued status in society and, in the case of speech, certainly still carry the major load of communication.

The terms in that new theory that I will consider – even if only briefly – are inevitably a selection of those that one ought to look at. I have selected those which most prominently, obviously, tellingly, show a necessary new way of thinking about literacy. There is, first and foremost, the concept of *meaning*, and associated concepts such as *learning* and *creativity*. Something needs to be said about *semiotics* and *semiosis*. Clearly, the concept of *mode* is crucial in a multi-modal theory of literacy, and so are associated concepts such as inherent and culturally made *affordance*, *modal specialisation*, *functional load* and *materiality*. In a semiotic theory the foundational concept is that of the *sign*; associated with that are concepts such as *interest*, *analogy*, and *metaphor*. In my conception of *sign* it is both *motivated* and *conventional*, which is certainly not the position taken in the mainstream of thinking. In a semiotic theory, concepts such as *representation* and *communication*, and *interpretation* and *articulation*, are clearly right in the centre of attention.

A new theory of meaning cannot do without the concept of *transformation*; it explains how the modal resources provide users of the resource with the ability to reshape the (form of the) resources at all times in relation to the needs of the interests of the sign-maker. Transformation needs to be complemented by the concept of *transduction*. While transformation operates on the forms and struc-tures within a mode, transduction accounts for the shift of 'semiotic material' – for want of a better word – across modes. This relates entirely to the (psycho-logical) processes of synaesthesia, which clearly have a semiotic analogue. It is in the realm of synaesthesia, seen semiotically as transduction and transforma-tion, that much of what we regard as 'creativity' happens. A theory that deals with multimodality comes up against the need for a usable definition of *text*, given that our present sense of text comes from the era of the dominance of the mode of writing, and the dominance of the medium of the book. We need to become clear how we wish to use the term text and the units internal to it; we need at the same time to be clear about the principles of organisation and shap-ing of text, such as *coherence* and *cohesion*. There are then the other principles of organisation which shape text, above all *genre* and *discourse*. And in a way that was not obvious before the era of the new media of information and communi-cation, it is absolutely essential now to consider the *sites and media of the appearance* of text, above all the *page* and the *screen*.

So something needs to be there in the theory about the (*new* and the *old*) *media of information and communication*, and their *facilities*. The world of communi-cation is now constituted in ways that make it imperative to highlight the concept of *design*, rather than of concepts such as acquisition, or competence, or critique. This is particularly essential given new requirements of education – even if these are not at the moment (officially) recognised. It is no longer responsible to let children experience school without basing schooling on an understanding of the shift from competent performance to design as the foundational fact of contemporary social and economic life. The world of the new economies that I have earlier alluded to makes that an essential requirement. In multimodal communication, the concept of design is the sine qua non of informed, reflective and productive practice. The opposition between the linked terms of *knowledge* and *information* hovers around here, and within these there is something about mode, ontology and *epistemology*, and about *modality* in the more traditional sense of 'proximity to truth'. Many other terms are significant, but among these none more so than that of *reading path*: it plays hugely into older and newer conceptions of the processes and the real tasks of reading. Because the present state and the likely future of literacy causes such anxiety – at times at least partially justified – I want to say something briefly about the affordances of writing and image, and perhaps of speech as well. This may be useful in countering some of what seem to me unjustified outbursts of cultural pessimism around the move from writing to image.

A 'toolkit'

The concept of *meaning* has been difficult enough to grapple with in the modes of speech and writing, and the subdisciplines of linguistics such as semantics and pragmatics set up specifically to deal with a basic flaw in most theories of language have not – unsurprisingly – been able to provide satisfactory accounts. In a multimodal framework the general questions remain, though the approach, given the semiotic framework, differs. There is no question of separating form from meaning; the sign is always meaning-as-form and form-as-meaning. The means of dealing with meaning are different; we need to understand how meanings are made as signs in distinct ways in specific modes, as the result of the interest of the maker of the sign, and we have to find ways of understanding and describing the integration of such meanings across modes, into coherent wholes, into texts.

Meaning is the result of (semiotic) work, whether as *articulation* in the outwardly made sign, as in writing, or as *interpretation* in the inwardly made sign, as in reading. The semiotic work done in the reading of text in alphabetic writing is twofold. It is the work of filling the elements of writing with content. In fact the task resembles that of forming hypotheses about the 'content' of these elements, and it is the work of making sense of these elements in all the possible combinations which they can contract with each other in the text. These elements may be sentences (though they may also be units above the sentence, whether several tightly or loosely connected sentences, or the unit of the paragraph), or clauses, or phrases, or words in phrases.

My comment about 'filling with content' is a contentious view of the lexical element 'word'. It assumes that words are signifiers, not signs – that is, that they are forms with potentials for becoming signs. The 'filling with content' is then based on our prior experience of such elements. Say that I have encountered the signifier *tree* many times; each time I have encountered it, it was as a sign made by someone. I will have used it many times, and each time I used it, it was as a sign: the joining of a form with my meaning of that moment. I have a history of encountering the element *tree*, which helps me – as does the environment in which it is used – in forming a hypothesis about what the signified might be on this occasion. The word/sign *tree* uttered on a walk in the sandstone landscapes around Sydney will have a different signified (a somewhat stunted, twisted, gnarled, olive green, though beautiful plant) than it will have uttered in the forests of southern Finland (a regularly shaped, deep green, tall, impressive, rather than beautiful, plant). *Reading as interpretation* is the making of a new sign from the sign that I have received as a signifier. I fill that signifier with my meaning. In *articulation* I use a signifier, say *tree*, and fill it with my meaning; on this occasion it might be some stunted thing in a large pot in a front garden, that I need to speak or write about: 'Your tree isn't looking all that healthy. Don't you think it'd do better if you'd put it in the ground?' Someone else might not be prepared to use the signifier *tree* for this plant; having lived all their life in the splendid forests of central Europe; their experience of the signifier *tree* rules it out as a possibility.

Much the same considerations apply to knowledge about the syntactic (and grammatical) status of the elements of writing – we know that this word functions as a *noun*, as a *subject* or an *object noun*, this word functions as an *adjective*, and we know what these functions mean. We draw on this as on other kinds of knowledge to hypothesise about the significance of the combinations in which the elements occur.

To put this very simply, when I read in my newspaper on 1 February 2002, 'Capricorn: Good news, good news, good news. Four delightful contacts from four gorgeous planets are making things a little easier than of late, actually a lot easier', I need to know what 'news' means – not something like 'the news on the radio', and that 'good news' means something like 'feel happy' rather than 'the scriptures according to St John the Evangelist'. I would want to know what 'contacts' in 'four delightful contacts' might mean, and I would need to assess just how large or small 'little' was in 'a little easier' and so on. I would also need to know that the repetition of 'good news' is a form of intensification, a kind of 'very'; that there is an implied 'for you' in 'are making things a little easier than of late' and so on. This may seem too banal to mention even, though I believe it is not; we have learned to assume that these things are obvious and unproblematic, though for every reader who pays even slight attention to the horoscope 'little' is likely to have a different meaning, depending on just how good or bad their day has been up to this moment.

Of course we do have a sense of what 'little' can mean, because of what it has meant in all the instances in which we have encountered it before. The hypotheses which we form in reading as to what a word, a phrase, a clause, might mean proceed on the basis of the outward 'look' of that element as we have met it many times before – whether it is the 'lexical form', the word 'look' or the abstract grammatical or syntactic or textual form. Whatever that form or element might be – a genre, a sentence type, a grammatical category, a word – it is the best available indicator to the meaning of the element.

These hypotheses are based on the experience of the reader, available to her or him usually as implicit knowledge about the shape and the previous meanings of the elements encountered. The taking of information or meaning from the text is therefore always an approximation. When as a reader I see a word, a phrase, a genre, I say to myself, 'I have encountered this before and it has meant these things; it is likely to mean something broadly in that same range.' From the perspective of the text-*maker*, the reader's meanings are always approximations. As I said, in reading, the reader 'fills' the form with her or his meaning, hence the form as interpreted by the reader is always a transformation of the maker's meaning. The result of that transformation is then available to the reader as (new) information or knowledge about the world, and is assimilated in its transformed shape into the reader's existent knowledge. Its assimilation or integration into the reader's existent knowledge produces a re-arrangement of all the elements there – however infinitesimally slight that rearrangement might be – amounting to a transformation of all the meanings of all the elements and of their interrelations. Getting meaning from reading is the effect of a process something like this, and meaning 'is taken' at the moment when the 'taken meaning' is integrated into the existing totality of all meaning in the brain. At that point I, the reader, know 'the meaning' of what I have read, for myself. Indeed, meaning cannot ever be other or more than meaning for myself.

In writing, meaning is made at the moment when 'that which is to be meant' is fused with 'that which can mean it', that is, when a meaning is matched with a form/signifier by the writer, in the most apt fashion possible. That meaning is complex, because it is both that which the 'meaner' wishes to mean, as her or his interest in meaning, and the manner in which she or he knows that they have to produce their meaning as an appropriate shaping of that meaning for the social environment in which the meaner's meaning is to be communicated. In other words, the meaning to be expressed has to be shaped to its social environment to make it suit the maker's sense of the needs of the environment of communication. For instance, I know that I need to speak to the powerful in a certain way, or write to them in a certain way, distinctly different to the way in which I speak or write to someone who is not as powerful as I am.

In both writing and reading, meaning is the result of (semiotic) work. Work always changes those who do the work, and it changes that which is worked on. The resources through which meaning is made are changed in the process of meaning-making, but so is the inner disposition of those who have made that meaning inwardly in interpretation or outwardly in articulation. The process of inward meaning-making and the resultant change to the state of an inner semiotic resource is called *learning*. However, the process of outward meaning-making also has a transformative effect. Again, the signmaker's resources have been changed, because the sign made outwardly is a new sign, and even though it is made from existing meaning-resources, it is nevertheless made into a new sign by the conjunction of an existing form with the new meaning; a conjunction which, it is safe to say, will never have been made in that way before. The inner transformations produce *learning*, and learning is the shaping of the subjectivity of the maker of signs. The transformations that are part of outward articulation produce new syntactic, textual or lexical forms, which play their role, however slightly, in changing the resource which was used in making meaning. This is how *semiotic change* happens – whether a change to writing, to speech, to gesture. But it is also the way in which that semiotic change, the change in the modal resources, always reflects and tracks the values, structures and meanings of the social and cultural world of the meaning-maker and of the socio-cultural group in which they are.

Learning is not a term that belongs in semiotics; sign-making is. However, learning and sign-making are two sides of one sheet of paper as Saussure might have said; which side we choose to look at depends on the perspective from which we are looking. Both learning and sign-making are dynamic processes which change the resources through which the processes take place – whether as *concepts* in psychology or as *signs* in semiotics – and change those who are involved in the processes. This makes both learning and representing/communicating into dynamic active processes, far removed from inert notions such as 'acquisition'.

The process of sign-making that I have outlined here entails that the sign is always new, whether it is the sign made in interpretation or the sign made in articulation. This is far removed from notions of language *use* in which a stable system with stable elements is *used* by the language *user* but not changed by her or him. In that approach to semiosis – and of course this would be the case with all modes – creativity is rare, it is special and exceptional, allowed to special individuals – poets, painters, musicians. In my approach, *creativity* is ordinary, normal; it is the everyday process of semiotic work as making meaning. Such an approach has, I believe, vast pedagogical, social and political consequences. From this new perspective it is possible to see that until now we have viewed human semiotic work in a way which is distorting: seen from the older perspective this now normal creative activity is classified as deviation or error; that which is most characteristically human is ruled out of court, not admissible.

Semiotics is the science of the life of signs in society, according to Saussure. The move from linguistics to semiotics is first and foremost a move from a primary concern with form to a concern with form-and-meaning; it is a move from a concern with form in one mode – if we see language-as-such as a mode, or two modes – if we see speech and writing as distinct modes (as I do), to a concern with form-and-meaning in many modes. The move is away from a theory in which form is dealt with separately from meaning. It is also a move from the assumption – implicitly or explicitly held – that linguistic theory can provide a satisfactory and generally applicable account of representation and communication, to the realisation that we need a theory which is not specific to, or derived from, one mode but which applies to all modes. Mainstream linguistics has largely focused on form – in semiotic terms, the signifier; meaning had been exported to peripheral disciplines – semantics, pragmatics, socio-linguistics, stylistics. For most of the twentieth century, linguistics has been the science of the signifier. Semiotics by contrast is the science of the sign, a fusion of form/signifier and meaning/signified. Semiotics promises to provide categories which apply to representation and communication in all modes equally. At the same time, that semiotic theory will tell us that when we deal with a mode at a more specific level we need to use terms and descriptions which pertain to that specific mode. But the terms that deal with a specific mode – let us say writing – will still be *semiotic terms*, not the terms of linguistic theories. There is no switching of theories as we move from one level – of multimodal description – to another – of specific mode description.

Semiotics has been the domain of two large schools of thought; one deriving from the work of the Swiss linguist Ferdinand de Saussure, the other deriving from the work of the American philosopher Charles Sanders Peirce. The semiotics of Saussure bears recognisable traces of its origins in the historical linguistics of the nineteenth century. In it, the sign is taken to be an arbitrary combination of form and meaning, of *signifier* and *signified*, a combination which is sustained by the force of social convention. In the example usually quoted, Saussure said that even though the object in the world referred to by the word *tree* in English or *arbre* in French is the same object, the sound-forms which represent this same object in the two languages are very different, proving that the relation of form and meaning was an arbitrary one. This embodies a fundamental error, a confusion which has gone unrecognised by and large, and endlessly repeated. It is a mistake about levels and forms: *the level of the signified tree – the meaning – is matched by the level at which the signifier is lexical form – the word*: not phonetic or phonological form as Saussure is said to have stated. In Saussure's formulation the level of meaning is mismatched with the level of sound; meaning is thought to be realised in sound. But the matching of signified with signifier is always like with like, and realisation is like with like. The signifier/form for the signified/meaning *tree* is the lexical form/signifier 'tree'.

In Peirce's semiotics the focus is less on the internal constitution of the sign than on the uses of the sign by readers/users, and on the relation of the sign to that which it represents. Peirce focused on what the sign represented, on the object/*referent* in the world, on how it was interpreted, assuming that there was no meaning until there was an interpretation. This he called the *interpretant*. He focused on the sign-characteristics from the point of view of the type of relation between signifier and that which it represented, something that seems to have been of only marginal interest to Saussure. Peirce consequently distinguishes between *iconic signs*, which in their form parallel the meaning of the signified – the drawing of flames to mean fire; *indexical signs*, in which there is a relation of 'consequence', as in smoke signalling combustion; and *symbolic signs*, where the relation between form and meaning was largely sustained by convention – the red cross of the Red Cross. Hence there is a distinct difference in focus between the two theorists, which could be taken to mean that they had produced distinct and potentially irreconcilable theories. In fact, the two theories are compatible and complementary, if one accepts their different foci.

In my use of the concept of sign I reject the idea of arbitrariness. I assume that the relation between signifier and signified is always motivated, that is, that the shape of the signifier, its 'form', materially or abstractly considered, is chosen because of its *aptness* for expressing that which is to be signified. That is, the shape of the signifier offers itself in its material 'shape' as an *apt* expression for that which is to be signified. In effect, I take Peirce's iconic sign as the model of all relations of signs to their referents. The example which I have used on a number of occasions is that of a drawing by a three-year-old boy (see Figure 4.1).

The three-year-old drew this, sitting on my lap. As he was drawing he said, 'Do you want to watch me? I'll make a car . . . got two wheels . . . and two

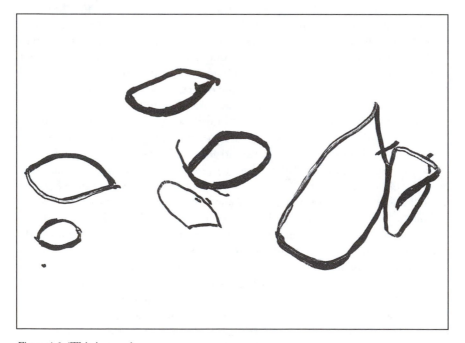

Figure 4.1 'This is a car'

42

wheels at the back . . . and two wheels here . . . that's a funny wheel.' When he had finished he said, 'This is a car.' This was the first time he had named a drawing – rather than, as frequently until then, providing a running account of what he was drawing. Had he not provided the 'key' himself, I might still be puzzling – or rather, I would hardly have remembered this example. A car was defined by him by the criterial characteristic of 'having wheels', and his representation focused on that which he wanted to represent: 'wheelness'. To a three-year-old that may well be the most significant thing about a car, whether in looking from his position in the world at the (wheels of the) car, or in the action of wheels. The three-year-old's *interest* is most plausibly condensed into and expressed as 'wheels'. Wheels are themselves plausibly and aptly represented by circles, both because of their look and because of their motion.

This sign is a double sign: once circles as signifying 'wheel', and once as wheels signifying 'car'. But each of the two signs is not an arbitrary conjunction of signifier (circle) with signified (wheel), and signifier (wheels) with signified (car). The relation is – thinking in terms of 'shapes' – iconic, or – thinking in terms of the principles of the connection – motivated. 'Principles of connection' for me is the principle of *analogy*, itself the principle of the formation of metaphor. Circles are apt forms for meaning wheels; 'circles are (like) wheels' – the principle of analogy, so circle is a metaphor for wheel; 'wheels are like cars', so wheels here is a metaphor for car. 'Many wheels' is an apt way – particularly if you are three years old – for meaning car. Whether we see this as a motivated sign or as a metaphor – it is both – it is the interest of the sign-maker at the moment of making the sign that leads to the selection of the criteria for representing that which is to be represented – 'wheel-ness' and 'car-ness' here, and for selecting the signifier which most aptly, most plausibly represents it.

Since I first used this example I have been shown other instances of wheel-cars; sometimes they have been steering wheels, or the wheels surrounding logos, or the actual wheels. What that shows is that there is, clearly, a quite general feature here, one which can become the principal criterion for representation. Two points follow from this. One, there are other possible criteria of course for representing 'car': the sound of the engine, for instance, is one; and later shape, colour, speed and power, become significant, as does imagined use. Gender plays its part early on, and imagined use combined with gendered imagination produces its specific forms – cars to be comfortably sociable in, or cars for mowing down pedestrians. Two, representation as sign is always partial: that which the sign-maker regards as criterial about the thing signified forms the basis of the sign. There is no means of knowing – other than broad cultural tendencies – what will be chosen as criterial, and so there is no way of predicting absolutely what the sign for an object or phenomenon will be. However, the signifier(s) chosen will always be apt for the signifieds. So the signs will never be an arbitrary conjunction of form and meaning, and from the shape of the signifier the reader/viewer/hearer will form their hypothesis about the sign as a whole.

This is the approach to sign, in any mode and at any level, which I adopt. It applies to writing and speech no less than to image. It means that signs are always meaningful conjunctions of signifiers and signifieds; it means that we can look at the signifiers and make hypotheses about what they might be signifying in any one instance, because we know that the form chosen was the most apt expression of that which was to be signified. The theory demands that we assume that all aspects of a sign represent their maker's interest in representing that which they regarded as most salient, at this moment, about the object or phenomenon to be represented. It entails that all aspects of form are meaningful, and that all aspects of form must be read with equal care: nothing can be disregarded. In a multimodal approach to writing this is essential. In social semiotics this is the key to unlocking meaning.

The making of signs, outwardly as articulation or inwardly as interpretation, complex or simple, large or small, in the socially shaped environments of everyday lives, is the process of *semiosis*. That process is ceaseless, and for most of the time the process is invisible. At particular moments it does become noticeable – visible, audible, tangible, tasteable – when there is an occasion to make signs outwardly. There is at that moment a decision about the mode in which the meaning which is to be made should be realised. I have used the metaphor of *fixing*, as in the (now old-fashioned) chemical process of developing photographs. It matters which mode, and therefore which materiality, is used to 'fix' the meanings. Of course, for most of these moments the mode in which that fixing is to happen is already settled: news appears in print, in sound, in sound and image, in sound, image and writing. Ph.D. theses by and large still appear in print; fashion magazines as much as Playstation magazines appear in print and image – with colour a foregrounded mode. But at other times there is the possibility of choice – how much writing, if any, to use on a website, how much image, what colour, whether soundtrack and moving image. In fact in the present period these possibilities of choice are increasing, which constitutes an important reason for a focus on design.

This approach to signs entails that *representation* is always 'engaged', it is never neutral: that which is represented in the sign, or in sign complexes, realises the interests, the perspectives, the positions and values, of those who make signs. The outwardly made sign, the sign made in the process of *articulation*, functions in *communication*, and so it must necessarily fit into the structures of power which characterise situations of communication. The sign-maker must factor that into the making of the sign – it must be fit for its role in the social field of communication. Communication is 'outward'; *interpretation* is inward. The sign that comes to the receiver in communication is taken by her or him as an object for interpretation; in the act of interpretation, a new sign is formed. Interpretation is of course also 'interested'; the receiver of the sign treats the sign as a prompt for interpretation, not for decoding even though that is the popularly accepted assumption. The receiver sees, hears or feels only the form, the signifiers, and from their 'shape' and on the basis of her or his knowledge of the social place where the sign/message has come from, and on the basis of her or his *interest*, will produce a signified and hence a sign as her or his meaning from it. This is Peirce's *interpretant*. There is a chain of semiosis in which the sign leads to an interpretant, which itself becomes an object/referent for a new sign in communication, which is the basis for the forming of yet another interpretant. Through conventions of many kinds, society keeps this process relatively firmly controlled, sometimes and in some domains very much so, sometimes and in some domains hardly at all, not least by conventions around what may be thought and communicated. If that were not the case communicability would be lessened or threatened.

In the era of the new technologies of information and communication, mode and choice of mode is a significant issue. *Mode* is the name for a culturally and socially fashioned resource for representation and communication. Mode has material aspects, and it bears everywhere the stamp of past cultural work, among other things the stamp of regularities of organisation. These regularities are what has traditionally been referred to as a grammar and syntax. In the high era of the book, of writing and of print, choice of mode was not an issue, or seemed far less so: books were covered in print, though of course, images of various kinds could also appear. Walls of churches were covered with images, and there were spaces specially made for statuary. The relation of mode and medium – writing and book, painting and wall – was then nearly invisible, through the naturalising effects of long-standing convention. When we can choose mode easily, as we now can through the facilities of the new media, questions about the characteristics of mode arise, in ways that they had not really done before: what can a specific mode do? What are its limitations and potentials? What are the *affordances* of a mode? The *materiality* of mode, for instance the material of *sound* in *speech* or in *music*, of *graphic matter* and *light* in *image*, or of the *motion of parts of the body* in *gesture*, holds specific potentials for representation, and at the same time brings certain limitations. Cultures work with these material affordances in ways which arise from and reflect their concerns, values and meanings.

One fundamental distinction brought with the materiality of mode is that of space and of time. Time-based modes – *speech, dance, gesture, action, music* – have potentials for representation which differ from space-based modes – *image, sculpture* and other *3D forms* such as *layout, architectural arrangement, streetscape*. The fundamental logics of the two types of mode differ. The logic of space leads to the spatial distribution of simultaneously present significant elements; and both the elements and the relations of the elements are resources for meaning. The logic of time leads to temporal succession of elements, and the elements and their place in a sequence constitute a resource for meaning. Each of these leads, in the culturally and socially valued modes such as speech and writing and image, to preferred textual/generic forms: *narrative* in speech and in writing, and *display* in visual modes.

Some modes – gesture, but writing also – are mixed, in that they participate in both logics: gesture is in the logic of space and of time; writing to some extent also. It leans heavily still – in alphabetically recorded languages – on the temporality of speech but has begun to make use of spatial resources, both actually and virtually: actually in spacings (spaces between letters, words), line forms, paragraphs, but also with other spatial features such as indents, bullet points, blocks of writing; and virtually, in the hierarchical structures of the syntax of writing. But mixed logics are, above all, a feature of *multimodal texts*, that is, texts made up of elements of modes which are based on different logics. Mixed logics pose new questions: of reading, but also of *design* in writing.

The distinct representational and communicational affordances of modes lead to their *functional specialisation*, either over time, by repeated uses in a culture, or by the interested use of the individual sign-maker/designer. That is, if writing is better for representing events in sequence, and image is better for representing the relation of elements in space, then it is likely that each will be chosen according to what it is best for. There is no inevitability about that, however: for a long period in the 'West', writing was used for tasks for which image is now beginning to be more commonly used. A culture can work with or against affordances, for reasons that lie with concerns other than representation. In multimodal texts, information may be carried largely in one mode, more than in others. There will therefore be a difference in the *functional load* which each mode carries. In school textbooks of thirty, forty years ago, most of the functional load was carried by writing; now that relation has become inverted, and much or most of the load is carried by images of various kinds. This varies from school-subject to school-subject, as it varies from social domain to social domain.

The materiality of modes has, as one other consequence, the effect of mode in relation to the physiology of bodily reception and production of meaning. Sound has its physiological channels of reception, as does sight, and so of course do all modes, through touch and feel, smell, taste. Each of these sensory channels is capable in principle of being developed culturally for full communication and representation – as touch is in Braille, for instance, for the sight-impaired. But beyond that, the bodilyness of mode has quite other implications which have to be considered in a new theory of meaning. The affective affordances of sound are entirely different to those of sight or those of touch; sound is more immediately tangibly felt in the body than is sight, but certainly differently felt. A theory of meaning that is inattentive to these will not be able to provide fully satisfactory accounts of the new communicational forms.

Human semiosis is constantly and ceaselessly engaged in representing the world, with resources which are never fully adequate to this task. For that reason, the process of *transformation* is central: that which is not adequate is transformed in the processes of writing and of reading – and in other processes – into something that is more nearly adequate. At the same time, transformation is a much better explanation of processes of apperception and of integration – as in reading for instance – than are notions such as acquisition.

Transformation works at every level and in every mode, though in the theoretical framework here, I use the term for processes operating within the one mode only. Transformation is a resource for establishing links between categories, and for producing new resources out of existing resources. I treat transformation strictly as a process which works on a given structure and its elements, and changes that structure and its elements in specific describable ways.

For operations which involve shifts across modes, I use the term *transduction*. When a science teacher asks a class to 'write a story' of the movement of a red blood cell around the body, he is asking the class to perform a task in which 'knowledge' presented in the modes of (a mix of) image, 3D model, speech, gesture and writing is to be re-presented in one mode, that of writing. In this task, knowledge which was configured through the affordances of the various modes is 'drawn across' into one, often a different, mode. This is not the process of transformation, the process which works on a structure and its elements in one mode, but of transduction, a process in which something which has been configured or shaped in one or more modes is *re*configured, *re*shaped according to the affordances of a quite different mode. It is a change of a different order, a more thoroughgoing change.

Communication – whatever the mode – always happens as *text*. The 'stuff' of our communication needs to be fixed, in the sense of my metaphor above, in a mode: knowledge or information has no outward existence other than in such modal fixing. This fixing provides the material resource through which or in which it is to be materialised. It does not provide the shape that it is to have. That shape is textual. Text is the result of social action, of work: it is work with representational resources which realise social matters. Two of these are crucial in my approach. First, the matter of the social relations of participants in social events – who is involved, with what purposes, what roles, what power, in what environments. The expression of these social matters gives one kind of shape to text, namely that of *genre*. Second, the social matter of 'what is at issue', 'what is being talked about'. Following the work of Michel Foucault, I call this *discourse*. Here the assumption is that that which is talked about is not simply there, but is shaped in specific ways in social institutions, whose meanings shape that which is at issue. When I talk to my neighbour about a complaint that I have, I do this in my everyday way of talking; when I see 'my' doctor, she or he will immediately talk about the 'same thing' in quite other ways, ways that are formed in the institution of Western medicine. If I talk to another neighbour, he or she might recast what I am saying in yet other ways, because they might be followers of some form of alternative medicine – 'natural healing', perhaps. Nothing escapes the shaping influence of discourse, though any text is likely to be the site of emergence of a number of discourses at the same time, more or less effectively interwoven.

There is an important question of naming and definition to be dealt with around the term *text*. Does it refer to linguistically realised entities alone? Or only to those realised in writing? Can it include message entities which consist of image and writing? And if it can, do we then refer to the written part of the text differently than we do to the visual? One reason for the long use of 'text' for written entities alone was of course the fact that there had been no possibility of a record of spoken realisations until relatively recently; it is only over the last fifty years or so that records of speech could be made with some ease. Once these means had become available, the term 'text' began to be used for (recorded and/or transcribed) spoken entities as much as for written entities. The video recorder has begun to have a similar effect for other modes – movement, gesture, position in space. The accident of the availability of technologies for recording is just that – an accident, even if an important accident. The technologies should not cloud the broader theoretical issue. I will use the term *text* for any instance of communication in any mode or in any combination of modes, whether recorded or not. If it happened as communication it will have been 'recorded' in any case by the participants in that communicational event. And if this 'recording' is partial, as inevitably it must be, then it is simply differently partial than is the case with recordings made with contemporary technological means.

Texts have a *site of appearance*: simply, they have to appear somewhere. These sites of appearance have their inherent and culturally produced orderings and regularities, which have effects on the texts which appear in these sites. We cannot afford to overlook these effects. The *screen* is the currently dominant site of appearance of text, but screen is the site which is organised by the logic of image. Hence the logic of image orders the appearance of texts – whatever their modal realisation – on the screen. Until the last two or three decades, the page – usually as a part of the medium of the book – was the dominant site of appearance of text. The *page* was ordered by the logic of writing, even though it often contained images. But when images appeared on the page, they appeared subject to the logic of writing. Clearly the dominance of the screen and the fact that the logic of image dominates there does not mean that written texts (or writing in any form) cannot appear on the screen; they do, in enormous numbers. What it does mean is that the logic of image comes to dominate the ordering, shape, appearance and uses of writing. Writing will be subordinated to the logic of the screen, to the spatial logic of the image. Writing will inevitably become more image-like, and will be shaped by that logic. It then remains to understand what it will mean for writing to become image-like.

There is a further effect, in that the order and logic of the dominant site of appearance, the screen, comes to affect the site of the page, as of all other sites of communication. It is and has been apparent for a while now that pages are coming to resemble screens, both in terms of a much greater prevalence of images on the page as well as the appearance of the order of the screen in the layout of pages. In other words, even if we were to constrain our attention to pages alone, it would not be possible to ignore the effect of the ordering principles of the screen in their effects on writing.

The *new media of information* and *communication* have facilities which differ from those of the *older media of book* and *page*. Above all these consist in the potentials for action by writers and readers, makers of texts and remakers of texts, the matter, so called, of interactivity; they consist also, and as importantly, in the hugely greater facility for using a number of modes in the making of texts. This facility, the ready, easy use of images, means that image is readily available for representation and communication. I do not wish to argue that the technological facility is leading the change, not at all. But the technological facility coincides with social, cultural, economic and political changes, all of which together are producing and pushing that change.

Older aims in relation to literacy are simply no longer sufficient. In the era of the modernist state, of its secondary industries of mass-production, of the mass-organisation of that state's bureaucracy and economy, competent use of a resource, whatever it might have been, was prized. Competent use envisaged both a stable system of resources for representing – 'the' grammar of 'the' language – and a user of that system who was content with being able to use this resource competently. He or she would 'acquire' that grammar – whether as a first speaker of the language or as a learner of the resource as a foreign language to a level where competent use could be more or less guaranteed – at least at the level required, hence the notion of functional literacy.

This was never really a plausible model of language, of literacy, or of human beings as learners, though in a world of relative stability the fiction projected by the model could be sustained, even if with some effort, because of its utility in those circumstances. But the demands of communication now are such that something else is needed. In a world of stability, the competence of reliable reproduction was not just sufficient, but of the essence – on the production line as much as at the writing desk. In a world of instability, reproduction is no longer an issue: what is required now is the ability to assess what is needed in this situation now, for these conditions, these purposes, this audience – all of which will be differently configured for the next task.

What is required is the facility for *design*. Design does not ask, 'what was done before, how, for whom, with what?' Design asks, 'what is needed now, in this one situation, with this configuration of purposes, aims, audience, *and with these resources*, and given *my* interests in this situation?' This corresponds in any case to the dominant – that is, mythically leading – social, cultural and economic environment at the moment. In a multimodal environment the realisations of this are aided by the varying affordances of the modes and the facilities of the new media of information and communication. It is possible to choose, not merely with full competence within one mode – where of course design decisions were made even if they were not called that but were called 'stylistic choices' – but with full awareness of the affordances of many modes and of the media and their sites of appearance. Anything and everything is now subject to design: that which is to be communicated (in an educational context, the 'curriculum'; in other contexts, the 'message'); the modal realisation of the curriculum or of the message – as word, as image, as word and image, as colour, as moving image and sound; the site of appearance – the book or the screen, and if the screen, the website page or the CD-ROM?

This is an aim which encompasses and exceeds competence, and it encompasses and exceeds critique. Awareness of the affordances of modes and the facilities of media provides competence, but design crucially introduces the interest and the desire of the maker of the message/text. On the part of the reader, awareness of the affordances of mode and facilities of media allows her or him to know what prior uses there have been of the affordances of the resource in the message he or she is engaging with. That allows them to form their hypotheses about the purposes which may have given rise to this use of the resources. Critique is anchored to the ground of someone's past agendas; design projects the purposes, interests and desires of the maker into the future. Design is prospective not retrospective, constructive not deconstructive, utopian and not nostalgic.

Among the many things that are subject to design is the *reading path* of the text. In the traditional written text this was 'taken care of' by convention, though it could of course, and still can, be interrupted or disturbed if that was desired, either by the maker of the text or by its reader. By contrast, in Western images of most kinds the reading path is not automatically given or readily recoverable. It may be constructed by the maker of the image through the many devices that are available to her or him, but the viewer might still not notice it, may in any case not wish to follow it, in part because convention has not regulated the viewing of image as strongly as it has the reading of written text. The reading path provides more than just a kind of handy rope or guide-rail along a difficult path; it marks the line along which a text is to be read 'properly'. I give examples which show that to follow different reading paths is to construct profoundly differing readings, epistemologically speaking. The new opposition which I describe in the chapter on reading is that between reading the world as told – *reading as interpretation* – and reading the world as shown – reading as imposing salience and order, *reading as design*. The former tends to go with the established reading path of the traditional written text, the latter with the to-be-constructed reading path of the image, or the to-be-constructed reading path of the multimodally constructed text.

It is becoming clear, unsurprisingly, that the affordances of different modes (together with matters such as generic form) have profound effects on that which is to be realised in the mode. This is the insight gained from the 'linguistic turn' of the 1970s, which showed that language was not a neutral vehicle for representation. All modes have that effect. Knowledge changes its shape when it is realised in the different modal material. Multimodality, and multimodal design, has therefore deep epistemological effects. The scientific entity *blood circulation* has a different *ontological 'shape'* represented in writing through the genre of diary, say, than represented in the spatial display of a concept map. The one is about movement in time from significant episode to significant episode; the other is about (in one such map that I have before me) relations of centrality

50

and marginality of concepts. Other modal effects have to do with factuality or non-factuality, with different forms of realism and naturalism, that is, they have effects on judgements about the 'truth' of a text. *Modality* in that sense is an issue that is very closely connected to modal choice, to design decisions, to the constructions of reading paths.

The 'decline of writing' and cultural pessimism: means for conducting a debate

Writing is such a potent metaphor for culture in general, that the move in the current landscape of communication from the dominance of writing to the dominance of image in many domains has given rise, understandably, to much anguish, soul-searching and deeply pessimistic predictions about the future welfare of civilisation. The approach through multimodality offers one means for conducting a debate about what is a deeply significant issue. The concept of affordance gives us the means to ask about the potentials and limitations of the different modes, and at least to begin to examine what might be real or potential losses, and what might be real gains in this move, and in what areas they might occur. This might allow us – cultural pessimists or not – to say, 'these are things which we ought not to give up, and for these reasons'. This book is not the place to conduct this debate in any extended fashion, but it can be the place for starting it in a way that goes beyond mere polemic, and might suggest the framework within which a productive argument might be conducted around this question.

Modes and fitness for purpose

Let me start with a simple example. I have here a no-smoking sign, from a coffee bar that a colleague and I visit frequently (Figure 4.2 overleaf). On the one side is the image with the caption, and on the other side is the detail of the smoking policy of the institution in which the coffee bar is located. The sign is placed on each table, in a hard plastic stand, so that both sides are visible. We might ask the question of gains and losses, of modes suited and not suited to specific tasks. What is quite clear is that while the two sides are both instructions or rules not to smoke, the two sides actually do quite different things. The image is clear and unambiguous: it says, 'do not smoke'. The other, the institution's 'smoking policy', is much more hedged, and even after several readings it is just about impossible to know when you can or cannot smoke.

It is clear that image would be extremely bad for communicating the detail of the written version; and it seems equally clear that the written version is just about useless as an easily read, quickly apprehended and clear sign to act in a particular way. The social life of this institution is obviously a complex one, particularly around the issue of smoking, and so the detail recorded here is no doubt the imperfect resolution of long debates. Nevertheless, if your life

NO SMOKING

RADA

SMOKING POLICY

In the RADA Bar ...

Smoking is restricted to the two designated smoking tables through the day from 9am to 6pm

On non-performance days all smoking restrictions are lifted between 6pm to 11pm, except for Foyer Events when the artistes have requested a smoke free environment

During performance days, smoking is not permitted between 6pm and 7.30pm when pre-show suppers are being served

Between 7.30pm and the end of the performance smoking is restricted to the two designated smoking tables.

All smoking restrictions are lifted at the end of the performance

YOUR COOPERATION IS APPRECIATED

Figure 4.2 No smoking sign

depended on it, you would want to have the image; if you were litigious, the image would be useless and the written text essential. In the overall context of institutional life here, it is also clear that the two modes perform complementary functions. If there was only the written version, the place would be full of smoke; if there was only the image, there would be fierce arguments by smokers insisting on their rights. (There is a discussion of just this kind of text in the chapter on genre, so I will not bother to do any further analysis here.)

What *is* clear, even from this extremely cursory discussion, is that the two modes have different affordances, and therefore each might fit more readily into one social situation than another. That would be something to investigate: which type of situation does each of these fit best; which of these situations occurs in what domains? Which is increasing; which is diminishing? There are many questions in this direction.

Modes and the shaping of knowledge

Let me move to my next example, which contrasts a written with a visual representation of 'the same phenomenon': blood circulation. The teacher had, in the one instance, asked the children to write a 'story' of the journey of a red blood cell around the body. In the other case the teacher had asked groups of children, two or three in each case, to construct 'concept maps', also of blood circulation. Apart from the fact that the children responded in the most varied ways to the generically vague term 'story' – from diary, as here (see Figure 4.3), to fairy tale, to James Bond thriller, to scientific report – and that each of these generic forms in itself has affordances in respect to this task, I want to focus on the affordances of the mode of writing and the mode of image, in the genre represented here.

In this brief analysis I will focus on the notion of movement. In the written mode, there is a requirement to lexicalise movement, to name it. That is, the writer has to find words to represent movement – *leave, come, squeeze, drop off, enter*. This requirement for naming is, from the point of view of the exercise set here, an irrelevance, an accident, a kind of 'noise'. The scientific account is interested in the abstracted notion of 'movement' and not in any of the specific lexicalisations of it; it is not interested in the meanings of the various words. They are a kind of unrequired by-product of using writing. And yet, if this

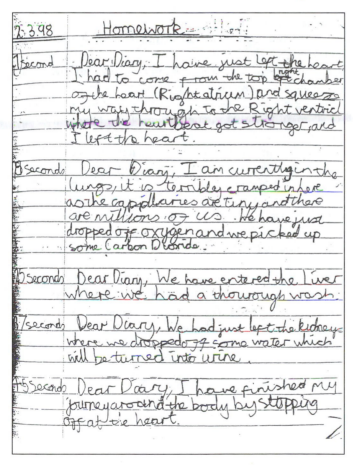

Figure 4.3 'Diary': a day in the life of a red blood cell

writer were to use the word 'move' constantly, he would feel uncomfortable, and even the science teacher might say, 'can't you find some different words, this is a bit repetitive'. This is a further accident, not a part of the mode but a part of the conventions of the use of the mode, namely that there should be variety.

The generic aspect of the text, namely that there are identifiable chunks of time, is again accidental, but this accident works well in this case – it corresponds to one manner in which the teacher had taught this phenomenon: the blood cells moving from 'organ' to 'organ' as a motion from one place to another place, doing their specific task at each, or having things done to them. But the epistemological commitment which the mode of writing demands, namely the (various) naming of the process 'moving', is not something that is part of the curriculum. The fact that each clause reports movement, in some way, with an agent that moves, and a location where it moves from or to, is also useful. So is the fact that the clauses are in temporal sequence, and that the chunks of time of the diary also stand in sequence. The genre *diary* was well chosen, and some of the affordances of writing – though definitely not all – serve the purposes of the task well.

In the concept map, by contrast, movement is indicated in a much sparser, less diverse, more abstracted way, as vectors with directionality or direction, that is, through arrows pointing from one 'place' to another. Of course, 'direction' is also a lexicalisation, a visual metaphor, in fact. Direction is not movement; it indicates the vector of movement. But here 'movement' is sparsely lexicalised, and each 'lexical item' carries just the one single meaning, whereas 'squeezed', for instance, carries meanings of movement, of constraint, and an evaluation of negativeness, and 'left' and 'came' carry indications of direction, 'from' and 'to'. Here there is just one lexical accident, not many as in the written text. Importantly, in the visual mode, repetition carries no stigma. In fact, were the arrow-shafts to be of various thicknesses, or of noticeably varied length, broken or dotted, these would be read as deliberate means of indicating different meanings.

One basic accident of the visual representation is the fact that whether wanted or not, meaning has to be expressed as spatial relations. A particular spatial ordering with its meanings has to be chosen; students chose different arrangements for their concept maps; as in Figures 4.4 and 4.5, for instance.

In the map in Figure 4.5, directionality is indicated in the left-to-right arrangement of the 'concepts', suggesting movement from left to right, by analogy with the reading direction of Western alphabetic writing. There are negative consequences of expressing meaning through spatial relations. Not only is it the case that one specific organisation has to be chosen – centrality and marginality; or central and concentric; or left as origin and movement to the right as destination – but also every instance of a particular relation means the same. The meaning necessarily dictated by choosing one element as central – as blood is in Figure 4.4 – means that other elements cannot be. But that

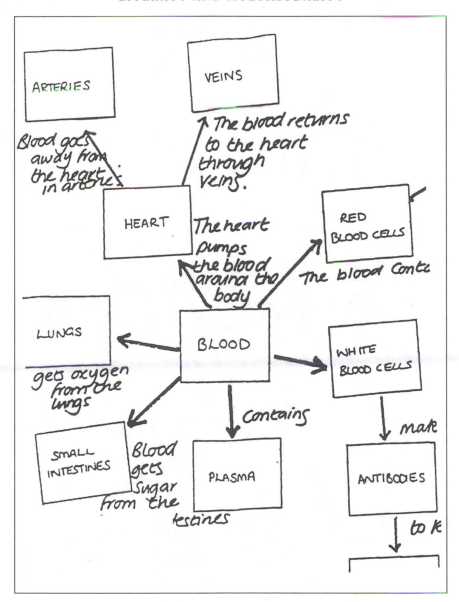

Figure 4.4 Concept map 1: blood circulation

might not be what the maker of the concept map intended. He might not have wished to make a choice; something of that is indicated in Figure 4.5, where there are two starting points, the heart and the lungs.

The problem of the single meaning of the relation has obviously struck the makers of these maps, who feel the need to supplement the arrows and lines

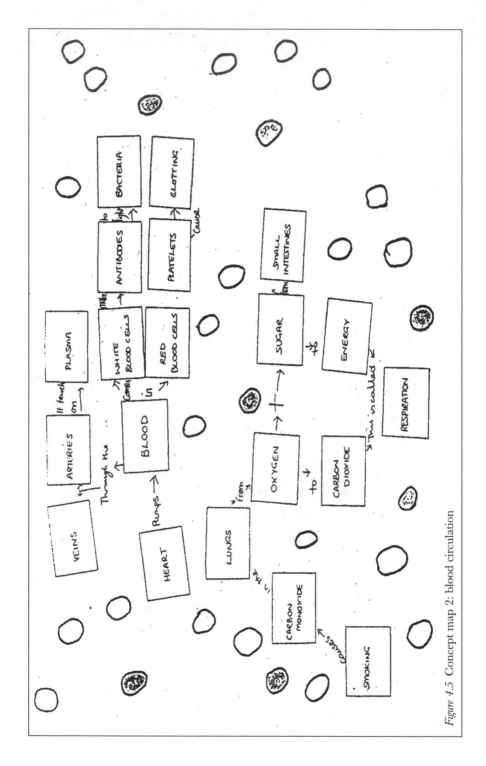

Figure 4.5 Concept map 2: blood circulation

with written labels of various kinds, indicating that in fact the different lines and arrows mean different things. Of course this may be an effect of the maker's relative incompetence in constructing such maps, or the relative unsuitability of the genre for this task – something that is not uncommon in demands made by teachers – but it does show a limitation of this mode in this genre.

Mode and epistemological commitment

Each mode demands what I shall call epistemological commitments. If I say 'a plant cell has a nucleus', I have been forced by the mode to provide a name for the relation between the cell and the nucleus. I have named it as a relation of possession, 'have'. If I draw the cell, and have been asked to indicate the nucleus, my drawing requires me to place the element that indicates the nucleus somewhere; I cannot avoid that epistemological commitment. Whether I actually think that it is just there, or whether I wanted to indicate a special place, I cannot avoid placing it somewhere. A viewer of my drawing is entitled to assume that 'there' is where it is supposed to be. My drawing, however, does not require me to say anything about possession, just as the writing did not require me to say where in the cell the nucleus is located.

Mode and causality

Causality may be one of the most significant of such accidents. If, in the diary, we read 'I . . . squeezed my way through', we know that the agent that did the squeezing is the agent who caused this action. Causation is just about built into clauses in languages such as English, with their noun-subject–verb–object structures, where noun-subject carries more or less implicitly the meaning of agentive cause. Sequence of events as represented in sequences of clauses is often open to a causal interpretation: 'we have just dropped off oxygen and we picked up some carbon dioxide' – 'because we had dropped off oxygen, we (could/did) pick up carbon dioxide'; or, 'we have entered the liver where we had a thorough wash'. At times the lexically expressed relations – as, and (because) – do this job of suggesting causality: 'it is terribly cramped in here, as [because] the capillaries are tiny and [because] there are millions of us. In the visual mode there are no implications of cause. In the case of the concept map, movement suggested by the arrows means 'point of origin' and 'point of destination', or it may mean origin and succession. Causality is not or only very weakly implied, if at all.

Spatial relations are not oriented to causality; no doubt causality can be conveyed by visual means, but more semiotic work needs to be done to achieve it. Temporal (sequential) relations, on the other hand, seem to be strongly oriented in that way. The (lexical) naming seems, from that point of view, to be a cultural strengthening of an affordance already inherently present for human interpreters in this mode.

Mode and conceptual-cognitive complexity

The move to multimodal representation, though I suspect as part of a much more widely ramified set of social processes, has given rise to a change in the mode of writing which can be variously described either as a move to simpler syntax, or as a move towards a more speech-like clausal syntax. Let me contrast two bits of writing from science textbooks for the same age-group – 12- to 13-year-olds – by focusing on the characteristics of sentences. 'One of the problems to which man has been turning his wits from earliest times is how to increase the comparatively small force which he can exert with his muscles into forces large enough to give him mastery over his environment' and 'In your first circuits you used torch bulbs joined with wires. Modern electrical equipment uses the same basic ideas. But if you look inside a computer there are not many wires or torch bulbs.' Apart from the noticeable difference in gendered aspects of language, we can see that the first sentence is syntactically complex; it consists of five clauses: 'man has been turning his wits'; 'the problem is . . .'; 'how to increase the small force'; 'he can exert'; 'give him mastery . . .' This kind of syntax is entirely usual for written texts in that period, the 1950s. By contrast, the sentences from the later text, from 1988, have one or two clauses, never more.

The definition of what a sentence is has proved notoriously elusive; my definition here is intended to serve my argument about gains and losses. If we take a clause as the report of an event or of a state of affairs in the world, a sentence is then a unit in which one or more such reports are unified into one complex representational and communicational entity. Simple things are joined, in often complex ways, to become complex things. A sentence, by its structure, says 'these things all belong closely together as one conceptual whole'. Seen in that light, the move from complex sentence-syntax to the simpler sentence-syntax of the more recent example gives away the means for constructing conceptually complex things. It is at this point that I believe the argument starts: what kind of use(fulness) attaches to such forms? Can we imagine a cultural world in which we do not have the means of making such complexes? Of course we can imagine humans not trained in the conceptual complexities of such forms, and not able to produce them – those who live largely in the world of speech do; they have forms which have constructed different means of being complex. But still, this is a resource which can be available to all. What cognitive and cultural consequences follow if that resource is no longer available?

At the same time, the page where the simple sentences quoted above occur is multimodally constructed (see Figure 9.7). A part of the task of reading that page is to make meaning from the two modes independently and in conjunction. This is a conceptually new task, and though we do not at the moment have the means for comparing the two kinds of task, we can tell they are different. In terms of 'reading', the one, with the complex syntax, asks that the reader follow the pre-given complexitites of the syntactic reading path; the other asks that the reader establish a reading path on the basis of criteria of her or his relevance. At the moment it is too difficult to know just what the conceptual-cognitive gains and losses are. It is, however, possible to say, with considerable certainty, that the tasks of reading the multimodal texts are entirely in line with tasks in quite other domains, where what is at issue is also the establishing of ordering on the basis of criteria of salience or relevance brought to the text by the reader, planner, designer and so on. The economy at large seems to be organised in this manner, from the micro-levels to the largest levels of organisation.

Mode, imagination and design

It seems obvious to me that mode is inseparable from cultural and from social but also – and especially because of its material aspects – from affective and cognitive matters. One truly profound question in the shifts in the modal uses in a culture will be that of the effect on forms of imagination. We all know the experience of having read a novel only to be utterly disappointed by seeing the film. 'The interpretation' of the director – to focus on just one figure – has clearly been entirely at odds with ours. This points straight at the basic task in reading written text: words in combination are not much more than rough out-lines waiting for us the readers to colour them in. What the written text provides is words in a clear order. Each word asks to be filled with meaning, a meaning that comes from our past experience of that word in our social lives. All our social lives – where we have lived them in broadly the same society – are shaped by the similarity of experiences, something that is much in the fore-ground, and shaped by the myriad of differences, something we need to leave in the background in everyday communication and interaction, but differences which are there, and are real. Writing provides relatively clear structures through syntactically and textually marked reading paths, for instance, along which are entities needing to be filled with meaning. This is the space for imagi-nation created by writing, by and large.

Of course, the possibilities of connections across elements, neither given nor constrained by a reading path, are myriad too, and they too provide the space for imagination. But this form of reading is already moving in the direction of the new forms of reading, as I will say several times in the book, where the reader imposes her or his ordering on a weakly ordered structure, or an entity with no clearly imposed order.

We are used to imagination of the one kind: receiving ordered structures, the elements of which need to be filled with our meanings. We are already in an era which may be defining imagination more actively, as the making of orders of our design out of elements weakly organised, and sought out by us in relation to our designs. In this, too, there is a relation between representation, communica-tion and the rest of the social and cultural world. Imagination in the sense that it was produced by engagement with the written text was a move towards an inner world; imagination in the sense that is required by the demands of design – the imposition of order on the representational world – is a move towards action in the outer world. One was the move towards contemplation; the other is a move towards outward action.

5

WHAT IS LITERACY?

Resources of the mode of writing

'Writing' or 'literacy'?

In the era of the screen and of multimodality some fundamental changes are inevitable as far as forms, functions and uses of writing are concerned. Maybe first and foremost there is the question of how the modes of image and writing appear together, how they are designed to appear together and how they are to be read together. There is the question then – a real question – in what direction writing is likely to move: will it move back towards speech-like forms, and become mere transcription of speech again, or will it move back in the direction of its image origins? And there is the old question of the resources of the mode of writing. In this book I cannot provide a grammar of writing, so in this chapter I focus on two aspects of this resource: the (relation of clause and) sentence, and the processes of transformation which operate at all levels, in forming sentences, in forming below-sentence structures, and in forming word-like entities. My purpose is to indicate two broad features or elements of writing, and to give a sense of the productive or generative potentials of the mode.

Whenever there are two terms that seem to name the same thing, it is worth asking whether there is after all some difference. Perhaps the terms describe the issue from different perspectives, or maybe we really do have an instance of that mythical thing, a synonym. So far I have insisted that a writing system, or writing itself, is not necessarily the same as 'literacy', which is – for me – writing with letters. The history of the word *writing* (the word is *writan* in Old English) is revealing in that respect. Its etymology shows that it belongs to a family of words which no longer has any relatives in contemporary English, but does in languages such as German, Dutch and Swedish, with words such as *reissen*, to tear, or *ritzen*, to scratch, in German; *rita*, to draw, in Swedish; and *rijten*, to tear, in Dutch. Writing, in the earlier history of the people of that part of northern Europe, was to scratch marks, the runes, into thin boards of soft beech-wood, or into stone. The word named the act of scratching, of scoring, of engraving, just as the word *grammar* – Greek in origin – comes from a root, *graphein*, which also has the meaning of scratch, mark, engrave, still present in English words such as *graphic*.

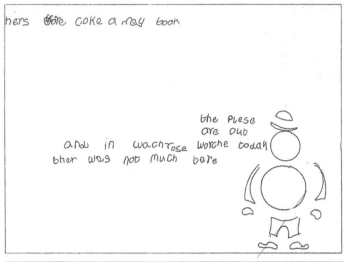

in the top box
Hers yore coke a rey book/Here's your cookery book
the plese are oud worche today/the police are out watching today
and in Wachrose ther was not much tere/and in Waitrose there was not much there

in the box below
thes a coo a reybook in the nwsepaper today/there's a cookery book in the newspaper today
Monday is a bisyday/Monday is a busy day
Mums and dads are rosheg to wrko/Mums and dads are rushing to work

in the speech-bubble
today is the frst of setabar/today is the first of September
its my birthday/its my birthday

Figure 5.1 Child's drawing: 'cookery book'

Writing, we might note at this point, is to make marks on a surface, in order to record something. What the marks are is not initially the issue – runes, letters, images, visual designs, characters. It may be useful to keep in mind and to make the distinction between a writing system using letters – for which the term 'literacy' is entirely apt, and writing systems which do not use letters, such as those of China ('characters'), Japan ('characters' and syllable signs); in the past those of Central America (petroglyphs), South America, Egypt (hieroglyphs), and elsewhere in the world even now, such as the recording systems of Australian aboriginal people. That distinction makes it possible to study the characteristics of each writing/recording system on its own terms, a step which is essential if we are to get near to an understanding of what human cultures have done and do now. It also avoids using 'literacy' as a 'concessive' term, trying to ensure that no negative judgements are made on people who do not use lettered writing. Clearly it is not at all essential to have the alphabet in order to have a writing system. What is essential is to know what each system can do and does do, what the affordances of each system are.

This book deals with a writing system founded on the alphabet in its Roman form, so called. Writing, whether it is represented by letters or by other means, is a *graphic* matter, a matter of sight rather than of sound, of marks made on a surface, a kind of image in two-dimensional space rather than a sound (sequence) in time. In the first place, writing is marks on a surface, in orders of a specific kind; it is a visual matter. For instance, we are used to recognising words in alphabetic writing because sequences of letters are marked off on each side by empty space from other sequences of letters. This is a visual convention. In medieval times and even into early modern Europe, writing did not have spaces to mark off words from each other – knowing the words of writing came from knowing the words in language-as-speech. The framing conventions and devices of speech were then so tangibly present and felt, in the transliterations of speech which writing then was, that words needed no graphic boundaries.

The early writing of children provides very good insights in this respect. Some of their early writing shows how they attend to visual aspects: often it consists of nonsense sequences of letters with spaces between them. These show that children recognise 'words' as visual units – I use the scare-quotes here to indicate that we cannot actually know whether these units have any of the significance of 'word' for the child-writers. What is clear is that they see them as significant visual entities.

Similarly, their transliterations of sound-sequences into lettered form show that this question of word-boundaries is a convention and has to be learned; they often have great difficulty in knowing what the graphic units/words are.

There are other visual units in writing: the *line*, for instance, is significant in many forms of writing; the paragraph is a visual unit as much as a meaning unit within the text.

Of course, *letters* and arrangement of letters as words (whether as approximate transcription of sounds or as the transcription of 'ideas' directly through the resource of writing) either in alphabetic writing, or broadly in character-based scripts, are just one aspect of what writing is. In large part this chapter will deal with entities which are definitional of the resource of writing with the Roman alphabet.

Writing as transcription

In previous chapters I have asked about the alphabet as a transcription system: what does it transcribe, sounds or meanings? Here I want to ask that question of writing-as-such, as a resource for transcribing, though I will also want to consider writing as a resource for new making. What does writing transcribe? Is it the means of transcribing the sounds of speech, or transcribing that which has already been articulated silently in speech, even if not uttered? Is it the means for the transcription of ideas, even complex ideas which get expressed in sentences? And does this happen more or less directly? That is, is the *graphic word* directly a transcription of the mentally held 'concept'? Is the clause a transcription of an event, directly, not via the intervention of intermediary elements? And the same questions need to be asked of all the units of writing – of phrases, clauses, sentences, even of the largest-level textual entities.

But in order to answer these questions we need a careful look at the resources of writing *as a mode* for representation and communication, and at the affordances of this mode. To do this, I will look at (just) some of the major elements of that mode and some of the major processes in that mode, asking what their potentials are. The element that I will focus on in the main is the sentence, and an entity which stands on the border of word and syntax, the 'nominal (phrase)'. Looking at that means looking at the process of transformation, for it is that process which is productive, is generative, in forming the units that writers need in their writing to answer the needs of the moment. Throughout, I will try to keep in mind the question or how and where speech and writing relate closely enough for us to feel justified in maintaining the idea that they both are part of a thing such as 'language'.

So, in looking at the affordances of the resource of alphabetic writing – what you can and cannot easily do with this resource – the elements that I will look at closely are *words* and the changes which words undergo; *clauses* and their relation both to 'word'-nominal, through transformations, and to the sentence; and *texts* and larger textual elements. I will look at the relations which these elements contract with each other, and the processes in which they are involved. This means looking at syntax in its triple role: as it relates to the making of words and to their arrangements; as it works internal to the clause and to the phrase; and in its role in the 'external relations' of clauses as they appear in sentences. Writing is quintessentially about the making of texts, that is, units which are complete in terms of their social environment, and complete in terms of their internal cohesion and coherence. So I will look also at *textual processes*.

The use of the resources depends of course on social factors, as I have mentioned. For instance, if social power is now no longer as strongly asserted as it was twenty years ago, then levels of formality in writing will change. That has its effects on the use of the resources and their involvement in syntactic processes and transformations. Writing, like meaning-making in any mode, always happens in a particular social domain. The meanings of that domain, as they are projected in texts by writers, shape the resources in its use. Hence specific morphological and syntactic arrangements can become characteristic of the use of the resource of writing in a particular domain. The social configuration of a group and its concerns, the social meanings and values of that group, have their effects on the habitual uses of the resource and, in this way, in the longer-term shaping of the resource in that domain.

Writing in the age of the screen: aspects of visual grammar

Had I been writing this chapter ten years ago, I would have felt that, by and large, that was more or less what there was to think and say about the matter: the question of what the resources of writing are, and of how people use them. Of course, even within that framework there are many things to explore. But writing the chapter now I am aware that things are very different. The screen more than the page is now the dominant site of representation and communication in general, so that even in writing, things cannot be left there. As I have said, what is fundamental is that the screen is the site of the image, and the logic of the image dominates the semiotic organisation of the screen.

This happens in at least two ways. First, the screen, and whatever appears on it, is treated as a *visual entity*. Even though the graphic marks, the graphic stuff, may be those of letters, that stuff is organised – potentially or actually, more or less – as visual stuff. It is 'laid out' according to principles which are visual principles: bullet-points are an instance; so are spacings, indenting, treatment of margins, of white space as visual framing. The written text now has to *look* good. Of course, aesthetic principles governed the look of the page: but that was then a matter for those professionals whose jobs were associated with writing: from 'typists' to typesetters and printers. Now everyone can and really needs to 'play about' with such matters. Added to this are other graphic or visual effects, such as bolding, differentiations in size and type of fonts, and so on. These make writing as a whole and letter in particular into visual entities, adding meanings of the visual modes to those of writing. On the screen, the *textual entity* is treated as a *visual entity* in ways in which the page never was.

Second, a significant organisational feature is that writing, whether on the screen or on the page, is accompanied more and more by image, whether as 'picture', diagram or map. In these writing/image ensembles *placement*, the spatial positioning of the mode-elements, matters, it has meaning-effects. The placing of the elements of image and writing on the space of the screen (or of the page) matters because that placing expresses principles of visual grammar through which this now visual entity is organised. A simple example is the 'caption', where it clearly matters whether the verbal caption is placed *near* to the visual element or more *distantly*, or whether it is placed at the *top*, at the *bottom*, to the *left* or to the *right*, *within* the same frame, *within* the visual element or *outside*.

It is now important to focus on each kind of element with equal attention at some level: on the *letter* as much as on *word*, *sentence* or *complete text*. But not just that: the placement of letter or word, the shape of the letter or its size, all these now need to be treated as *signs*. Now that the logic of image dominates on the screen certainly but increasingly also on the page, and now that frequently the elements of writing occur in a subsidiary role to image, it may be the case that a letter in itself has significance at the visual level, or that a word occurs simply as a subsidiary part of an image, a caption. Figure 5.2 is an instance of such a word–image relation.

On this 'page' writing is very much the subsidiary mode, and it is reduced to the function of label. Here the caption at the highest textual level is bolded, its significance is marked by visual means; it is placed close to the item for which it acts as label, so spacing – also an aspect of the visual – indicates that meaning.

In the high era of writing, when the logic of writing dominated the page, the organisation of the page was not an issue. Now that organisation has become one resource for the meaning of the new textual ensembles. These meanings derive from the meanings of the mode of the visual, from the meanings of visual 'grammar'. It becomes necessary therefore to say something about visual grammar. My brief excursion into etymology at the start of the chapter indicates why I am happy to use the term *grammar*, despite the danger of being accused of applying linguistic terminology to images. I feel confident about reappropriating the word for a much wider use in *semiotic* discussion of all modes of meaning-making, where the term can have real uses. In that new sense *grammar* is for me the overarching term that can describe the regularities of a particular mode which a culture has produced, be it writing, image, gesture, music or others.

The points made here draw directly on the grammar of images set out in *Reading Images: The Grammar of Visual Design*. The assumption – following the *semiotic* theory of Michael Halliday – is that any fully functioning human semiotic resource must have the potential to meet three demands: to represent states of affairs or events in the world – the ideational function; to represent the social relations between the participants in the process of communication – the interpersonal function; and to represent all that as a message-entity, a 'text' which is internally coherent and which coheres with its environment – the textual function.

Take, as an example, the utterance 'it's cold in here'. The state of affairs it represents or reports is about temperature in an enclosed space. Grammatically it is a declarative, so something is being declared by someone to someone else; semantically it is a statement, something is being stated by someone to someone else. Both of these produce a specific *social* relation: of someone who can declare

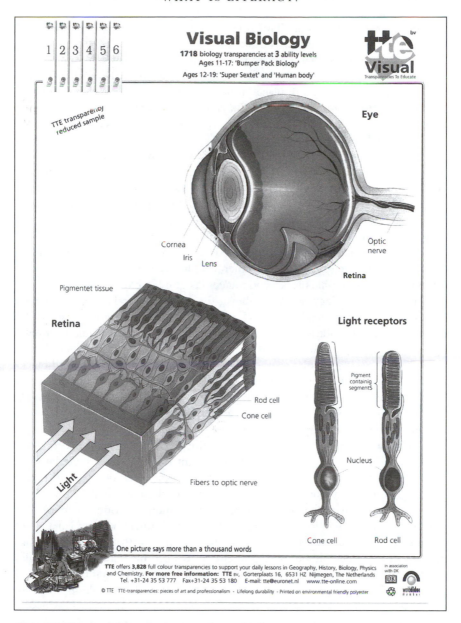

Figure 5.2 The eye: biology in the secondary school

or has something to state, to someone who is, by that utterance, cast as someone who may want or need such information. An interrogative, or question, by contrast – 'is it cold in here?' – produces a different social relation, a different assignation of roles of someone who might confirm or disconfirm, and someone who needs that confirmation. The utterance reports something, and does so in the so-called present tense, which has the effect of suggesting 'this is', rather than 'it might feel like that (because you're sitting still)'. Lastly, the utterance is internally coherent, for instance in the sense that the statement 'it's cold' coheres with the adverbial of place 'in here'; and it coheres (or does not!) with the immediate environment both of the conversation (say, a preceding 'I think I'll put on something warm'), and of the physical environment, the room in which it is spoken.

For the purposes of thinking about written word/image ensembles, only one of these needs to be considered at the moment. That is the textual function: how do the elements which make up the text-ensemble cohere in the space of page or screen, and what meaning attaches to their spatially constructed relations? Traditionally, this is what is meant by 'layout', though layout tended not to be seen in terms of making a contribution to meaning. The questions are, 'how are they placed together, and how do they cohere?', and 'what meaning derives from this particular arrangement?' This is the level at which word arrangements (as graphic blocks) and images (as graphic blocks) interact.

In the 'Visual Biology' example above, the lower-level relations are marked by connecting lines, the higher-level ones use *proximity*. There is use of the device of *bolding* to indicate salience, as a means of indicating semiotic equivalence – equivalence in the sense of 'elements operating at the same level'. In a page from a geology textbook, the relations might exist between word-blocks and image-blocks. It is of course strange to think of a *block* of written text as a 'graphic block'. But in these new textual arrangements that is what they are. At the first level of analysis, whether the formal analysis of theoretical work or the informal analysis of everyday reading and viewing, we are dealing with the mode of layout and its elements. These entities exist as 'graphic blocks', elements in the mode of layout. The 'blocks' might be realised by material from any other mode: writing, image, diagram. At the next level 'down' we then ask questions about the mode-specific characteristics of these elements. At this level we are concerned with the blocks in terms of their mode – writing or image.

It may seem strange to think in terms of 'blocks' rather than immediately of meanings; it is in fact no different than when we play with syntactic meanings in speech or writing, without paying attention to word-meaning. If I say 'oggles igged twuddles' everyone who understands English will know that the oggles did something that affected the twuddles. From there I would be able to say, 'Oh, you mean the twuddles were igged, then?' I would know that on this occasion at least, the oggles were iggers of twuddles, and so on. There are structural relations which have a regularity and have a meaning. The relations and the regularity together ensure the meaning – in speech, in writing, in image, in gesture and, here, in layout.

For all modes, the regularities are culture-specific. Image is not directly and transparently a representation of the world which is represented. My comments apply broadly to those Western cultures that I know – Germany, Australia,

France, the UK, the USA – even though there are differences between these that need to be explored. In general, because of the long history of cultural trade between cultures in Europe, these regularities have relative validity across many European cultures, though the further one travels from the north-west of Europe to the south-east, the less that is likely to be the case.

The resource which is used for making meaning in the visual mode is that of (*position in*) *space*. In a framed space, say the rectangular space of the page or the screen, elements can be placed at the bottom or at the top, to the left or to the right, or in the centre. These positions have meaning-potential. In Western visual tradition, though perhaps much more widely, given our body's position-ing in space ('feet on the ground', 'head in the air') and the meanings which attach to that, the meaning-potential of 'bottom of the visual space' and 'top of the visual space' are broadly those of 'grounded', 'of this earth', 'the empirical' – meanings which might be characterised as 'real'. The meaning-potential of 'top of the space' has broadly opposite values: 'not of this earth', 'that which is desired' – meanings which might be characterised as 'ideal'. These are *meaning-potentials*, not meanings: literally, they are potentials for making meaning. 'Real' in a sixteenth-century religious painting may mean 'of the earth' or 'secular', whereas in a contemporary advertisement it might mean 'what the commodity is actually like' and while in a scientific diagram it might mean 'the empirically real'. 'Top' in the religious painting may mean 'of Heaven', 'divine'; in the advertisement the meaning might be 'the benefits that you might get through the use of the commodity'; in the scientific diagram it might mean 'the abstract', 'the theoretical', 'the general'.

In Western alphabetic cultures – not, however, in alphabetic cultures such as Arabic or Hebrew – the reading direction of written texts is from left to right. This means that 'left' has a culturally different meaning-potential to 'right' (though it may be the case that left and right, just like top and bottom, derive their meaning from historically earlier, semiotically and perhaps physiologically more basic organisations). The left is 'where we start from', whether that is the chapter or the line; it is 'the starting point'. The right is then 'the point to which we are moving', 'where we will get to'. If the left is the starting point, it is also where 'we' all are to begin with, it is the place 'we' know, and information that is placed there is shared, known, 'given' in the (Hallidayan) terminology of *Reading Images*.

This gives rise to a quadrant of differing meaning-potential as in Figure 5.3 (overleaf). Moving from bottom-left in clockwise direction, the meanings are given/real, given/ideal, new/ideal and new/real. Placing elements in these quad-rants has significant effects. It makes a difference whether an image is to be read, in a geography textbook, say, as 'new' and 'real', or as 'given' and 'ideal'. New and real could be an image showing a geological formation after a process of faulting, with the formation as it was prior to the process of faulting on the left, as given and real. 'Given and ideal' might be an abstract formulation, a depiction of a theoretical formulation in science; in fact in a school textbook it corresponds to

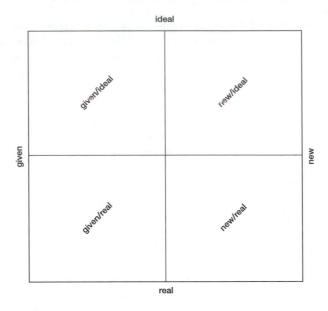

Figure 5.3 Quadrant of spatial meaning potential in 'Western' images

the placing of the diagrams and photographs of folding and faulting above the photograph of the mountain (Ingleborough in North Yorkshire) and the caption accompanying it. Placement in this scheme leads to particular readings; in the case just mentioned precisely that of the 'empirically real (the photograph of the mountain)' and the 'scientifically ideal' (the diagrammatic/theoretical account). These potentials for meaning play a part in the multiplicity of ways in which word and image interact.

To a common-sense view, trained in seeing meaning in language but not in image or in layout, this might seem implausible, and the question 'but how do you know?' poses itself. Making use of the meaning-potential of space is no different in its principle to making use of the meaning-potential of sequence in the case of speech. To go back to my earlier examples, in 'Mary married Bill' the meaning differs from that of 'Bill married Mary'. The first is said by someone who is likely to focus on Mary more than on Bill, for whatever reason – maybe they are closer friends; the second is likely to be said by someone whose focus is more on Bill. That meaning is carried by the affordance of sequence, of sequence in time as a signifier. And if I say 'Bill and Mary married', then this differs in ways which we understand, because I am attempting to overcome the meaning of sequence by constructing a joint entity 'MaryandBill'. The principles at issue here are semiotic principles of great generality: whatever is available for making meaning in the culture, in this mode, can be and will be used, if it serves the needs of the maker of the message.

Let me give one last example which shows the resource of spatial placement

used for meanings which may be directly political – it is of course, like all representation, always ideological. In 1997 sovereignty over the then Crown Colony
of Hong Kong reverted to the government of the People's Republic of China.
We know that semiotic resources are culturally shaped, placement in space
being no exception. One feature of this is the directionality of writing systems.
Chinese was traditionally written in columns from top to bottom and from right
to left. More recently, under the influence of 'the West' this has changed somewhat, in places like Taiwan, Hong Kong (in Japan also), so that in these places
the semiotics of directionality of 'West' and 'East' coexist and intermingle.
Anyone who looks at advertisements while waiting for the underground train in
Hong Kong will quickly notice this.

It would be reasonable to assume that as with other semiotic resources, this
would be used in accordance with the structures of power, so that while Hong
Kong was under British rule the spatial semiotics of the colonial rulers might
rule also. Here is a sign from a road that runs at the top of the Peak, a highly
select residential area of Hong Kong (see Figure 5.4).

My assumption was – I took the photograph in early 1999, some two years
after the 'changeover' – that this was the semiotic system of the colonial rulers,
among whom some of the best off lived in houses on the Peak. Figure 5.5 (overleaf) shows a sign from the walking path that circles the Peak. My assumption
was that here we have the Chinese spatial semiotic system at work.

This is reinforced by the appearance of what may be the Cantonese deixis of
take/bring in the English version of the message. The mixing of semiotic
resources is evident in many of the signs on the Peak, as indeed everywhere in
Hong Kong. Along this path (which connects with an extensive network of trails
on the island), popular with locals who come up for a few hours, are distance
markers. The Chinese semiotic dominates in the directionality of the figure of
the walker Figure 5.6 (overleaf). On signs in England he would be walking from
left to right. The Western semiotic dominates the numerical indicator, and the
English writing, and the Chinese writing, when horizontally written, also runs
from left to right. I cannot tell whether the Chinese or the English semiotic
rules in the placement of figures and other information: a western reading
would say that the 'real' information is at the bottom, and that the 'ideal' is represented by the figure of the walker. I can imagine that a Chinese reading
might differ from that.

Figure 5.4 Lugard Road: road sign, Hong Kong

71

Figure 5.5 Sign on a walking trail, The Peak, Hong Kong

Figure 5.6 Distance post: The Peak, Hong Kong

In the subtle and complex politics of the recent history of Hong Kong one could undertake an archaeology of power and shifts in power by looking at these signs – whether on the Peak Tram, in the Zoological and Botanical Gardens, or the signs on public buildings; wherever public declarations are made which need to be sensitive to such matters. In the era of multimodality these issues have come to the fore, though as the signs from Hong Kong show, these resources were always present and used.

So what is writing?

The question of what writing is has occupied linguists for some time. The answers have ranged from 'writing is a transcription of speech, it is speech made visible and permanent' (broadly the position adopted in mainstream Western linguistics since Bloomfield) to 'writing is a discrete system of representation, with its own historical origins, derived from image-based representation' (broadly a position such as that of Roy Harris). The answer to this question remains crucially important, as it shapes thinking about writing, how it is to be approached (in contemporary Britain and in the USA the Bloomfieldian position is dominant in education, so that the learning of writing in early years of schooling is based on 'phonics', which treats the sound–alphabet relation as the key to the learning of writing). The answer is important also in that it always reflects social issues: who is in control, what is being controlled and what is that control being used for?

Given that, in the era of image, writing is both frequently in the context of image, and that image is itself a 'writing system' in that more abstract sense, there is a need for some discussion of the different conceptions of language and writing deriving from the distinction between alphabetic and image-based writing systems. This is even more urgent given that in these new environments, writing is likely to move in the direction of its image origins. The alphabet disposes its users towards a view of language which foregrounds sound: 'Language is sound and combinations of sounds. Meanings can be attached to combinations of sounds. Sounds can be represented by letters'. Image-based systems are likely to dispose their users differently: 'Language is meaning and combinations of meaning. Meanings can be represented by (conventionalised) images, however abstract. Sounds can be attached to images'.

There is also the question to what extent we are entitled to speak of that abstraction, 'language', rather than of the modes of speech and writing more specifically. If we think that there is 'language' we may not want to treat speech and writing as distinct modes. Each position will have quite specific consequences, for pedagogies of writing, for instance. In cultures with alphabetic writing systems, speech and writing are linked by the sound–letter connection (only the most literate readers do not 'subvocalise' in some noticeable way, even if noticeable only to themselves).

However, the major relation between the two modes rests on the unit of the clause, and on what speech and writing each do syntactically/textually with the clause. I will give an example of writing in English from the seventeenth century, showing how the syntax/textuality of writing both drew on (as it still does) and 'freed' itself from that of speech, and how that relation is newly becoming problematic in the environment of the new technologies of information and communication. This is most frequently talked about in relation to e-mail and the forms of writing which it produces. In the new environment, the always present image-like quality of writing is coming much more to the fore, in many different ways, given the affordances of this technology.

My assumption is that syntactically and textually writing may be becoming more speech-like once again, while in its visual/graphic/spatial dimensions there is a move in the opposite direction, away from speech. As always (as I will show in my 'historical' discussion of the clause/sentence in this chapter) this is a matter regulated in the end by social and not by technological factors.

Two examples of 'transformation'

I will now discuss two examples of how I see the resources of writing, starting with the process of transformation. The first (Example 1) is a brief extract from a history of Australia, *A Land Half Won*, written by an Australian historian, Geoffrey Blainey, in 1972.

> In Central Australia . . . the Pitjantjatjarra were driven by drought to expand into the territory of a neighbour.
>
> Several of these invasions might be partly explained by a domino theory: the coastal invasion of the whites initially pushing over one black domino which in turn pushed down outer dominoes. But it would be sensible to believe that dominoes were also rising and falling occasionally during the centuries of black history. We should also be wary of whitewashing the white invasions. We should also be wary of the idea that Australia knew no black invasions.
>
> Even when Aboriginal tribes clung to their traditional territory, fatal fighting within the same tribe or between members of hostile tribes was common. It is possible that many tribes suffered more deaths through tribal fighting than through warfare with the British colonists in the 19th century.
>
> (Blainey, 1972)

A number of points could be discussed here: the then current Western ideology of the 'domino theory' ('if one country in South-East Asia turns communist, all will'), the a-causal nature of these dominoes rising and falling by themselves, the 'history' of aboriginal Australians, and so on. Blainey was, at that time, regarded as a politically progressive historian, and so he did not wish to perpetuate the formulation that had been used earlier to name the process of dispossession and colonisation, namely 'settlement'. That term, with its implication that there had been an empty land just waiting for its settlers, had of course been used in Ireland much earlier, as it had in North America.

The term which had then come into use to name the reality of that history was that of 'invasion': a hostile, violent, aggressive act against people and their land. Blainey softens that term in two directions (apart from implicating black Australians in the process also), by introducing the much more neutral terms 'expansion' and 'expand' to gloss 'invasion' ('expand into the territory'), and by altering the more usual syntax of the verb *invade*, and of the noun *invasion*. In the more usual usage, *invade* takes as an object-noun a word that stands for a political or social entity of some kind. I can invade something which belongs to someone politically or socially: I can invade someone's property, land, territory or privacy, or the pitch at a cricket game. But I cannot, in normal usage, *invade* something that has no borders, is open, is not owned, belongs to everyone, and is natural rather than social.

That is what Blainey does: 'the coastal invasion of the whites' is changing the grammatical/syntactic scope of the verb *invade* and of its noun *invasion*, derived from the clause 'the whites invaded the coast'. It is now an act ('the whites invaded the coast') which can take place in relation to a new category: 'invade' has been deprived of its political force, it has been made innocuous. It is something done to something which is merely a geographical, a natural, thing, not a political or social entity. (This view was lampooned years later in a film, 'Barbequearea', produced by aboriginal film-makers, in which a group of black people in the costumes of Hanoverian guards arrive in a boat at a picnic ground, ask a family of whites who are engaged in preparing their Sunday barbie what the area is called, to be told 'barbequearea', a land which they then proceed to 'invade'.) Similarly, to use a descriptive adjective such as *white* with the word *invasion* has the effect both of obscuring real agency (not 'the British invasion'). It permits the ideologically convenient act of equating white and black invasions (where 'black invasions' had been caused by natural events, such as droughts, implying, perhaps, a natural cause for the 'white invasions' also).

The syntax of a small part of the language has been changed. The interest of the agent of these transformations, the historian, is quite clear. A historian who wished to appear as progressive politically, but whose instincts and interests were deeply against such a move (as became overtly evident in the mid-1980s), transforms the existing resources of the language to serve the directions of his interest. There is nothing at all unusual in this: however, it became visible to me only because an aboriginal Australian student used the example for work he did in a course I taught in Sydney. The normal invisibility of these processes should not deflect us from recognising their utter usuality, and their utter normality. Their invisibility is evidence of the ubiquity of the process.

My second example (Example 2) goes in a somewhat different direction. It consists of two linked texts: a position description and a job application based on that description.

RESPONSIBLE FOR: The supervision of office staff providing administrative services to the academic staff. The provision and coordination of all student and student related activities within the institute.

1 Coordination and supervision of the office staff providing administrative support.
2 Supervision of the attendance/flexitime system for all Institute staff.
3 Co-ordination of student enquiries and related activities.
4 Assist in the organization of student admission/enrolment/registration/assessment.
5 Prepare documentation for submission to the Institute's Admission and Progression Committee and act as an Executive Officer to the Committee.
6 Ensure the accurate maintenance of student records.

7   Preparation of correspondence relating student records/progression/transcripts.

Example 2: position description

In all positions held, good oral and written communication skills have been essential in satisfying job requirements. Communication at all levels from students to company executives, to College Principals has required clear concise expression together with attention to confidentiality and sensitivity.

Supervisory and management skills have been developed over my career. Most recently in Student Administration, it has been my responsibility to form work teams, oversee work flow and set short term goals to meet deadlines. Immediate responsiveness to client/student enquiries has been required in previous positions, whilst the planning and organisation of day to day business was carried out. Skills of resource organisation and decision-making were quickly acquired.

Experience with computer systems has been gained whilst working with . . .

Example 2: job application

The points I wish to make here are about the productive potential of the resources of the language; the near reproduction of the resources in the form in which they have been received, and what that might mean; and the role of power in this.

To take the first point first, the PD is an example par excellence of the heavy, nominalised (that is, noun-like static, frozen forms derived from full clauses with actional verbs) language, with nouns/nominals of inordinate length and complexity. The opening nominal is the best (or worst) example: 'The supervision of office staff providing administrative services to the academic staff' is one single nominal, that is, a syntactic element which acts as a single noun. Other examples abound: 'co-ordination and supervision of the office staff providing administrative support'. These are noun-entities formed by a productive linguistic process, in response to an environment of certain social processes and structures. Where these occur regularly and frequently over a period, they come to seem not like new events each time but as the existence of a stable phenomenon outside time – something which is always like that, best represented by a noun-like linguistic entity (nouns being the linguistic category for entities, objects, phenomena, outside time).

A more event-like representation might be something like this: 'The successful applicant will supervise those staff who work in the office, who provide services (services in which staff administer certain areas) to the academic staff'. This description is not particularly elegant (I have not aimed for elegance but rather for getting all the actions drawn out overtly again), but nor is it very much longer than the original nominal form.

76

I mention that because 'efficiency' of space, a reason usually given, seems not plausible here. However, the nominal form has much more authority, because it is the name of something which exists as a thing (rather than in the more verb-like form which is a description of events that happen and which may, therefore also not happen). But, above all, as a stable thing it can be administered, something which is difficult to do with events.

Here the productive potential of the resources of writing lies in being able to turn event-in-time into object-out-of-time; to turn events with human participants into entities with no overt trace of human presence; to turn the world of human social endeavour into the world of general categories. We might feel that the word 'productive' is somewhat misapplied here, but the point is that that would not be the bureaucrat's view of it. This is the technology that enables the bureaucrat (and many others – the scientist, the policy-maker as much as the law-maker) to turn the messy world of events and actions into the stable, unchanging, orderly world of entities. It is and has been an essential technology in the era of the industrialised economies and of their social and political structures. The applicant for the job has a difficult task; she recognises, from the language of the PD, how this institution represents itself, and feels that she needs to approximate to that language in her application – to show that she understands and is in sympathy with this institution. At the same time she needs to show some signs of 'individuality', which is, on the face of it at any rate, one of the characteristics looked for: nobody wants (nobody wants to admit that they want) an employee who is merely a clone of the institutional structure. She must therefore show some signs of this individuality while giving the impression that she will fit in without causing a ripple.

Her strategy is to move a little way back from the heavily nominalised forms towards the more event-like structure. She uses the resources of the language innovatively, even in this difficult situation of what must seem, to her, extreme constraint. She uses transformational means to unmake and move away from, some of the heaviest of the bureaucratic language. So 'supervision of all office staff' becomes 'supervisory skills have been developed'. She does not name herself directly – either, as here, by deleting the subject/agent of the passive, or by eliding the subject nouns of verbs; nor does she make herself the agent of any action. She suggests her own agency by the use of the possessive pronoun *my*, as in the first sentence of the second paragraph, 'skills have been developed over *my* career' (rather than 'I developed skills for my . . .'), and by the use of the active verbal form (but with an inanimate agent-noun): 'Communication at all levels . . . has required' (rather than 'communication at all levels required me to . . .', or 'I responded to the demands of communication by . . .', or even 'when I was required to . . . I responded').

When I saw this text some years ago (it comes from an academic institution in Australia, *circa* 1988) I felt that it showed the power of language, of bureaucratic discourse, that is, the world organised and represented through the lens of the bureaucratic institution. I thought that the applicant felt constrained to replicate the language of the institution and to fit herself to it. When I look at this text now – through my now somewhat changed lens of a view of grammar as a resource for new meanings that I outlined earlier – I still see the power of the linguistic resources, of the discourse, and of the institution, but I also see the attempt by the 'applicant' to show herself as somewhat, somehow, distinct from the institutional forms, as speaking in her own way, through the use she makes of the resources of the language. She has changed the heavily nominalised language of the original (which had been sent out with the further particulars) into a direction where she can appear, however faintly, in the way I have outlined.

In this text I now think there is both the power of the language and of the institution from which it comes. Of course, this applies not only to this institution: it has allowed itself to move into a discourse of this kind, no doubt because it was seen at the time as good management, as good 'human resources' practice. At the same time there is the power of the individual to transform the resources in the direction of her own interests, a power of which she avails herself. These interests, as always, include a complex of issues, and after all if one wants the job that one is applying for, it includes an attempt to present oneself as though one already has the shape that fits in with the purposes of the institution. This job application seems to be saying: 'I am (already) the position you are seeking to fill'.

Sentence, texts and the social environment

The major resource which the job applicant draws on is that of transformation of elements of sentences. Now I will discuss the sentence, from two perspectives: its constitution as the result of textual processes which combine clauses; and in terms of the social production of the sentence, a question of its 'origins'. The examples both come from the seventeenth century, a time when English had been the written language of formal public life for not much more than a century – whether at the court, in the judiciary, in commerce, in public administration, in some areas of intellectual life or, for that matter, in literary prose. My reason for choosing examples from that period is that it is still possible to see, in writing from that time, the social–cultural making of writing as a mode. A hundred or a hundred and fifty years before then English was used in writing – the Paston letters, written by members of an important aristocratic East Anglian family to others in the family, are one well-known example. But that writing was very much closer to transcription of speech.

Inevitably it was the forms of the educated elites and of their *public forms* of speech which became the basis for their writing. The nearly half-page-long paragraphs of the writings of Bacon, Hobbes, Newton or Milton, with their paragraph-long 'sentences', were the result of the mixing of two resources – the 'learned' grammars of Greek and Latin and its structures of public oratory with English speech.

The first example comes from John Milton's tract against censorship, *Areopa-*

gitica. Its sentence-structures and cadences are influenced by the structures of written Greek and Latin, both of which an educated person was expected to be competent in, but these sentence forms come from the forms of speech as public oratory.

> Good and evill we know in the field of this World grow
> up together almost inseparably; and the knowledge of
> good is so involved and interwoven with the knowledge
> of evill, and in so many cunning resemblances hardly
> to be discern'd, that those confused seeds which were
> impos'd on *Psyche* as an incessant labour to cull out,
> and sort asunder, were not more intermixt. It was
> from out the rinde of one apple tasted, that the
> knowledge of good and evill as two twins cleaving
> together leapt forth into the World. And perhaps this
> is that doom which *Adam* fell into of knowing good and
> evill, that is to say of knowing good by evill. As
> therefore the state of man now is; what wisdome can
> there be to choose what continence to forbeare without
> the knowledge of evill? He that can apprehend and
> consider vice with all her baits and seeming pleasures,
> and yet abstain, and yet distinguish, and yet prefer that
> which is truly better, he is the true warfaring Christian.
> I cannot praise a fugitive and cloisterd vertue,
> unexercis'd & unbreath'd, that never sallies out and
> sees her adversary, but slinks out of the race, where
> that immortall garland is to be run for, not without
> dust and heat. Assuredly we bring not innocence into
> the world, we bring impurity much rather: that which
> purifies us is triall, and triall is by what is contrary.
> That vertue therefore which is but a youngling in the
> contemplation of evill, and knows not the utmost that
> vice promises to her followers, and rejects it, is but
> a blank vertue, not a pure; her whitenesse is but an
> excrementall whitenesse; which was the reason why our
> sage and serious Poet *Spencer*, whom I dare be known
> to think a better teacher than *Scotus* or *Aquinas*,
> describing true temperance under the person of *Guion*,
> brings him in with his palmer through the cave of
> Mammon, and the bowr of earthly blisse that he might
> see and know, and yet abstain. Since therefore the
> knowledge and survay of vice is in this world so
> necessary to the constituting of human vertue, and
> the scanning of error to the confirmation of truth,

how can we more safely, and with lesse danger scout
into the regions of sin and falsity then by reading
all manner of tractats, and hearing all manner of
reason?

(Milton, *Areopagitica*)

This is writing in which the 'raw material', the 'stuff' of English words and clauses, is shaped by the demands of classical rhetoric, itself influenced by the grammar of the rhetorically trained elites of classical antiquity. What dominates here, and provides the structure of the text, is a specific conception of the structure of argument; the structure of sentences follows from that. Sentence-syntax is shaped by the needs of the textual structures which fulfil the social need to 'show learnedness'. The demands of that rhetoric are to pile point on point in an argument, and to contrast the edifice of piled-on points with an edifice of equal weight as counters to these points.

The clause-structure of the sentences is hugely complex. The opening sentence of this passage contains ten clauses: 'we know . . . good and evill grow up together . . . the knowledge of good is involved . . . and interwoven . . . the knowledge is to be discerned . . . those seeds were confused . . . which were imposed . . . psyche culls out seeds . . . and psyche sorts them asunder . . . the seeds were intermixed'. Sentence and clause internal structures are complex; for instance, the conjoined subject noun of the second clause − 'good and evill . . . grow up together' − is transformationally 'raised' or 'fronted' before the subject of the sentence to become the theme of the sentence 'good and evill we know . . . ' In this process 'good and evill' take on the feel of being the object of the first sentence, 'we know good and evill'.

This is not a structure derived from everyday interaction. It is one specialised form of an elite social group − of the academies and of those not just trained there but seeking 'preferment' from there − speaking and writing in highly specific environments; it is not their language of the everyday. The textuality of the writing, and deriving from this textual structure the syntax of sentences, both had specific social origin and motivation.

Here, simply for comparison, and to show that this had become the regularity of a resource, is an extract from Bacon's long essay *The Advancement of Learning*.

Surely, like as many substances in nature which are solid do putrify and corrupt into worms; so it is the property of good and sound knowledge to putrify and dissolve into a number of subtle, idle, unwholesom, and (as I may term them) vermiculate questions, which have indeed a kind of quickness and life of spirit, but no soundness of matter or goodness of quality. This kind of degenerate learning did chiefly reign amongst the schoolmen: who having sharp and strong wits, and abundance of leisure, and small variety of reading, but their wits being shut up in the cells of a few authors (chiefly Aristotle their dictator) as their persons were shut up in the cells of monasteries and colleges, and knowing little history, either of nature or time, did out of no great quantity of matter and infinite agitation of wit spin out unto us those laborous webs of learning which are extant in their books. For the wit and mind of man, if it work upon matter, which is the contemplation of the creatures of God, worketh according to the stuff and is limited thereby; but if it work upon itself, as the spider worketh his web, then it is endless, and brings forth indeed cobwebs of learning, admirable for the fineness of thread and work; but of no substance or profit.

Bacon, The Advancement of Learning, I.iv.5

By the time of Milton's writing, printing presses had become ubiquitous in cities like London – one of the reasons why the government of the day attempted to control their use, and the reason for Milton's pamphlet. And so this now no longer so new and certainly no longer so elite medium could become available to the lower classes, as a means for their expression, representation and communication. Here is a brief example, a religious rather than a political tract this time, roughly contemporaneous with Milton's text. However this is written by someone not trained in Greek and Latin, and not versed in the elite forms of public oratory.

Like Milton, Trapnell draws on the resources which were available to her: they are all forms which she knows as speech (though she would also have *read*

A m *Anna Trapnel*, the daughter of *William Trapnel*, Shipwright, who lived in *Poplar*, in *Stepney* Parish; my father and mother living and dying in the profession of the Lord Jesus; my mother died nine years ago, the last words she uttered upon her death-bed, were these to the Lord for her daughter. Lord! Double thy Spirit upon my child; These words she uttered with much eagerness three times, and spoke no more; I was trained up to my book and writing, I have walked in fellowship with the Church-meeting at *All-hallows*, (whereof Mr. *John Simpson* is a Member) for the space of about four years; I am well known to him and that whole Society, also to Mr, *Greenhil* Preacher at *Stepney*, and most of that society, to Mr. *Henry Jesse*, and most of his society, to Mr. *Venning* Preacher at *Olaves* in *Southwark*, and most of his society, to Mr. *Knollis*, and most of his society, who have knowledge of me, and of my conversation; If any desire to be satisfied of it, they can give testimony of me, and of my walking in times past.

Figure 5.7 The concept of 'sentence': a seventeenth-century religious tract

the Bible). In the extract (Figure 5.7) we can discern a lower-class English, the speech of her parents perhaps: 'my mother died nine years ago . . . I was trained up to my book and writing'; the speech of the preacher: 'my father and mother living and dying in the profession of the Lord Jesus', heavily influenced by the Bible; and the speech of the religious community of which she had become a member: 'the last words she uttered on her death bed were these to the Lord for her daughter'. What is clear is that diverse social domains and the forms of speech of those domains are drawn on here. Anna Trapnell's sentence is a device for bringing such diversity into at least temporary conjunction. Out of such temporary conjunction longer-term semiotic forms might then emerge – the prose forms of Aphra Behn in the same century, or those of Daniel Defoe some decades later. In this extract there are just two 'sentences'; if anything it is clearer here than in the prose of John Milton, that the concept of sentence has a different meaning for Anna Trapnell than it does for us. Like Milton's sentences these are socially determined, and textually motivated. Socially, they are groupings of clauses which seem to belong to what Trapnell considers relevant social categories: 'my biography', 'my credentials'. Textually, they are chunks of linguistic material related by their form and function in the text-as-genre. Unlike Milton's sentences, which derived their organisations from (adherence to) the rules of a well-understood rhetoric, Trapnell's sentences derive their organisation from principles of her own making, which themselves may have come from criteria understood by and active in her community.

The point that I wish to make here is that we always draw on the resources which we have available to us, for the purposes of making the representations that we wish or need to make. In the process the existing resources are transformed, reshaped in the direction of the requirements of the environment of communication and by the interests of the maker of that message or representation. That applied to Milton as much as to Trapnell, even though the resources available to them in the same 'language' were entirely different, and the social valuations of these resources unequal. Nevertheless, the *processes* were the same for both, as they still are the same for anyone engaged in communication. In both texts, that of Milton and that of Trapnell, we see the emergence of the written sentence, out of the socially distinct resources of speech of different kinds (and of the grammars of Greek and Latin in the case of Milton). It would be a revealing study to attempt to see whose language, whose resources, had the greater effect.

Simply for effect I will produce two kinds of sentence which I discuss elsewhere in the book: both are from science textbooks. One is from 1936, the other example from 1988.

When a current is passed through the coil in the direction indicated in the figure we can show, by applying Fleming's left-hand rule, that the left-hand side of the coil will tend to move down and the right hand side to move up.

In your first circuits you used torch bulbs joined with wires. Modern electrical equipment uses the same basic ideas.

Of course I would not say that there is anything resembling the rhetoric of Milton's sentence in the example from 1936 (written for 13-year-old students); there is something of the syntactic complexity. And there is nothing of the social diversity of Trapnell's sentences in the 1988 example (also written for 13-year-olds) but there is something of the syntax. What all the examples illustrate is the responsiveness of the resource to the needs of the writers in their social and cultural environments, and the socially shaped characteristic of that often too abstractly thought about notion of the sentence.

There are two other points to be made here. One concerns technology and its effects and influences. By the time of Milton and Trapnell, the printing press, with its movable type, had superseded the scribe and his practices, but the traditions left by the scribe and the forms of both the elites and the non-elites immediately colonised the new technology and the medium. The other point goes somewhat in the opposite direction: yes, the old resources colonised the new technology, but at the same time the affordances offered by the new technology reshaped the resources. The printing press had its effects on writing and on the sentence. The written sentence as we still know it is as much an effect of the affordances of that technology in interaction with the users and the environments of use as it is an effect of the resources which had been brought from the past to writing for print. These are essential points to be borne in mind in thinking about literacy at a time when the effects of technology are again overwhelmingly present.

At a time of deep change it may be necessary to look at both past and future. What were the shapes of the past brought forward into the era of the printing press? And what shapes are we carrying forward, unbeknown to ourselves? What are the discernible shapes of the near future? It is clear, as I have suggested, that we are moving out of an era of relative stability of a very long duration. In debates on literacy we tend to be focused even now – often entirely implicitly – on the industrial revolution and its effects in so many ways. But we also know that the invention of the printing press predates the early period of industrialisation by a good two centuries, and indeed it is often held that the invention of printing by using movable type represents the first stage in the process of mass industrial production. The significant point, however, is that when the printing press became commonly available, and replaced the medieval scribe – whether at the court or in the church – it was the *forms of writing* of the medieval scribe which came to dominate the new technology. What lessons are to be learned from that?

6

A SOCIAL THEORY OF TEXT

Genre

Genre in theorising about literacy: some introductory remarks

In Chapter 4 I discussed some theoretical concepts we need in order to provide a full account of literacy. I said that *text* as the product of social action was the starting point. However, we need categories that will help us understand what text *is*, how it is constituted and, above all, what text *does*. Again, the starting point is social action. Who acts, with what purposes and around what issues? Clearly, in social action there are issues; they may be exceedingly trivial, or they may be significant. *Issues* are one reason for action. Where there are no issues, there is no action. In earlier formulations (1984/1989) I used the notion of *difference* to explain the coming into being of text; difference not in the sense that Derrida has used it but in the sense in which we explain lightning: a potential for a current to flow due to a difference in electrical charge. The current is made possible by that difference, with a flow from negative charge to positive charge. In semiosis that difference can be about anything: about who is to act, about purposes, about knowledge, about issues of any kind. Difference as such is itself an issue. In this book I want to use *issue* to refer to *content*, to what something is *about*. In the social semiotic theory that I use, this is dealt with by the category of *discourse*. It deals with the social provenance, production and organisation of content, following from the work of Michel Foucault.

Genre, by contrast, deals not with what is talked about, what is represented in the sense of what issues, but with *who acts* (and) *in relation to whom*, with the question of purposes. This is directly in the domain of social interaction: the questions that arise are questions such as 'who are the participants involved in the social action as it takes place?' and 'what are their social relations with each other?' Such interactions have structure and shape, which is reflected in or realised in the representational practices that are part of such actions, or which constitute such actions. When that social action is looked at from the point of view of representation, we invoke the category of text. Text is the result of the social semiotic action of representation. We say that a text was produced. Whether that text was recorded or not is not the issue. If it has been recorded we can go back over it and reflect in various ways on aspects of the text – we can do text-analysis. But even if there is no record of that action, there will nevertheless have been a text, though as with most social action, the traces of it are likely to be slight and difficult to recover. When the action has taken place predominantly via graphic modes – rather than as speech or as bodily action – we have a tangible trace, a 'written text', or a text using a number of modes, a 'multimodal text'. This text is more immediately amenable to reflection and analysis, a fact which has led many commentators to speculate that writing is crucial to the development of certain forms of intellection. Of course, even when there is such a graphic trace, the actions which produced it will have been accompanied by other actions, and will have taken place in specific environments, many of which will have shaped, without leaving directly recoverable traces, the text.

The significant point is that social actions shape the text that is a result of such actions. If the actions are relatively stable and persistent, then the textual forms will become relatively stable and persistent. At that point generic shape becomes apparent; we can see more or less instantly what genre is invoked, what generic occasion we are involved in. At that point, too, convention becomes significant, in that it becomes essential to take account of what conventions are at work in that domain of practice; if I am not aware, I will commit errors which will be noticed by those who are in the community that observes that convention. There will be penalties for not observing, or not being able to observe, the conventions. This is the point at which there is a pedagogic interest. In as far as the school sees it as its task to provide young people with the resources to act in their societies with maximal potential for autonomous action, the young will need to understand the constraints and limitations as well as the potentials and possibilities for action. A full knowledge of genre conventions – by which I mean knowledge of the socially generative conditions and their realisation – is one part of such knowledge in the domain of written representation.

Social practices take place in fields of power, and so the genres which are characteristic of a social group are not just expressions of such power, they are also arranged in hierarchies of power. To be aware of the genres, their constitutive principles, their valuations in hierarchies of power, and above all to be able to produce them, in variations which are fully adequate to the writer's interests at the moment of writing, becomes both the sine qua non of fully literate practice and the condition for full participation in social life. It is then inescapable that genre-knowledge – among others, of course – needs to form part of the curriculum of literate practice. For me this is beyond question. The really important questions arise at a different point: are genres to be taught as ideal and stable forms? Are the genres which are most powerful in a society to be taught in preference to others? Are the genres of marginal groups – whatever the reasons for their marginality – also to be included in the curriculum? In part I have already indicated my answer. For me the focus will need to be on the social principles that generate the textual forms. If we place the emphasis there, then there is no issue about teaching stable types: we would already have shown that the stability or instability of textual form derives from somewhere else. It comes from the social arrangements in which actions take place and, to some extent – but always present – the interest of the text-maker in closely or not so closely adhering to what they understand the reasons for the conventions to be. This approach also answers the questions about non-powerful genres: we would always need to focus on the question of power; it would be in focus. And because the curriculum would show that generic configuration derives from social/cultural configuration, the question would be, do we want to learn from and about the cultural configurations of all groups in the society, do we want to benefit from the experiences of all cultures as they are coded in genre, or do we wish to neglect that knowledge? The question would then be a profoundly political one, to which the literacy curriculum would provide both access and key.

One other question remains at this point. This *is* a book about alphabetic writing, but a book about that topic in the age of the new media. So in a real sense the question of the coexistence, the cofunctioning of modes of representation is central: not just alphabetic writing, but alphabetic writing in the environment of other, co-occurring modes, importantly, in the environment of the new media. Here the question of genre takes on two forms. One is about the origins of our theory, and whether it is adequate to an account of writing in a multimodal and multimedial world. We might suspect that, in this case particularly, all the debates have been shaped by linguistic theorisings, so that the categories that we have may be the wrong ones for what we wish to do. The other is the suspicion that maybe genre is a category which belongs only to linguistic modes – speech and writing – or perhaps to temporally organised modes, which would bring in gesture, dance, image-in-motion and so on. Maybe genre is neither appropriate as a category for spatially organised modes, nor appropriate therefore in a theory of multimodality. However important the social world which is realised in genre is, it may be that it has no possibility of realisation in spatial modes, no existence there. That would give language a privileged place indeed, the place it has held for the last few centuries. I will deal with that question in the next chapter. It might be useful to say two things now: clearly if we do extend the category of genre to modes other than linguistic ones, it will need to be defined in non-mode-specific ways. If genre-in-language does realise significant social relations then we would need to show how and why it is irrelevant to realise that such social relations are, in texts, constituted in other modes, how it could be that these social facts were not present and realised in such texts. I leave that at this point as a question to bear in mind.

The introduction of the concept of genre into theories of literacy entails that we see *text* – not letter, not word, not clause or sentence – as the central category in literacy. Text is the result of social action, and so the centrality of text means that literacy is always seen as a matter of social action and social forces, and all aspects of literacy are seen as deriving from these actions and forces.

The shift to the centrality of text is essential and its consequences are far-reaching. It challenges ingrained, common-sense theories of how we make and communicate meanings. It insists that language-use is one kind of social action among others, and that texts are the result of these social actions. This provides the relevant frame in which to pose the question of genre: within a broad framework of text as the result of constant making (in writing or speaking) and remaking (in reading or hearing) of accounts of the place of writers and readers in the world, providing us with the sense of who we think we are.

Genre is a category that orients attention to the social world. To employ it is to accept that language-use is one kind of social action, shaped by social structures and habituated practices of greater or lesser stability and persistence. In social action, the text-maker shapes language into text-as-genre. But 'text' is a material entity, drawing on the resources of the mode of writing to realise the significant features of the social environment in which texts were made, shaped and organised. In this manner, texts realise the significant features of the environment in which they were formed. Above all, these include the interrelations of the social actors involved in the social event of which the text production is one part and the dissemination of the text another. Some social events, rituals of state or religion for instance, have great stability; after all, the stability of the ritual signals and guarantees the stability of the institution. In as much as the emphasis in research has been on genres of power, it has inevitably also been on genres of greater stability, and this, somewhat inadvertently, has led to an emphasis, in theory, on the stability, even the fixity, of genre as a category. Some social events have relatively little stability. The stability or otherwise of the social situation of which the genre is the textual trace leads to the greater or lesser stability of genres themselves. It may be, as a general rule, that public events have greater stability than private events, so that public genres would be both more stable and more subject to control.

Take job interviews as an example. When I was interviewed for my first (very junior) job in a university in England in 1966, the interviewing panel consisted of at least ten people. The arrangement of the room was highly formal, with the panel ranged on one side of the room and myself opposite the panel, at some distance. That is a very unlikely scenario now. The panel would be smaller, the arrangement more 'friendly', and the formality much lessened. That change is inevitably realised in the genre of job interview. Job interviews are now closer to 'conversations' than to 'interrogations' as they were then. In periods of great social flux, the degree of dynamism, the rate of change, can lead to a sense that there is in fact no such stability to social-textual forms.

The present period is one in which, as I said earlier, the formerly stable framings in all sorts of significant areas are weakening or have already disappeared. This leads on the one hand to rejection of the notion of genre as not conforming to how things are, and to an attempt therefore to reimpose social control at the level of text. On the other hand it leads to an emphasis on blending, and on hybridisation – and to insistence that there are no longer any pure genre categories, only flux. Mixed genres are seen as evidence of the absence of genres. At one level this is of course odd; one cannot mix what does not exist in the first place. Nor can one blend things which are not initially distinct or discrete. It is not necessary to throw the baby of a useful category out with the bathwater of a theory of doubtful validity.

The mixing of genre has to be a reality, simply as an effect of our ordinary normal social lives and our ordinary normal use of language; constant change has to be seen as entirely normal as an effect of a social theory of language. In learning language as much as in our everyday lives, we encounter language in its social use, that is, as text-in-the-making and as text. Both as text-in-the-making and as text, language is always socially/generically formed. Therefore we always encounter language as genre; it cannot be otherwise. That means that every bit, every strand of language-as-text which we encounter is generically shaped. When we use language in our new making of texts, in social situations which are always at the same time recognisably like others and always new, we use generically shaped strands to make our new generically shaped texts.

These new texts-as-genres cannot therefore be other than generically mixed, even though we are using the generically shaped strands to make texts which realise both the new and old social givens of the situation in which we are making the text. Similarly with the question of fluidity and change. Even in periods of the strictest policing of generic norms, makers of texts have to make texts which fit the changing social situations in which the texts are made. And even though there may be periods in which there are stringent attempts through the exercise of power to keep the social immobile, that is always something aimed for but never achieved. Human semiotic action just like human social action is ceaselessly changing. Views to the contrary are the dreams of ideologues.

Nevertheless, there are periods of greater and periods of lesser change, for whatever reason. The last two hundred years of 'Western' history, despite being marked by cataclysmic events, has in some profound respects been a period of great social stability. The political systems of 1945 were not that different to the political systems of 1918, nor for that matter to those of 1871. To speak personally for a moment, the life lived by my grandmother, who was born in 1884, was and remained recognisable to me as the life I knew as a child, even into my adolescence in the early 1950s, despite some significant – yet I would say, superficial – differences. And indeed, the values which I attempt, now, to pass on to our children – entirely unsuccessfully – are recognisably those which I know stem from the life of my grandmother. The major force for stability was of course that of the economy of industrial mass-production, and the social and cultural forms which it produced. These lasted well into the 1950s, in Germany as much as in the UK or in Australia, or indeed in the USA. It is no wonder that social/cultural forms such as genres should come to be seen as stable.

The genre debates

One of the ironies of the still current debate around genre – in the UK it has now made its furtive appearance in the National Literacy Strategy – is that the category re-emerged into theoretical prominence, and in particular as 'stable type', just at the time when its social life had become precarious, when the 'security' of the category had come very much into crisis, towards the end of the 1970s.

Genre – the term means, simply, 'kind' – has a history as long as the western literary tradition. Aristotle used the term to distinguish major literary forms. In more recent history it has come, by and large, to be used to name 'established' literary forms – the novel, the sonnet, the epic, the tragedy – in a somewhat timeless fashion, as forms which existed out of history. Since the mid-1960s, a rapidly increasing academic interest in popular culture – film, popular print fiction (Radway, 1987), music and so on – has led to the use of the category as a device for classifying the many objects of popular culture. Here it has come to take on meanings of 'heavily stereotypical form'. The distinguishing feature of such texts was seen to be their strict adherence to convention rather than any disposition or potential to variability, unconventionality or 'creativity'. In this context 'genre-fiction' or 'genre-writing' had come to be used as a marker to distinguish between texts of high culture (not stereotyped; not, in that sense, 'generic') and popular or low culture. By extension that became a means of distinguishing between kinds of reader, namely those who seek predictability, repeatability, and those who look for the new, the unconventional, the unpredictable.

Needless to say, these are classifications made from the 'outside', judgements made by those who inhabit high culture. The users of 'genre-fiction' are fully aware of nuanced variation, and assign precise valuations to these. Nevertheless, this external – and disdainful – valuation is important to bear in mind in relation to the debate which developed around the introduction and use of the term genre in (literacy) education.

From the early 1980s the concept of genre began to be used in educational contexts in Australia. The argument in Australia went broadly like this: if there was a predictability and recognisability of text-forms, then these were important facts about writing, and competence in writing, and it was knowledge that should be made available explicitly for all learners in school. This was both a political and a pedagogical move. On the political side it seemed clear that access and equity depended on this knowledge and the possibilities of its use. On the pedagogical side the idea seemed incontestable that writing could be taught better if the characteristics of textual forms were understood, described and therefore available for explicit teaching. More than that, it was clear that an explicit curriculum was the essential prerequisite and underpinning of an equitable curriculum. In a culturally and linguistically plural society it could not be assumed that all children would come to school with the same background knowledge, culturally and linguistically; with the same cultural capital, to use the terminology of Pierre Bourdieu. Hence the language curriculum – and that of writing in particular – would have to make all that knowledge essential for any student to achieve a full competence in writing available in explicit form.

On the face of it this seemed unexceptionable as an educational aim. In fact it gave rise to a quite ferocious debate. The goal of explicit teaching of writing touched, perhaps unwittingly, a number of raw nerves. First and foremost it touched the nerve of writing as personal expression. This was the expression, in the curriculum of the school-subject English – whether in England or in Australia – of the egalitarian politics of the mid-1960s to early 1970s, which wanted to value all experience and all expression equally. That politics was the response to Stalinist and McCarthyist authoritarian repression, in the 'West' as in the 'East'. In a closely related manner it touched, equally unwittingly, the nerve of the idea which was implicit in that politics, namely that of a culturally homogeneous society. However, it did so in the face of an unrecognised change in the reality of those societies, namely that they had, in the meantime, become the culturally plural societies of the post-industrial 'West'. So what was intended as an egalitarian move could only have been that in a culturally homogeneous society, where everyone could be assumed to come with the same cultural resources into the school. It could not achieve that aim in a culturally plural society, where it is often the case that young people come into the school with cultural resources entirely unequal to those of others in the same classroom.

Let me explain. English had, in England as in Australia, become, post the 'Dartmouth Conference' in the mid-1960s, the school-subject which saw it as its aim to foster the development of the full human being, through facilitating expression of the person's individuality. 'Authenticity' was seen as one of the most important features of 'good' writing. The moral and pedagogic purpose of this approach was to foster 'authenticity', a kind of being-held-to-account for one's (actions in) writing in terms of truth to personal experience. This was a plausible goal (leaving aside the ethical considerations of this inspectorial/inquisitorial attitude (which still leaves me highly uneasy) just so long as all the members of a school-class came from, at least broadly, the same social and cultural background. If that condition was met, it might then be more confidently assumed that they would come with the same knowledges and skills around language and writing – not to mention culture much more generally.

The fact is that this approach to language and writing assumed that all students shared a homogeneous social background. It was only with that assumption that it could be thought that all members of a classroom could express their individual meanings fully, happily or competently, using the resources of representation of the dominant group. After all, it is impossible to be authentically 'me' in my writing if I do not have anything resembling real command of the resources of writing which are held to be adequate, in this language.

So two, perhaps *the* two, central supports of previous approaches to writing (*authenticity* of meaning in writing, and *writing as individual expression in a culturally homogeneous society*) were simultaneously challenged in the severest fashion by genre theory in its new form. In that new form, genres were seen as forms which had come into being as the result of social action and which, in and through all aspects of their form, represent the central characteristics of the social occasion in which they are produced. Let me go back to the simple example of the interview. It is a text in a generic form; it comes into being in a particular social situation. In that situation people come together, usually in the context of some institutional framework (work, entertainment), with specific purposes and intentions, with quite well-understood expectations, rights and duties. These are all reflected in different ways in the structure of the interview: who can ask questions, when, of what kind; who cannot ask questions; how long questions and answers may be; how direct or indirect ('polite' or 'impolite'). These forms and structures – from rules about turn-taking to finely articulated conventions of politeness – are coded with absolute precision in the language/text of the interview: whether as 'would you mind repeating that question, please?' or as 'look, we really need you to answer this point!'

But this move makes language-use, whether in writing or, as in this case, talking, no longer an individual expressive act, but a social act performed by an individual, any individual, within conventions which are clearly enough there. The action is conventional, even though I argue in this book that conventional actions are nevertheless still new and innovative. But the ability of the individual to express himself or herself as he or she wishes, as it had been seen in English pedagogy, has evaporated. We can go a step further, and say something more about convention, for it can now be seen that writing (or talking) always happens in a situation where *power* is the defining characteristic for potentials for action, and not *desire* as in the earlier pedagogic approach. Convention has two aspects: on the one hand it is that which names the results of actions undertaken in structures marked by persistence of power, so that members of a group acquiesce in or simply accept certain forms of action. These are structures that we regard as 'conventional'. On the other hand, to act within convention is to accept to a certain degree (it always is 'to a certain degree') the structures which exist, and use them as the basis for new action. The individual who acts 'conventionally' is seen as fitting into the pre-given structures of power and power-difference through their realisation, whether in forms of action or in forms of text. In that approach, the impulse for writing has shifted from desire to power, from the individual to the social, from expression to communication, from creativity to conventionality, from authenticity (a question of fit with personal truth) to appropriateness (a question of fit with social truth). No wonder there was a debate, and a fierce debate at that. Genre theory threatened to unmake everything that the subject English thought it had stood for over the preceding twenty years.

The case made by the Australian proponents of genre theory went one step further: it said that in any one society there are social situations in which the effects of power are such that not to have access to the generic forms through which power is coded is to suffer exclusion from participation in public life, to be denied criterial elements of social, economic and cultural goods. Hence access to the genres of power was seen as crucial for full, active participation – and hence for a literacy curriculum that would do its part to ensure equitable social outcomes.

There were two major foci of critique of this position. First, it was suggested, a literacy pedagogy based on this version of genre theory would ask young writers to fit their writing to pre-existing schemata, and turn their writing into the mechanical performance of an acquired rigidly adhered-to competence. This would produce the antithesis of 'lively', 'authentic', 'dynamic' writing, and would encourage stability to the point of stasis. Second, the emphasis on access to the genres of power would lead to a spurious kind of equity, in which there was no challenge to the existing status quo of social arrangements: inequitable social arrangements were not threatened or subverted, but were confirmed and, if anything, strengthened by the teaching of these forms. The proponents of genre theory by and large countered that the first critique could no longer be valid in a society in which the major requirement made of education systems was to provide equity of access to all. While it might be fine for those who already had linguistic (as well as social, cultural, economic) access to complain about the requirement to adapt to rigid schemata, for those who had no access – which included many non-middle-class white children as well – the provision of explicit knowledge was an absolutely essential step towards equitable conditions and outcomes in school. Among other things, even secure access to the curriculum of the school itself was in doubt without such knowledge. As for the argument that teaching the genres of power would leave skewed power arrangements firmly in place, the answer given tended to be that once access was available to many, then that would of itself alter the distribution of power fundamentally.

These debates, it has to be remembered, took place in the mid-to-late 1980s. In my view they reflect, without the participants on either side being particularly aware of this, conceptions taken for granted in an earlier era, in which stabilities of social and linguistic kinds had shaped the thinking of everyone, myself of course included. With the benefit of hindsight it can now be seen that the real conditions of political and social life, and of linguistic and other forms of representation, had already moved somewhere else: away, decisively, from the stabilities which made the proponents of the project utterly certain and its opponents deeply furious in equal measure.

What, then, is genre? What does it look like?

So far I have presented the picture as though there is, broadly, agreement about what genre is. Now I have to declare my own position and say that within a large frame of broad agreement within the 'Australian genre school' there were at times wide theoretical differences among those who use this category. And indeed it has to be said that this is so with other proponents of the idea of genre, the work of scholars from North America such as Miller, Swales, Bazerman, Freedman, Medway; scholars such as Bhatia and Hyland working in Hong Kong; Ongstad, Berge in Norway, and others elsewhere. In my account I am not concerned to give a survey; I am more concerned with sketching out principles of approach in which I will foreground my own.

Let me construct one other example to illustrate the range of views within the 'Australian school'. Let us say that the interview which I talked about in the preceding section was an interview with a politician, on television, and that it is just one part of a programme devoted to, say, youth unemployment. However, in an English lesson it is the programme as a whole, the whole text of the programme, that I might be interested in. The interview is merely one part of it. The text as a whole consists of genres of several kinds – there might be a panel discussion, a bit of documentary film of unemployed young people somewhere in the city, some vox pop. The text overall consists of segments which are generically distinct, but which together make up this text. Therefore we can say that 'genre' and 'text' are not the same thing; on the one hand, the latter includes the former, the former is an aspect of textual organisation; on the other hand, they are categories of different kinds. Text is the category which refers to the material aspects of language, the tangible phenomenon; genre refers to aspects of the organisation of the text, an intangible phenomenon. The two are not coextensive with each other. However, it needs to be added, there is no text or textual element that is not generically formed. Here is one point of theoretical difference: for some theorists text and genre are identical; for others, myself included, they are not.

I might be watching TV the next night and be surprised that the programme I am watching has pretty well the same structure as the one that I saw the previous evening. Tonight the topic is 'Drugs in the Inner City'. Again it has the interview with the politician, the panel discussion and so on. Generically the programme/text has stayed recognisably the same, yet in terms of its issues of concern – what it is about – it is different. The one was about unemployment, this is about drugs. This makes it clear that there is more to the make-up of text than generic organisation alone. This text is different in *discourse* from that of the evening before, even though generically it has stayed the same. Genre stays constant across these two texts, but the issues vary. In this lies another point of theoretical difference. For some theorists text is not fully explicable or describable through the category of genre alone; for others genre subsumes all there is to say about text – the two are coextensive.

Genre as sequence: temporality

One of the best known definitions of genre is that of Jim Martin (1993): 'Genres are staged, goal-oriented social processes which integrate field mode and tenor choices in predictable ways'. 'Field' is the term used to describe the 'social goings on, what the text is about'; 'mode' is the term which is used to describe the realisational mode through which the text finds its material form; and 'tenor' describes the social relations of the participants in all this. Clearly, in this definition everything that goes on in the text is included in the definition of genre, though the initial focus is on the 'staged, goal-oriented processes', that is, an emphasis on the social goal that is to be achieved by means of the genre. Most other definitions of the term tend to be equally inclusive, even though the emphases may differ somewhat.

In my approach to genre I take it to be one of three significant factors (there are others) in the constitution of text, along with *discourse* and *mode*. For me the term is best used to describe one aspect of textual organisation, namely that which realises and allows us to understand the social relations of the participants in the making, the reception and the reading/interpretation of the text. Equally central is what I have referred to as 'issues' above, and call, following the work of the French philosopher Michel Foucault (1959), *discourse* – the organisation of content/material from a particular institutional point of view, as in 'legal discourse', 'religious discourse', 'sexist discourse'. Beyond this we need to attend to realisational mode, for instance the form of language we are dealing with: is it speech or is it writing, or in multimodal contetxs, is it writing and image, or combinations of other modes? Each leads to differently organised textual and grammatical forms. Some of the other matters that are important in understanding text are questions such as dialect for instance, age, gender – the facts of biology which make men's and women's voices differ. And while these factors may not affect the overall organisation of a text, all these make spoken or written texts importantly different.

In other words, text is, for me, a large category, and it is text which needs to be understood, whether you are an English teacher, a linguist/academic, or, increasingly, a teacher of any subject in the school, in England certainly. And as I will say in this chapter as elsewhere in this book, text and the design of text needs to be newly understood in multimodal communication. However, I now want to be more specific about genre and what it is. I will look at three texts which I consider to be – broadly – in the same genre, which I shall call 'rules and regulations'. The focus here is to see in aspects of the texts traces of the social relations of the participants in the production of the text. Here is the first text:

Swimming club rules

1   Parents must accompany and take responsibility for their children at all times, unless the child is in the water in an instructed class. *Note* – In most cases this will mean one adult enrolling with one child, or, if they so wish one adult with more than one child provided it is understood they are responsible for them.

2   Being absent for more than three consecutive sessions without explanation to the membership secretary means automatic expulsion.

3   No outside shoes will be worn when in the pool area.
4   Please respect the facilities and equipment, and take particular care with untrained children.
5   The age limits of the club are six months to eight years. For the six to eight years old instruction will be provided. Children may remain members for the completed term in which their eighth birthday falls.
6   There must be no more than twenty-four bodies in the pool at any one time.
7   Membership cards must always be carried and shown on request.

(Norwich, England, 1974)

To start with, we can note that the rules are numbered. While the sequence of rules seems to have some meaning – for instance, the rule-makers seem to have been concerned to foreground 'parental responsibility' – the ordering seems more to be about how many rules there are than about a strict sequence in which the rules are to apply, and more about showing that there is 'an order' than about some principle of ordering. Rule 7 for instance might appear as rule 2 and so on without any great disturbance to the meaning of the text. The idea of 'staged process' is very weakly present.

The rule-makers, or the authority from which the rules issue, are not named, and with one exception those to whom the rules are addressed are not directly addressed; the exception being rule 4. That is, the participants are in fact not or hardly named or identified; they are assumed to 'know who they are'. The social relations between them are represented as distanced, via three mechanisms: the use of third person terms of address: 'parents' (rather than 'you'); the use of agentless passives – 'cards must be carried' (rather than 'please always carry your card'); and the quite pronounced use of nominalisations – 'an instructed class', 'being absent for more than three consecutive days without explanation to the membership secretary', 'untrained children' (rather than the form with the verb: 'children who are not yet (toilet-)trained'). The first makes the people involved talked about rather than talked to; the second deletes mention of those who are responsible for actions; and the last shifts focus from *actions* in time, to *states of affairs* or *object-like phenomena* out of time.

A rule is both a command and an instruction indicating how action is to be performed. In these 'rules' commands are represented either as 'meanings' – 'being absent means expulsion' – or as classifications – 'the age limits are six months to eight years'. That is, interpersonal relations are re-presented either as a meaning relation or as a relation of classification, that is, as ideational relations: 'being absent . . . *means* automatic expulsion', 'in most cases this will mean one adult enrolling', 'no outside shoes will be worn', 'the age limits are six months to eight years', 'there must be no more than twenty-four bodies in the pool'.

Overall there is a strong sense of uncertainty and insecurity about social relations, indicated as much by a wavering between the aspiration to total control through total knowledge – 'no outside shoes will be worn when in the pool area' to the anxiously nervous 'please . . . take particular care with untrained children' – as by the over-formal syntax. Much could be said about the social world and its relations that has given rise to and is reflected in the generic form of this text. It may be enough to say that it was produced by a group of young women, mothers who knew each other socially, who were unpractised rule-makers. They needed to produce rules that might guide the safe conduct of a new water babies swimming club, and clearly felt uncomfortably lodged between the attempt to impose authority and the reality of friendly social relations. My point is to show just how precisely these social facts are reflected in the generic form of the text.

As I have indicated, in some approaches to genre, (temporal) sequence figures significantly as one definitional criterion: 'staged, goal-oriented social processes'. In the approach that I take, sequence can have its role, in those genres in which the unfolding of social action is significant. Certainly that is the case, for instance, in a *procedure*, such as a recipe for instance. In other cases, the rules here being one example, social relations are not expressed through the sequenced ordering of action but through factors that focus on aspects of power. Sequence forms no part of the definition of genre in this case. This matter will be important to bear in mind when I come to discuss the question of genre in spatially displayed representation.

My second example comes from a different place and a different time, not from Norwich in the England of 1973, but from the far north coast of New South Wales, in the Australia of *circa* 1988.

Beach house holiday units

This unit accommodates 5 persons only. Extra persons will be charged a nightly rate. Unit to be vacated by 10 am. on the day of departure.

Only soft toilet paper to be used in septic toilet & please do not dispose of sanitary pads in toilet.

Garbage bags to be placed out on concrete near barbecue each MONDAY before 7 pm.

Barbecue is available for your use. Utensils in laundry.

No pets allowed.

No fish to be cleaned on premises.

For safety reasons please turn off heaters and fans when unit is unoccupied.

Thank you

Brian and Norma Denny (Prop.)

PLEASE DO NOT PUT GARBAGE IN COUNCIL BINS

Holiday flat rules (Red Rock, Yamba, Australia, 1988)

To start with, we note that these rules are not numbered. Here too the sequence of rules has the meaning of foregrounding those issues which seem to have proved most worrysome to the rule-makers in their weary experience – too many people cramming into their flats, blocked toilets, uncollected rotting garbage, and so on. It seems that fish-scales on the concrete near the back door are more problematic than heaters left on for hours. Here the rule-makers, or the authority from which the rules issue, are named at the end of the text, though as in the previous set they are not named in the rules themselves: not 'we ask you to place your garbage out on the concrete'. With one exception, those for whom the rules are intended are not directly addressed: not 'you are kindly requested not to use newspaper in the toilets'; the exception being the fourth rule. So, as with the previous set, the participants are not or are hardly named. The relations between the proprietors/rule-makers and the addressees of the rules are represented as distanced, via three mechanisms: the avoidance of terms of address – with the exception of 'persons' and 'your'; the use of agentless passives – 'no fish to be cleaned'; and the pervasive use of negation – *only, no, not.*

There are therefore clear similarities and clear differences between the sets of rules – similarities both at the level of strategies, such as *distancing*, and of actual realisations, such as the agentless passives, third person address, avoidance of naming. The similarities guarantee the recognisability of the genre – no one would mistake it as a genre of a different kind – and the differences are evidence of the constant shifts in form in response to variabilities in the social relations.

It might be of interest to pick on just one of the differences, in order to explore the very close link between social relations and linguistic realisation. The second set of rules has five overt negatives, counting *only* as one of these (*only* five = *not more* than five); although there are also several covert negatives *vacate (not stay), turn off (not leave on), unoccupied (not occupy)*. In the much longer Swimming Club text there are only two overt negations, though there are several covert ones as well. The social situation of the one genre is such that the rule-makers can assume that prohibitions are, by and large, internalised to such an extent that either they need not to be stated, or they can be left as covert negatives. This is a social group that accepts that 'X means Y' means 'X cannot mean other than Y'. It is a group that has agreed to internalise prohibition as tacit consent. That can seemingly not be the basis for action of the proprietors of the holiday flats. Their clientele is not socially unified enough to permit such an assumption. They can assume that their guests will not light a fire on the living-room floor, but they cannot assume a range of other things; they are not addressing a social group which is unified in that respect.

This is more apparent still in the third example. It comes from an Aboriginal community in Northern Australia; Wollondilly, the name of the community, is fictional.

Toyota Law

Wollondilly Health Council

1 NO GROG at all in ambulances.
2 NO EATING at all in ambulances.
3 Ambulances must be cleaned by drivers when returned.
4 Ambulances for HEALTH business only – NOT FOR COMMU-
NITY AND OTHER MEETINGS.
5 NO SHOPPING.
6 NO KANGAROO HUNTING.
7 Only for sick ones. – Not too many family. – Hospital and Health
business only.
8 No private use by staff on weekends, except when used for clinic
business.
9 One car for sorry business only.
10 Only CLOSE family to go with patients to town. Not big mobs of
the one family. (Ambulance drivers need to be strong.)
11 Not more than eleven (11) passengers.

SIGNED: [10 signatories]

MEMBERS OF THE HEALTH COUNCIL
(Northern Territory, Australia, 1992)

There are similarities to the preceding two sets of rules; clearly these are rules. I
am so unfamiliar with the social lives of the people involved here that I cannot
say, with the relative confidence that I expressed before that the ordering of the
rules either is or is not significant. In other words, one has to be at least relatively inward with a social group and its lived day-to-day experience to
understand such a thing – whether at the social level or at the generic. There is
only one passive here, but there is an overwhelming use of negation. Prohibition on action has to be made explicit. That much one can say from the form of
the genre. It is a society in which these things cannot be taken for granted.

The point that I wish to make is that there is an entire link and an extremely
close link between the social organisation and the social relations of social actors
involved in the making and receiving or interpretation of texts, and the realisational forms of the texts. It is the social givens which shape the generic form of
the text. Genre is a response to the social givens. This is clear enough, and
counters any assumptions about the complete stability, or the generality, of
genres. At the same time it does not undermine or negate the point of recognisability. The question that arises is, where are the recognisable similarities, and
the recognisable differences, and what do they reveal – at the level of the meaning of genre about the social organisation of this group and of its actions? At the
level of the forms of genre, we can see that variability within recognisability is
not an issue at all.

It is possible to add to this set, ad infinitum (and friends who know my fascination with this kind of text take delight in finding and sending me new examples, from Japanese hotels, from University changing rooms and so on). My three examples go across some fifteen years and two hemispheres. But just to show the ubiquity and stability of the form, here is one other – without discussion – from a Japanese hotel, *circa* 1999.

Since hotels are public service institutions and their doors are open to all guests at all times, we have to devise some rules and regulations to maintain the dignity of the hotel and the security of our guests. Therefore, we request you to observe the following regulations revised on the basis of Article 11 of the Provisions Governing Accommodations:

1 Kindly do not smoke in bed or any other place liable to catch fire.
2 Use of a heating apparatus, cooking appliance or an iron inside the hotel is prohibited.
3 Do not bring the following into the hotel:
   (a) Animals or any kinds of pets.
   (b) Any goods emitting foul odor.
   (c) Goods considerably large in number, quantity or size.
   (d) Inflammable powords, oils or dangerous goods.
   (e) Guns or swords not authorized for possession.
4 Moving about in the corridor or outside the guest rooms while in Yukata (informal kimono) or slippers is undesirable.
5 Please do not invite visitors to your room.
6 Refrain from making noise or singing loud enough to disturb other guests in the hotel.
7 Gambling or doing anything which is hostile to public morality in the hotel is highly objectionable.
8 Minors, who are not accompanied by their guardian, may be refused accommodation at the hotel.
9 The distribution and display of advertisements and the sale of goods inside the hotel are not allowed.
10 Outside orders for food and drinks are not accepted.
11 Attaching items to the windows which will spoil the outside appearance of this hotel is undesirable.
12 Please do not throw items out of the window.
13 The use, without permission, of hotel facilities and furnishings for purposes other than those originally intended is prohibited.
14 Do not transfer the hotel facilities and furnishings from one position to another or change their original positions without permission from the management.
   In case of non-conformity with the above regulations, the guest may be refused further accommodation and use of the hotel

facilities in accordance with Article 12 of the Provisions Governing Accommodations.

15 Upon check-in, please use the free deposit box located at the front cashier section for custody of your cash and other valuables. Should loss or theft of the guests cash or valuables occur from any other part of the hotel, the management will not be responsible for any of the lost or stolen articles.

16 The custody period of things received in the cloakroom will be three months from the date of receipt, unless otherwise specified.

17 Kindly deposit valuables in the safe custody of the cashier.

18 When the bill amount exceeds deposits, the guest will be asked for additional payment. In case of a long stay, weekly payment will be required.

19 Regarding payment of hotel charges as mentioned in Article 10 of the Provisions Governing Accommodations, the following rules will apply.
   (a) The guest may be asked to pay charges even during his stay in the hotel. When notified of such payment due, please comply immediately.
   (b) When a guest stays in the hotel for a long period of time, payment will be requested at seven-day intervals.
   (c) When changing the length of stay, payment to date will have to be made.

20 Pay telephones are located in the 1st and 2nd lobby area, and on the 3rd floor. A small service fee is charged for each outgoing call from your room phone.

Japanese hotel rules and regulations

The fact that we can add indefinitely many examples to this set shows several things. My friends recognise the 'kind'; that is, they know the genre; the genre occurs very widely – because the social situation in which it arises occurs ubiquitously around many parts of the world; the (four) texts here have similarities, and yet they are also very different. In other words, genre responds, flexibly, to social environment, because the makers of genre are immersed in the demands of social lives and are constantly responsive to these demands.

The first point demonstrates conclusively the reality of the concept: my friends are not linguists, they are, from that point of view, interested bystanders. The recognisability has to do with the similarity of the social organisation from which these texts come. The third point demonstrates that genre is social: it reflects, is structured by and projects those aspects of the social situation which focus on those involved and on the manner of their involvement. Genre is a social category: it is made by people in their social encounters, and when it has become text it gives us insight into the make-up of the social world in which it was made. This is precisely one of the central interests in texts of many people, whatever their professional or non-professional involvement with text of any kind – literary or televisual, popular or high cultural. The focus here concerns where we look and what we are looking at. The previous focus on text, historically, and one which is still that of common sense, was the interest more on what above I called 'the issues', the discursive aspects of text. In this new focus that interest remains, but now there is equal focus on how the social world is present in the very structure of the text.

To state this once more: both the 'Swimming Club Rules' and the 'Toyota Law' text focus on a prohibition on action. The most usual way to do this, in most instances, is to use a negation: 'no smoking' (or 'we thank you for not smoking'); 'please do not pick the flowers' and so on. In the Swimming Club Rules there are just three instances of negation: 'no outside shoes will be worn', 'no more than twenty-four bodies', and perhaps the 'embedded' negative in 'untrained children' (children who are not (yet) trained). By contrast, in the 'Toyota Law' text ('Toyota Law' because Toyota land-cruisers are the vehicles used as ambulances in this community), every one of the eleven rules uses a direct negative, with the exception of rule 3. What does this mean? Does it mean, simply, that there are more negations, and that there are more prohibitions to be made in the case of 'Toyota Law'? Hardly: every rule in the 'Swimming Club' text constitutes a prohibition, and has (or is) a (deeply) buried negation. 'Parents must accompany . . . .' is 'parents must not leave children unsupervised'; 'Being absent for more than three consecutive sessions means expulsion' is 'do not miss more than three consecutive sessions'. The verb 'mean' is used twice, tellingly: if you are told the meaning of something, then this is not simply to enrich your semantic repertoire ('"Liebe" means "love"'), nor is it simply an instruction ('if you want to mean "Liebe", then in English use "love"'); it is a prohibition ('if "Liebe" means "love", then do not use "affection" in your translation').

The texts project different social worlds; but that difference is not about more or less prohibition, it is about how members of two distinct social groups are socialised into prohibition and how prohibition is handled in these two worlds. One says that you provide 'meanings', which are so entirely internalised by all members of that group that no one will act outside of these meanings, and all of us know that we can rely on that. Prohibition has become invisible. This is one social implication of 'shared meanings'. The other says that if you want things done or not done, you say so, overtly; meanings are not internalised or at least you cannot rely on the internalisation of meanings by all members of the group. Prohibition is out there, for all to see. There are social implications both for the presence and for the absence of 'shared meanings'. The point is not to make value judgements on these worlds; the real problems of each are easy enough to see. My point is rather to show how generic organisation – realised in linguistic form – provides another, a powerful, way of 'reading' the meanings of the social worlds projected by these three texts.

In the three texts there are many other linguistic and textual features which have social import; in fact, all of them do. For instance, the heavily formal language of the 'Swimming Club Rules' speaks of the (borrowed) weight of bureaucratic language and the institutions in which it is produced. Look, as just one instance, at the subject noun-phrase 'being absent far more than three consecutive sessions without explanation to the membership secretary' or take the impersonality of the address to members. This text was written by a group of young mothers of very young children, all well-educated women, who knew each other socially and frequently met in each other's houses; a fact which shows the social significance of genre even more: to step into, to assume the forms of a genre, is to step into a specific social world with its vastly ramified values, practices and obligations.

The genre of rules and regulations is not all that easily accommodated in the broad classificatory schema of the generic types of the Australian genre school, though the genre of procedure may be relatively close to what is going on here. If you look at the 'beach house holiday units' text you get closer to a sense of that genre. Nevertheless my three examples present their rules in a relatively unordered fashion or, to put this more honestly, I cannot readily make out the principles of the ordering. I suspect that in all three cases there are principles of order: the rule about turning off heaters comes aptly at the end, as you leave the flat, so to speak. And maybe in the 'Swimming Club Rules' the writers did not want to start with the merely officious rule about carrying membership cards (this was 1974 after all), and felt that parental responsibilities should be the first concern. Procedural genres, like all genres, project a world with a larger order, a coherence: whether, as in the recipe for duck à l'orange, the necessary sequence of steps to achieve the perfect dish, or in the procedure through which a scientific experiment, an industrial process, or a social event is set out.

The important point is to be aware of the fundamental tension around genre, uneasily hovering between regularity and repeatability on the one hand – the effect of social stabilities and of regulations erected around text to keep them close to 'convention' – and the dynamic for constant flux and change on the other hand. These are the effect both of inevitable social change (even in the most conservatively stable societies) and of the constantly transformative action of people acting in ever-changing circumstances (even where the changes are of the subtlest kind). The current interest in genre may, paradoxically, be an effect of social, economic, political changes of the most far-reaching kind, which are precisely unmaking the conditions of stability, repeatabilty, recognisability. So just when the concept was introduced into education, in Australia in the mid-1980s – with a clear emphasis on stability – it had ceased to have the tight connection to social conditions which had given it (the appearance of) stability. In other words, in some senses the concept's potency was discovered in theory (and introduced into educational practice) just at the very moment when the social conditions had become such as to make the concept problematic.

I will discuss one other example, a different genre (Figure 6.1). It is a slight

Figure 6.1 'Annapelle': a multimodal promotional message

text, but I want to know what I can say about it generically. My own definition of genre remains as before: genre is that shaping of text which reflects and is brought into existence as a result of the social relations of the participants in the making (writing/speaking) and in the use (reading/hearing/interpretation) of a text. Here is a copy of the written part of the text:

> Annapelle is a 100% Australian owned company specialising in the manufacture and importing of quality handcrafted Leather handbags and accessories. This fine produce which is made in Italian Leather was manufactured in the People's Republic of China under strict supervision, and the packaging and quality inspection was carried out in Melbourne, Australia.
>
> (card supplied with leather purse)

The provenance of this text is as follows: it is a small card, about 5 x 10 cm, on quite firm 'cardboard', olive/eucalypt green. It came, together with two other cards exactly the same, in a leather purse, sent from Australia, in 1996 on the occasion of a birthday, sent as a gift and as a memento from 'home' to us, living now in England.

What can I say about this text from the point of view of genre? First, it informs me, it tells me things, and in this it suggests a social relationship between its makers and me: I am someone who may like (or need) to be told things; 'they' are someone who can tell me things. The text is laid out in what I take to be an aesthetically pleasing fashion – it is 'sculpted' (it reminds me of the shapes of poems by the seventeenth-century poet George Herbert). The makers of the card address me as someone who is interested in something beautiful, as someone who has taste. There is of course the logo (is it Renaissance Italy, or is it Australian art deco?). The language too strikes me as carefully 'crafted'; it uses adjectives such as 'fine'. The punctuation is sparse to the point of severity; I assume so as not to make the text look fussy. In its overall generic shape it is perhaps nearest to the report genre – leaning on the factual, the reporting of matters presented as fact.

Now the appearance of a report-genre (if that is what it is) in this shape, in this context, is for me quite unusual. I expect genres to occur in a certain place, and when they appear out of their place I wonder what is going on. This recontextualisation of a genre (to borrow a term from the theoretical work of Basil Bernstein) makes it quite different. 'Lifting' a genre from one context and putting it in another (lifting it out of its 'proper' social context and inserting it in another) is an innovative act, an act of creativity. It changes not just the genre, not just my relation to the text, but it changes also the new context in which it occurs. 'Why', I ask myself, 'am I being told these things?' I am happy just to have the purse, why the report?

The answers to that question are many. The work done by the card is semiotic work, it is the work which transforms the purse from something made from Italian leather (the text says '*in* Italian leather'), and made in China, into something which is 100 per cent Australian. That is why I am being given the report. In an economy and a society of consumer capitalism, in which consumption is the means for establishing 'who I am' through my lifestyle, the purse is no longer just a purse, it is something through which I can (re)connect to Australianness. Of course, in order to see how the card really does that, we need to focus on more than the features I have mentioned. In the text we need to focus on the discourses of nationalism, of (weakly articulated) racism, of taste, and of contemporary economies ('quality inspection'). Beyond the written text in that narrow sense, we need to focus on quite physical material features of the card. Generically, as card, it relates to business cards, and to the social relations of that type of card, the relations to visiting cards, credit cards and so on. In its colour it invokes both a certain idea of Italy, and the colour of the Australian bush. Australianness could have been signalled, of course, with the use of the Aboriginal flag, and its red, gold and black colours. But that would have jarred with the discourses present here, and with the generic construction of the rest of the card.

Are all of these features – whether generic or discursive – there by accident? Of course not: they are absolutely precise indicators of the assessment of the widest social, political and economic environments by the maker(s) of this object or text. That is the condition of all textual objects. The deep changes in that complex environment have given rise here to the production of a text which, in its generic, discursive features (realised in language but also in quite other semiotic modes: colour, paper, shape, image, layout) represents these features. This is, to me at least, an entirely novel text, and its novelty arises out of the innovative, transformative, creative response by its maker to the environment as she or he has perceived it.

Of course, in this we have at once also one feature of the new demands which are made on 'literacy' in the widest sense. Text is more than content or form, more than discourse or genre in my terms, but texts are also always more than language. This card (as indeed the rules and regulations texts) is a response to new demands, met out of a knowledge of what existing linguistic/semiotic resources are available – from punctuation to syntax, from layout to genre, from discourse to logo, from colour to prepositional usage, to thickness of card and size – and how they can be (re)shaped in response to the requirements as understood by the maker of this new text. This is a complex example of semiotic design: an awareness of what is to be represented, for whom, using modal resources available to serve the purposes of the designer. In this shift it becomes apparent that text is more than genre, that text is always more than language. We have moved from literacy as an enterprise founded on language to text-making as a matter of design, an enterprise founded on a variety of forms of representation and communication. From competence in use we have moved to competence in design and, with that, innovation and creativity (through the use of many modes) are now in the centre.

In this brief discussion I have tried to indicate that generic meanings are carried as much in prepositional usage as in the thickness of the card and its glossiness, as much as in the type of card as in the written text. All these point to social meanings, realised in genre. They are not, however, all tied in any way to temporality or to temporal sequence. The assumption that genre is a category tied to temporality and sequence seems to be an instance of a mode-specific meaning taken generally, an 'accident', we might say, of linguistic realisation.

7

MULTIMODALITY, MULTIMEDIA AND GENRE

A multimodal view of genre

So far I have treated the category of *genre* more or less as though it were obviously and naturally realised in language, either in speech or in writing. Much of the work done over the last twenty or thirty years assumes that genres are linguistic phenomena. Yes, film, or video and television, have been described by using this category, and of course they consist of much more than 'just' language. And literary texts have been described in genre-terms for a very long time. But in the broad area of literacy the work that underpins the interest in genre treats it as a purely linguistic phenomenon. This needs to be expanded a bit by saying that the assumption that genre is a linguistic category does not really surface into explicitness: it is simply there. Yet as so many of the text-objects in the contemporary world – as my example of the small card in the previous chapter – make use of modes other than speech or writing, or make use of many modes at the same time, the question must arise of whether 'genre' is a category that applies to texts or text-like objects realised in other modes, in image, gesture, 3D representations, or in relation to multi-modally constituted texts. Is genre a linguistic category first and foremost, or most plausibly? Or is it a category that applies to all forms of representation and communication?

The problem which arises is that the theoretical categories developed to understand and describe genre are linguistic categories, developed by linguistics for linguistically realised objects. The question then is whether categories that are specific to the modes of speech or writing, to texts which are (predominantly) linguistic, can be apt, appropriate or useful for describing texts which are realised in other modes. Does it matter if we use linguistic categories to describe visual or three-dimensional texts? Can that which is realised in language – that is, the kinds of meaning that I discussed in relation to written genres – be realised in other modes, in image, for instance, or in combinations of image and writing? Can the meanings of negation, overt and covert, that I discussed be realised other than in speech or writing? Or, to turn it the other way around, are there social meanings which can be realised in the mode of image but not in the mode of speech or of writing? We can make the question quite specific and ask, how do images represent social relations and social inter-actions?

The materiality of the different modes – sound for speech, light for image, body for dance – means that not everything can be realised in every mode with equal facility, and that we cannot transport mode-specific theories from one mode to another without producing severe distortions. This is somewhat diffi-cult to express clearly, because I want to say that meanings, in the broad sense, can be realised in any mode, but that when they are, they are realised in mode-specific articulations. This means that we need to attend to that which is mode-specific and to that which is not. Our past understanding of meaning has not raised that question, and therefore our attention does not go in that direc-tion. Rather we have been told that that which is meant is realised, and that that which is realised is that which has been meant. Instead we need to under-stand that meaning is articulated in this way in a specific mode, and in this other way in another mode. From here we have questions which go on the one hand in the direction of 'meaning', loosely speaking, and on the other hand in the direction of theory. From the point of view of meaning the question is, what is the meaning to be realised? From the point of view of theory one question is, what are the affordances of different modes, and how do different modes there-fore realise meanings of a certain kind? The other is about genre as a category: is it a mode-specific category or not?

The question about the social meaning is readily answered: it is not possible to imagine communication which does not encompass the meanings realised in genre. That is, no message or text is conceivable which does not respond to such social facts. Hence all representation and communication must be generi-cally shaped; it must carry these social meanings. 'Meaning' is inevitably and necessarily realised differently in different modes. And so the question here is, what is our sense of the social givens realised in genre, and how will they appear in this modal articulation? Does the category of genre remain impor-tant, useful, necessary; does it become more or less important in the era of multimodal communication? The answer is that the category of genre is essen-tial in all attempts to understand text, whatever its modal constitution. The point is to develop a theory and terms adequate to that.

The question is, what is it that we want to mean, and what modes and genres are best for realising that meaning? That leads us to the social givens which we want to realise in a genre, and a question more like, what social, representa-tional and communicative function do genres have? I will return to this throughout this discussion, but here I wish to make this concrete by looking at two texts.

The texts are entirely usual. They come from a science classroom in a sec-ondary school in inner-city London. The children in this class are in year 8, which means that they are 12 to 13 years of age. The series of lessons in which the texts were produced had as its topic 'plant cells'. Four children – all girls – had worked together in a group around a microscope, first preparing a slide with a piece of the epidermis of an onion, then looking at this slide through a microscope, and afterwards carrying out the task, given by the teacher, of 'doing a report'. Each had to 'record' the experiment: to draw what they had seen through the microscope and to write what they had done in conducting the experiment. The teacher had given them just two specific instructions: 'put your writing at the top of the page' (the teacher was anxious that the drawing should not take up too much of the space, so as to leave enough room for writing), and 'use only your lead pencil – do not use coloured pencils in your drawings' (to distinguish 'scientificness' – black-and-white drawing – from 'artisticness' – using colour pens – or from 'everyday realism'). Here I will look at two of the four texts produced. I am particularly interested in the meanings of formal aspects – the genre – of the texts.

The first example (Figure 7.1) has the drawing at the top of the page (as did another one of the four), and the written part of the text at the bottom. Image and writing are clearly separated on the page; each has its own, slightly differing, heading. The written text is in the generic form of a 'recount'. That is, it is a temporally ordered or sequenced presentation of events reported in sentences. The image part of the text has the form of a line-drawing; it is not clear that there is a suitable generic label available to name it.

Here I will first say something briefly about the written part of the text as a 'recount', then I will attempt to uncover the generic form of the visual part, and then speculate on the generic form of the text as a whole. My intention is to answer the question 'is the category "genre" useful in a multimodal text and, if so, how is it useful?'

As I have mentioned, I treat genre as that category which realises the social relations of the participants involved in the text as interaction. The social relations which are realised in the recount are of three types: first, those of the relations of the actors, objects and events which are *reported in* the recount; second, those of the relations between the participants in the act of communication, which are *implied by* the recount. The third type concerns the social world that is *represented in* the recount. The question here is, how is (the institution of) science represented or constructed as a social activity? Here we are in large part in the realm of the discursive organisation of the activity, in the sense of Foucault's use of 'discourse'.

The relations 'in' the recount are of actors acting in events with and on objects, either singly (I collected all the equipment) or jointly (we then sorted the microscope out). This is recounted 'realistically', that is, it is presented as being a recount of the actual, significant events, in the temporal sequence in which they happened, with a clear enough implication that no other (significant) events occurred. The recount is 'complete'; there is closure: it is a completed, finished, rounded-off textual entity. The recount, as genre, makes an implicit claim about the relation of the events or practices recounted to other practices in the world, and of the relation of the domain of the practices to other domains. It is the claim of realism, in the everyday world. It makes the

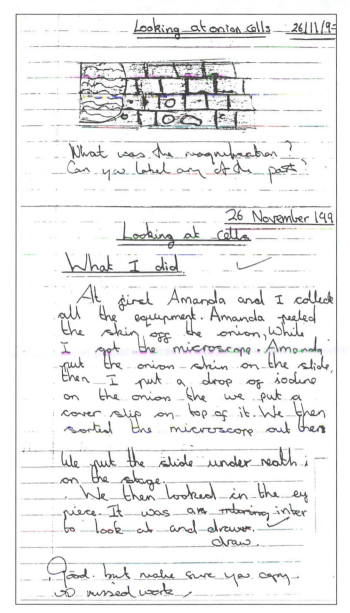

Figure 7.1 Student drawing of a plant cell 1: 'like a brick wall'

claims, implicitly: 'this is, simply, how it was; these were the main participants, the main events and they occurred in this order'. It claims, specifically, that 'practices in the science classroom are practices in the everyday world'. (A narrative, by contrast, makes a different claim: 'that is how I have (re)constructed the world for you', and 'practices in the everyday world may be different to the way they are narrated here'.)

The social roles and relations established and implied by the *genre of recount as message* (that is, genre oriented towards communication) are, if *I* am presenting the recount, those of 'recounter' – I am someone who knows that which is being recounted – and 'recountee' – you are someone whom I regard as wishing to have the events recounted to you. If I am receiving the recount, the roles are those of myself being someone who is interested in having these events recounted to me, in being the 'recountee', and accepting you as the 'recounter'. The recount presents a world of action/event, temporally ordered and complete.

In asking about the generic form of the drawing, we bump up against a problem: there are no genre-terms for describing what this drawing is or does, either in terms of the presentation of material – the content – or of its representation of the social relations between the 'participants' in the production and reproduction of the text, the participants in the communicational event. What are these relations, as they are realised in the drawing, as they appear here? (To some extent what appears here will become clearer by comparison with the next example.) In answering this I will make use of the same types of relation as I used just above. First, what is shown 'in' the drawing (analogous to what is shown 'in' the recount) and by the drawing as a whole? The drawing shows a rectangular block with clearly distinct elements within it. The block is strongly framed along the top and the bottom, but is 'open' at each end, suggesting that it is 'a part of', 'an extract from', 'a fragment of' a larger entity. This suggests that while the drawing is not textually complete, it is conceptually complete: any other part of the larger entity of which this is a fragment will also be like this fragment. The elements themselves are drawn as being broadly uniform in shape and size. One of the handouts used in the lead-up lessons had suggested to the students that they would see something resembling 'bricks in a brick-wall', and quite clearly that metaphor has guided this student's 'seeing'. On the left-most edge there is a large 'irregularity' – the circular shape – and there are small bubble-like elements within the bricks.

This is a structure of relatively uniform elements in regular arrangement: the blocks are arranged in even layers, arranged regularly. While the recount presents a world of *happenings*, of *actions* or *events*, what is displayed here is a world of *entities as they are*: static, stable, regular elements in regular arrangement. While the world of the recount is complete in that *it represents all there is to recount*, the world of this display is complete in that *it represents all there is to know* – to show more would be to show more of the same, and while the world of the recount is set in time and is completed – it has happened – the world of this display is out of time – it just *is* – and it is complete in *being*.

The relation between the participants in the act of communication is an 'objective' one. The viewer is presented with this text-element 'front on'. It is objectively there, with maximal 'involvement' of the viewer, that is, the viewer is positioned as confronting this image straight on, at eye-level. The positioning is neither to the side – which would indicate lesser involvement, nor is the viewer below or above the element shown, something that would indicate difference in power. The entity is presented to the viewer in a maximally neutral manner: it is simply 'there', *objectively*. Instead of the relations of 'recounter' and 'recountee' of that which is 'recounted', we have the relation of 'displayer' and 'viewer' of that which is 'displayed'.

At this stage we would need to look back at the written recount and attempt an assessment of kinds of involvement there. We can, however, make comments on the third level, the relation between the world of practices represented here and that of the everyday world. The mode of drawing is not a realist one: it is generalised away from everyday realism, both through the means of using the soft black pencil on the white page (rather than the use of colour, as in one of the other pieces of work) and the abstracting, diagrammatic form of representation. The former tells us that certain aspects of the everyday world, such as the colour of the viewed entity, are not relevant here, and similarly with other aspects, such as the actual, 'real' boundaries of the object. These all provide pointers to the kind of social world into which we are invited. 'Diagram' is closer to serving as a genre-label, in that it suggests both a particular social purpose, and social relations, of those who use the diagram and those who make it. 'Diagram' also suggests a particular coding-orientation: not the realism of the everyday world, but the realism of the scientific-technological world.

Meanings of genres in multimodal texts

So what is the genre of this text overall? And what consequences does all this have not just for a view of writing, but for the actual uses of writing, and for likely changes to the uses, forms and values of the technology of writing?

To answer the first question, we can say that there is a clear difference between the 'naturalism' (within the realism of everyday life) of the written genre of recount, and the abstraction (within the world of scientific theorising) of the visual genre of diagram-drawing. The first positions me as someone who hears an account of a completed, ordered, sequence of events, recounted as though they form part of my everyday life. That sense is reinforced by the syntax of the writing, which is close to the clausal structures of everyday speech, as is its use of words – 'we then *sorted* the microscope *out*' from a quite casual register. Doing science, in this account, is like doing cooking, or doing the dishes. The second form, the visual, positions me as someone who is given a view of a fragment of an entity, but understands that the fragment 'stands for' the structure of the whole entity, in a form which is not part of the everyday world. I am positioned in a different domain, out of time, in a world of regularity produced by the theory that I am applying.

The task of the science curriculum is, still, to induct young people into the practices that constitute 'doing science'. That practice is presented in two distinct ways here: 'doing science' in the recount presents me with a world of ordered actions or events which are like actions or events in the everyday world. 'Doing science' in the drawing/diagram is presented as being about another world, not one of actions and events, but of states of affairs with regularities, abstracted away from the everyday world. If this multimodal text-entity 'has' a genre, then it is a mixed genre, in which differently organised worlds appear differently: one a world of actions where the actors are like you and me, the other a world without actors, a world of things as they are. If one is the world of the everyday, then the other is the world of theory, abstraction. One draws me in by suggesting that I am like the actors in a world that is familiar to me. The other positions me as a neutral observer of an objectively present world, but an observer with a special status and a special lens.

This is the meaning of this genre; these are the social relations and the social roles of the participants projected by the combined genre. Of course, this is a genre produced by a non-expert. The fact that she mixes the social relations of the world of the everyday with the social relations of the world of scientific work may be an effect of the teaching that she has had, or it may be her response to what she has taken from that teaching. She is able to form her own generic response, to see science her way and to represent it her way: actions which are like those of the everyday, in relation to a world which is differently constituted. The genre overall seems to position her somewhere between the everyday and the special world of technical/theoretical endeavour.

Mixed genres are commonplace, though the kind of disjunction presented here would appear as a severe problem if both texts were written texts, or if this was the text of an expert. Because the two generic positions are realised in different modes, the disjunction is not readily apparent, or does not become a problem; it does not appear as a contradiction. In fact it may well be a very good representation of the social relations as they exist in the science teaching that she is experiencing. Is it a problem that we do not have labels for these 'mixes', or indeed do not have labels for many kinds of generic organisation? This is not, I think, the main issue at all; if we find that we need labels, we will make them up. What is important is to recognise that texts realise, among other things, the kinds of social relation pointed to here.

In this text too we see design at work. This young woman has made a number of design decisions in a multimodal representation: a decision about layout, in where to place which element; a decision about generic (epistemological) form – everyday or scientific – for each of the two elements; a decision about which mode to use for the realisation of each of the distinct positions; and no doubt others.

As far as labels for the mixes are concerned, my analysis of the next example (Figure 7.2) will show that this may be even less of a useful aim.

Several differences are immediately apparent. The 'diagram' (with the teacher's written comment, 'Diagram needs to be much larger') is below the written text, as the teacher had asked. There is a division between the written

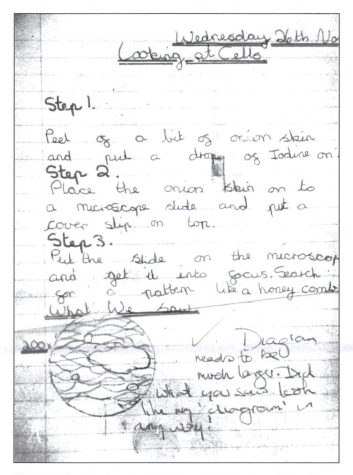

Figure 7.2 Student drawing of a plant cell 2: the lens of the microscope

part and the visual; they are separated by a heading – 'what we saw'. But the image partly protrudes into its heading, and the heading is very tightly linked to the written text, insisting, as it were, on a connectedness, even a unity, of writing and image. Where in the first example they had been clearly separate, here there is a real move physically to integrate them.

The genre of the written text is that of *procedure*: a sequence of distinct (in this case numbered) steps which, when followed, will lead to the achievement of the intended aim. The social relations expressed 'in' the procedure differ from those in the recount. The recount told what happened, and the assumption was that there might be those who would wish to reproduce those actions. Here there are those with the power or authority to order actions to be taken, and those who carry out the actions. This is very different to the recount. It is no longer the friendly telling of what happened so that you might do the same; this is

113

being told what to do. The claim made implicitly in the procedure is one of relations of power, actions and intended outcomes. This is not a realist genre in the manner of the recount; it is not a report of real events or actions of actual people, of events which have happened. It is a set of commands (in the syntactic form of imperatives) for actions that are to happen.

As in the first example, the written text-part is generically complete. Its relation to the world of the everyday is different; it is not the world of everyday happenings. This is a world in which power exists, and those with power can insist on actions being taken in a specific way and in a certain sequence. These are social relations of a very different kind. In the recount we could be sure that all the *significant* events were there, even though there might also be others. For instance, in the recount we are told that 'it was interesting to look at and draw'. In the procedure we have only those potential actions (as commands) which are essential to the carrying out of a task which already exists as a prestructured schema.

In terms of communicational roles, there is a big difference: the text overall is a set of instructions, and the individual segments are commands to carry out the instructions as they are indicated. Consequently, the roles here are of a different kind: to act in a world in accord with the commands of some other with power, with clear procedures and in accordance with those procedures. The reader is not in the world of their everyday life. My role is to carry out commands issued by some (institutional) authority.

That also describes the relation between the world of this written text and the everyday world: they are different. In this world I have less power than others. The manner in which I am drawn into the text is by command, by means of power, and not as before, by the pleasure or interest of the recount. The world projected here is the world of precise procedures which those who are a part of this world must follow. It is not the everyday world of these students: there is no (implicit) claim here that the world of scientific practices is like the world of their everyday practices.

The drawing differs from that in the first example. One clue is provided in the instructions: 'Search for pattern like a honeycomb'. In his talk the teacher had provided the metaphor, among others, of the honeycomb: 'it might look like a honeycomb'. In the case of both texts a metaphor provided in language – in writing in the one instance – 'what you will see will be like bricks in a brick wall' – and in talk in the other – has been transducted by the pupils into visual form. Let me follow the steps that I took in analysing both the written and the visual elements of the first example. The drawing shows a strongly delineated circle, with elements of different kinds contained in the circle. What is represented 'in' the image, and what is represented by the image overall, as a whole? Like her fellow students, this young woman saw air-bubbles, larger and smaller ones. However, the cell-entities which she saw are far less regular in shape, and their arrangement is not in any way as orderly as in the 'brick wall' example. Regularity of the elements or of their arrangements is not a feature of this image. The drawing differs from that in the first example in that what it shows is complete: here we have the whole world that is to be represented. The implication is that this is what she actually saw through the microscope: everything that was there to see is there, as she saw it. It is textually as well as representationally complete.

In the drawing in the first example scientificness lay in abstraction away from that which appeared in view in the microscope, abstraction in the direction of theory and generalisation. There was no representation of the lens of the microscope, and in fact no real pretence that the drawing represented what the 'eye' had seen. That drawing represented what the 'eye of theory' had seen. Here, by contrast, scientificness lies in the precision of representing that which is there in view, that which the human eye can see. In the first example truth is the truth of abstraction, the truth of theory; here truth is the truth of actuality, of that which is there, the truth of the empirically real world. We are shown not only what she saw, but the means by which she saw what she saw, hence we see the eyepiece through which the young woman looked – we see everything that she saw. For her, being scientific resides in the accuracy of observation and representation.

The relation of the written text and the image is inverted in relation to that in the first example. There the written text was broadly realistic and the visual broadly non-realistic, theoretical. Here the written text is not an account of events as they happened, but of a schema as it exists in the world of science, which might lead to a set of actions in that world. The visual part, by contrast, is realistic. The two aspects of the text jointly seem to suggest that the meaning of 'scientificness' here might be that the world of science is ordered by schemata for action which organise and underlie action, and that the essential task of science is to achieve an accurate account of the empirically real, aided by these schemata of actions.

If we contrast the two examples, they are nearly an inversion of each other: in the first, the written part of the text is realist; in the second it is schematic/theoretical; in the first text, the visual part is theoretical/abstract, while in the second it is empirical/realist. Scientificness is carried in distinctively different ways in the two cases. Underlying this is the action and the process of design of an overall message-entity.

What is the role of writing in these multimodal ensembles? Even though the written parts of the two ensembles are *generically* different from each other, they do share a significantly common feature: both are focused on action and event, even if differently so; both of the visual elements by contrast are focused on 'what is', the visual display of the world that is in focus. Each of the two texts overall is incomplete without both written and visual parts; each mode, writing and image, does distinctly different and specific things. The specificity is the same at one level: the affordance of the logic of time governs writing, and the affordance of the logic of space governs the image. Within that, there is the possibility of generic variation. And the generic variation of the ensembles, in each case, produce an overall difference of a significant kind.

Genre as design: text and the new media

As I suggested, the two texts that I have discussed here – as well as the Annapelle text earlier – are examples of *ensembles of modes*, brought together to realise particular meanings. The fact that the two school-texts are made by unpractised designers is in one way an advantage in that it shows how an untutored maker of such ensembles uses the affordances of the modes for their ends. The purpose of the science curriculum is, in one important way, to induct young people into the idea of scientificness. Here we see the response of two students to this demand, expressed through what we can see as design decisions in the realisation of that meaning. They are faced with the question of 'what is it to act or be scientific?' and each gives a distinct answer, which is expressed through choice of modes, and choice of genres, more than through what aspects of curriculum content to represent. Both students understand the affordances of writing – best of all it does the job of representing action and event – though of course the teacher's demands and previously encountered models will have given them resources in that respect. The teacher's inexplicit or 'open' framing of the task leaves much of the design decision to the students: how to interpret the relatively open request 'write what you did' in generically specific terms, and to do the same for the request 'draw what you saw'.

The first of the two examples shows a decision to go for realism in the written genre: to be truthful to science means that I am expected to report things as they were; I have to stay true to the empirically real. But this student also realised that science is about constructing general accounts of what this aspect of the world is (like), and she does that in her drawing: the truth of this world lies in this abstraction, which generalises away from the messiness of the empirical and to a general truth. The truth of actions is reached via the mode of writing, and the truth of how the world looks is reached via the mode of image.

For the second student there is a similar question, though she answers it differently: the truth of science lies in the generality of the procedures, in the generality of the practices, which must be the same each time they are performed and not open to the chance of contingent event. This truth is reached via the mode of writing. The truth of what the world is like is reached via the mode of image and the precise recording of what there actually is in that world, without concession to anything but strict observation.

These are epistemological decisions, but they are realised through design decisions focused on the use of modes and the truth they harbour, the use of genres and the truths that they contain. On the face of it, these decisions have nothing to do with the existence of the new information and communication media. In reality they absolutely do: the manner in which these young people encounter school science owes much to the revolution in representation which has already in their world altered the status, the function, the uses and the forms of writing. The 'books' which they use are transformed already by the joint effects of the emergence into central representational use of the mode of image, and the effect on the page of the organisations of the screens of the new media. The fact that there is now a design decision to be made, and that decisions about genre are now relatively open, is both a direct effect of the new media via their effect on the look of the page, and also an indirect effect of the new media in that teachers as much as designers of textbooks know that the young are attuned to a differently configured communicational world.

In that new communicational world there are now choices about how what is to be represented should be represented: in what mode, in what genre, in what ensembles of modes and genres and on what occasions. These were not decisions open to students (or teachers or textbook-makers) some twenty years earlier. Of course, with all this go questions not only of the potentials of the resources, but also of the new possibilities of arrangements, the new grammars of multimodal texts. These new grammars, barely coming into conventionality at the moment, and certainly very little understood, have effects in two ways at least. On the one hand they order the arrangements of the elements in the ensembles; on the other hand they design the functions that the different elements are to have in the ensembles. These are the kinds of decision that I pointed to: writing used for the representation of event structures, and image used for the representations of displays of aspects of the world. This is what I call the 'functional specialisation' of the modes, and that in turn has the profoundest effects on the inner organisation and development of the modes.

Where before, up until twenty or thirty years ago, writing carried all the communicational load of a message, and needed to have grammatical and syntactic structures that were equal to the complexities of that which had to be represented in that single mode, now there is a specialisation, which allows each of the modes to carry that part of the message for which it is best equipped. This brings with it the possibilities of great simplification of syntax for writing, for instance. It leads to some new questions, such as I have mentioned: what are the elements which come together in the multimodal ensembles? In the two text examples discussed above, there are image blocks and writing blocks, and it is these which form the first level of conjunction. At the first level of reading we note that the text is composed of 'blocks', and at that level it is not immediately relevant what modal realisation these elements have, whether they are image or writing. They are treated as elements of the same order. This is a bit like the analysis of a sentence where we might want to know what the main verb is, what its subject noun might be, and what complements – if any – there are. Reading at the next level down would then focus on the internal elements of these higher-level elements.

If we take Figure 5.2 (see Chapter 5) as an example, it is clear that there are three elements or blocks at the first level. These are predominantly visual, but the point is that in our first engagement with and analysis of ('scanning' might be another useful term) the page we note the three blocks. We then note that each image has accompanying it a written bolded label. So at the next level down our analysis reveals that each block consists of two elements, in a particular relation. That relation is in part defined in mode terms – large image, relatively small label – and in part by proximity – the label is at a certain distance from the image, indicating that it 'goes with' the image. At the third level down, the analysis reveals lower-level elements both in the visual mode and in writing, and here too the relation is that of labelling. Because the relationship is not so obvious – the elements are smaller, and the 'goes with' relation could be misinterpreted – it is indicated by a connecting line.

It is clear that here the question of genre no longer rests with the written mode. If we wish to understand the social relations realised in this text, we need to look predominantly at the visual mode. The verbal mode supplies text-elements, namely 'labels', and labels do of course also have generic effect – they supply the information of 'name', and supplying information is to take and assign a specific social role. In the original, the images are in heavily saturated colour, deep reds, purples, yellows, some green – all close to the primary part of the colour spectrum. We are not in the same domain as the black-and-white drawing of the students, nor in that of the student who used colour pencils. Nor are we in the coding orientation of the circuit diagrams in Chapter 9. This is the world of excitement, entertainment, pleasure, the world of consumer culture, and science has become a part of that. That is perhaps the first thing to note about this page/screen. We are shown the retina from the side, signalling lower involvement with what we are looking at than in either the onion-cell drawings, which were front-on, or the circuits, which also were. We are looking down on the square which is a hypothetical slice out of the retina. *Standing apart* (signalling low involvement) and *looking down on* (signalling greater power of the viewer) bring highly affective subjective elements into the social relation. These objects or entities do not demand our attention by the front-on objective demand – of the circuit diagram or of the onion-cell drawing. We, the viewers, are in control here, it is our will and our pleasure which dictates what we do. The distance at which these entities are presented is at mid-range: a distance which can signal some engagement, but not too close.

Generically this image suggests a social relation like that of the report; this is what there is; this is all there is; I have shown you all. However, the image, through its spatial affordances, can bring aspects of social relations into the text which might be problematic in a written genre in school science. For instance, there is a clear appeal to the viewer in the angles I mentioned, in the social domain signalled by the hyper-realist representation, including the intense saturation of the colours, and by the dynamism indicated by the angle of the retina segment. It is a 'display', but for a viewer with power – the power of the consumer in the market society.

Genre labels

These examples raise again something of a recurring problem: what do we call such 'mixed genres'? There is in any case the problem that there very few commonly used labels for genres; only really prominent ones have well-understood names – whether literary (the novel) or non-literary (the interview) or texts of popular culture (romance, film noir). That problem is somewhat compounded by the differences in theoretical practice – where genre can be used as the naming of the text as a whole or, as in my approach here, as the naming of an aspect of text. One of the solutions that has been adopted at times is that of inventing subcategories. So we have 'interview' but also then 'job-interview', 'media-interview', 'radio-interview' and so on. In these three cases the qualifying adjective names quite different things, a very good reason for avoiding this strategy. But even if we kept the categories steady, using one category, say 'what medium?' (radio, TV, newspaper and so on), we would end up proliferating types, and end up with an unprincipled list.

My preferred solution is to accept, to begin with, that *mixing* is normal, in whatever domain, and at whatever level. In writing we can have clauses functioning as subjects of a sentence, taking a quasi-noun role. We can have single words or two-word structures functioning as complete message units, taking a quasi-sentence role, and indeed functioning as complete texts – as in 'No' or 'No Smoking'. Mixed genres exist in written text, though they have been somewhat of a theoretical embarrassment. Mixed genres exist in multimodal, or mono-modal, non-verbal texts. The question is, what do we call generically mixed texts in writing? We have no problem accepting generically hugely mixed texts such as the novel as a genre. No one disputes that 'novel' is a genre label. Or is it perhaps a matter of the intensity and the degree of mixing? If all genres are mixed genres – as I suggested earlier – what is a 'genre', a pure genre; how and where would it occur; and how would we recognise it?

In my approach, where genre does not name the text, but an aspect of the text's organisation (though I am happy to name the whole text after its dominant generic features – as in 'interview'), there is no problem in saying that a text can be and in many cases will be generically mixed. If we see this as a matter of 'levels' then there is no problem at all: we have genres and generic fragments embedded in, forming a part of, the text overall. The real issue in any case is not really to have labels, though they can be useful devices, and it is clear that bad labels can be importantly misleading. The science teacher's use of the label 'diagram' might be one case in point. But the real issue is to understand the generic nature of the text – what meanings does the text realise, what social meanings are at issue?

Genre and educational strategies

The profound cultural diversity of all contemporary 'Western' post-industrial societies, as much as the new demands for education for participation in a fully globalised economy, has specific educational consequences. It means that an 'outcomes-based curriculum' or, to use a better formulation, a curriculum which focuses on skills, disposition, essential processes and understanding of resources for representing and communicating, may be what all of 'us' in the anglophone and ever more globalising world will need to consider urgently. This will be a curriculum which focuses above all on 'dispositions', a return to quite traditional notions of education – not training – on something akin to the German notion of *Bildung*, but refocused clearly on the real features of the new globalising world and its demands. I am not here thinking of the facile and deeply mistaken ideas around skills-training, but focusing rather on giving students a full awareness of what might be possible, beyond both the suggestions of current politics and the seductions of the market-led consumption. Such an education would provide them with the means both for setting their goals and for achieving them in the contexts of their lives. This is the ability for which I use the term 'design'. Much more goes with that change in curriculum from either content as stable knowledge or content as the training for skills, to dispositions to 'design'.

A new theory of text is essential to meet the demands of culturally plural societies in a globalising world. In my *Writing the Future: English and the Making of a Culture of Innovation* (1995) I suggested that the school-subject English needed an encompassing theory of text, in which the texts of high culture could be brought into productive conjunction with the banal texts of the everyday. If the literary texts which have been seen as 'the best' are to have real effects on all texts, they cannot be treated as separate. I suggested three categories of text, within the one theory: the aesthetically valued text – the texts treated by any one cultural group as the texts which embodied for them what they saw as best; the culturally salient text – texts which were significant for a society for any number of reasons, but which might not meet the criteria of aesthetic value; and the mundane text – texts of the everyday, entirely banal texts (the Annapelle text would be an example) which are significant because they constitute, reproduce and remake the 'everyday'. All these will have to be dealt with within one theory of text, within one culture, across cultures in one society and across historical periods. But what is quite clear is that even the production of the banal text – Annapelle – requires much more than competent knowledge. That text is based, however imperfectly, on the understandings of design: an understanding of what the social and cultural environment is into which my text is to fit, the purposes it is to achieve, the resources of all kinds that I have to implement and realise my design, and the awareness of the characteristics of the sites of appearance of that text.

That educational environment will deal with banal texts, culturally salient texts (from all the cultures represented in one society) and aesthetically valued texts, in all modes and in all kinds of modal combination. Translations, transformations and transductions will be entirely normal, and made more so by the affordances of the new information and communication technologies which make modal transformation and transduction, as well as the co-appearance of modes, entirely normal.

Theories of meaning will have to be rethought and remade. There is a reality to genre, but the conceptions from former social arrangements with their (relative) stabilities have left us with both the wrong theory and the wrong vocabulary. The wrong theory led us to believe that stability of language or of text-form (as indeed of other social phenomena) is a feature of texts, when it had always been – as it appears now – a feature of these phenomena in a particular historical period, when relative social stability had obtained. So, for instance, to speak of 'generic mixes' is really to conceive of genre in the older fashion – of stable genres which can be and are mixed. A newer way of thinking may be that within a general awareness of the range of genres, of their shapes and their contexts, speakers and writers newly make the generic forms out of available resources. This is a much more 'generative' notion of genre: not one where you learn the shapes of existing kinds of text alone, in order to replicate them, but where you learn the generative rules of the constitution of generic form within the power structures of a society. And you learn what the shapes of these texts are, coming out of those social conditions. That will permit (and account for) constant change, and makes the actions of the producer of the genre innovative and transformative. It encourages and normalises 'design' of text in response to the perceived needs of the maker of the text in a given environment. In such a theory all acts of representation are innovative, and creativity is the normal process of representation for all.

There will need to be a new evaluation and description of the resources for representation and communication, the means for making texts, which are available and in use in a particular society. For in a plural society the generic forms of all cultural groups will need to be brought into the market of communication.

Literacy and communication curricula rethought in this fashion offer an education in which creativity in different domains and at different levels of representation is well understood, in which both creativity and difference are seen as normal and as productive. The young who experienced that kind of curriculum might feel at ease in a world of incessant change. A social theory of genre is one essential element in bringing about that shift.

8

MEANING AND FRAMES
Punctuations of semiosis

Punctuation as a means for making meaning

My first serious encounter with the issue of punctuation dates from my second year of 'doing English' at a university in Australia. At the bottom of one of my essays appeared the following comment: 'If you don't know how to punctuate, at least learn to do it by rôte. 12/20'. I remember thinking that the circumflex on 'rôte' was placed there expressly to ensure that I could not mistake the tone, and feeling a deep annoyance at the lack of logic: if I did not know how to do it, how could I learn to do it by rôte? The tension in the comment between a view of punctuation as a system about which there was something to be known, and the view, simultaneously, of the system as entirely meaningless, occurred to me only a lot later.

The issue of punctuation in that narrow sense had vexed my tutor, but there is also punctuation as a means of 'framing' much more broadly. I will approach this from several angles. First I look at what punctuation in the more modest sense is and what it does; what frames it provides, in speech and writing; and what the elements are which punctuation produces. Even here punctuation is a dynamic, productive, generative resource, which we use to produce elements that we need rather than merely implementing rules with no sense of their purpose. Semiosis is ceaseless, and without fixing and framing we would have nothing tangible and graspable. Punctuation in that sense both fixes and frames elements, and framed elements can be units in larger structures: relations can be established between them, with larger-level frames making them in turn into elements. Without frames, no elements; without elements, no structures; and without structures, no meaning.

Frames can be concrete, material, such as a full stop or a semicolon, the space around a paragraph, or the space that frames a finished text. Frames can also be intangible; many or most social and cultural frames are of this kind – they hold us invisibly and inescapably in a place. Many such frames exist in semiosis, and I will look at their effects in a few cases, simply as exemplars, and look at what material manifestations they have – just as other frames have material manifestations.

What is framed can be linked, and linking can take many forms, from the simple act of placing one element next to another, to the much more complex act of integrating elements either of the same kind or of different kinds into each other. This is one task of punctuation, for instance in the very simple act of putting commas between items in a list, or the slightly more complex act of *inserting one element (such as here) into another element.* That act has many versions, concretely and more abstractly. Punctuations in that sense enable us both to produce, and to ratify and fix, conceptual arrangements of great complexity.

In a multimodal theory of literacy we need to be able to deal with textual entities which are constituted in several modes. In the chapter I deal with the interrelations of the modes of speech and writing, and across the modes of writing and image also. Many textual entities are now constituted in two or more modes. In a CD-ROM writing can occur with still or moving image, with speech, with soundtrack, with music. All these bring their meaning to the whole textual ensemble, and so have their effect on what writing is and what it does. This poses some new problems, though in principle these should be accommodated in the one theory.

What meanings does the system of punctuation allow us to produce? Can punctuation be thought and talked about meaningfully other than as an integral part of all the structuring systems of speech, of writing and of all other modes which occur on pages and screens? A much newer question now is, 'How does punctuation fit into a multimodal theory of literacy?' Framing marks off, but in doing so it establishes, at the same time, the elements which may be joined. A social semiotic approach to representation and communication sees all modes as meaning-making systems, all of which are integrally connected with social and cultural systems. The multiple and often contradictory logics of multimodal texts can be explained plausibly and satisfactorily only by bringing them into an integral relation with the logics of other social and cultural systems. And so I attempt to see punctuation as one among many devices for making meanings in the contradictory world of social and cultural matters.

Text as the domain of punctuation

Some sixteen years after that first unpleasant encounter, I came back to the question of punctuation in quite a new context. In the meantime I had come to know just how culturally shaped punctuation is and all sorts of framings are. I had come to understand that the framings of writing that I had absorbed as part of learning to speak and write German, as my first language, differed hugely from the framings of English. Sentences which stretch over three or four or five lines of a page, and paragraphs which go for a page and more, are not really favoured in English. It was that felt sense of the meaning of punctuation which I brought to an attempt to understand how children grapple with the difficult notion of the sentence in the early years of their learning to write. It seemed to me then, and I have not changed my mind since, that punctuation can give one kind of insight into a writer's sense of their place in the world, whether as a child or as an adult.

The elements which a writer establishes through the framing of punctuation are a precise indication of how she or he parcels up the conceptual world, putting their particular order on it. I felt, and am still convinced, that this approach is both more useful and more defensible than the approach that sees punctuation as a vacuous enterprise which must nevertheless be taught, learned and displayed, by rôte – with or without the accent circumflex. In the case of child writers I felt that their punctuation shows them at work with astonishing acuity and astuteness about the world, shows them struggling to make real sense, their sense, of the difficult matter of meaning. And I certainly did not think that it displayed incompetence in the use of an adult system, as is too often and too readily assumed.

When children learn to write, they move from the textual/syntactic structures of speech – the simple linking of clauses, in a chain-like manner – to the gradual inclusion of several clauses in a more complex unit, the sentence. Their punctuation shows an intense preoccupation with the characteristics of this complex unit: what is to be included in the sentence, what is not to be in it. The motivations for their decisions to put clauses together in one unit tend to be clearly textual motivations: what makes sense in terms of the overall coherence, structure and needs of their text. This childish sense has led me to see the sentence as always a textual rather than as a syntactic unit – even in the writing of a fully practised adult writer. The text derives its organisation from the social practices in which it is formed and of which it is a part; sentences are elements of these practices, and are motivated in their content, their form and their interconnections by the coherence of these practices.

Treating punctuation as a textually rather than as a primarily syntactically motivated matter involves looking with a much broader span than traditional or contemporary reference-grammars tend to do: they do treat punctuation in terms of the syntax of the sentence and of its internal structures.

Punctuation is a semiotic resource, available for making social meanings. So for me one question is, 'Who is punctuation for?' And of course, 'What is (counted as) punctuation?' Some of the topics I wish to focus on are the relations of speech and writing, textual and cross-textual structures, syntax and lexis, cognitive and conceptual issues, and interpersonal and social issues. I will analyse a number of examples, taken from writings (and in one case, the speech) of many different kinds of writers: an accomplished male academic writer of high status, the poet John Milton, a seventeenth-century woman pamphleteer, a girl in primary school, a young man and a young woman at the end of secondary school, a female 'middle manager', and, in the case of the spoken extract, a woman trade-unionist. But I will also look at punctuation as framing across modes, on the pages of magazines and on a website.

Some examples

I make the assumption that texts are the result of implicit or explicit structuring and planning. Implicit structuring in that the organisation of social systems – whether in overt interaction and dialogue or in seeming monologue – provides the overarching structuring frames, both the rules of generic organisation and the rules of thematic development. Explicit structuring in that it is actually displayed, whether in the orderly succession of questions and answers in interviews; or the regular organisation of any one of many genres; of paragraphing; of topic development handled syntactically; or indeed in the visual organisation of layout. Punctuation is one means for the overt marking of conceptual arrangements and dispositions. This marking must be clear enough to be apprehensible to the hearer, reader or viewer, so that the speaker, writer or image-maker knows that they can make their ordering communicable. In this sense, punctuation is for the maker of the message. It marks and ratifies a meaning-ordering already planned, and it is realised by many means. This is punctuation as design. But punctuation is also for the listener, reader or viewer. In as far as listening, reading or viewing represent a willingness on the receiver's part to engage with the text of the producer, it is an attempt by the viewer to enter into productive engagement with the text. Of course this does not exclude debate and argument with that text, or even severe remaking in the transformative reception of it, nor does it exclude rejection of the message and of its conceptual ordering in its entirety.

Punctuation as the framing of an overall organisation, and as the framing of different kinds of order, is a feature of all texts. It is a necessary condition of communication. 'Without framing, no meaning', we might say. Punctuation in the narrower sense is the overt, deliberate, appearance of 'directive markings' of this structuring, a guide and instruction to the viewer, reader or hearer towards recognition, perception and, if things go well, an acceptance by the reader of this disposition of material and this order.

Speech and writing

The mode of *alphabetic* writing is peculiar in that – to a significant extent – it stands in a close relation to the mode of speech. Sometimes it is a near transliteration, sometimes a translation, at times a transformation and at times a transduction of speech. In the latter case, writing as a mode is most independent of speech, whereas in the first case it is in effect the recording of the mode of speech in the graphic medium of letters. For practised writers, writing exists as a mode in its own right: there is no question of transliteration or even of transduction; it is a resource fully present in itself to the writer. Much or perhaps most writing resides somewhere between the two poles – of writing as translation or transformation and of writing as an independent mode. Transliteration exists really only for those who are specialists, who need transliterations for specialist 'forensic' tasks – whether the forensics of the court, or that of academic research. There are few instances of the truly unpractised writer – young learners excepted – whose writing is in fact transliteration. Transduction is, equally, rare: there are few occasions when ordinary writers are called on to turn their (or others') speech – however it has been recorded – into writing. Again, academics sometimes attempt it, and of course novelists constantly pretend to do it. In fact, the mode of writing has developed a range of devices for this – direct reported speech, indirect reported speech and various syntactic means for the more or less full integration of speech into the mode of writing. (The histories of reading, from reading aloud to silent reading, to suppressed reading aloud, as in sub-vocalisation in reading, are relevant here.)

I take it for granted that speech and writing are modally distinct. However, the relation between speech and writing is constantly present, is constantly active, and can constantly be activated in particular ways in relation to specific purposes. The new environments for writing, in which multimodality and the new dominance of the screen on the one hand and changes in social power on the other are pressing in on the organisation of writing as a mode, have as one consequence that the interrelations of speech and writing are newly put into flux. We need to understand what the principles of that relation are in order to focus on those which remain as constants. This will allow us to understand in what ways the principles are used now.

One significant dimension of punctuation is as the marker of the relations of speech and writing, whether as a translation, transformation or transduction from the one to the other. For those writers – I include myself among them – who have it as a social aim to write in a more speech-like manner, punctuation has a crucial place in translating from one system of framing, that of speech (through pacing, intonation, accent), to another system of framing, that of writing (through word-order, embedding, punctuation); this applies equally to those writers who write with the cadences of speech in mind while they are writing.

The shift from speech to writing involves a shift in 'logic': a shift from the logic of sequence in time to the logic of arrangements in (conceptual, visual and other) space. This necessarily involves a change in the resources of framing. I can also express this as a move from frames that rely predominantly on the use of the voice – as stress or rhythm, and as pitch or intonation – to frames that use the affordances of sequence – syntax. It is a move from clearly discrete linked clause-elements to (clauses in) highly integrated sentence structures. It is a move from the overt lexical (*and, so, then, therefore*), vocal and clausal framing of speech to the reduction of types of frame and the production of larger units which are syntactically and textually framed. The journey from speech to writing is marked by a number of closely related aspects:

1   from a linear, sequential order of simple clause following on simple clause in a chain-like structure, to a gradual 'fusion' of several clauses into one syntactic unit;

2 from horizontal connection to vertical hierarchy;
3 from simple linking to (complex) embedding;
4 from relations which are lexically and intonationally expressed, to relations which are syntactically expressed; and
5 from open syntactic structures to the fusion of closed lexical elements, as in nominalisations producing a new quasi-'word'.

Integration of clauses through syntactic fusions of various sorts, and the hierarchical subordination of a number of clauses to other clauses, produces the form of a full writing-like sentence.

To summarise, in speech the textual-syntactic framings of *clauses* are relatively clear; each one is discreet. The material means for framing are the voice, through pitch variation and through variations in energy; these become the modal means of intonation, which 'affords' pitch prominence and pitch contours, and rhythm, which 'affords' rhythmic structures, such as 'feet'. In writing, the textual-syntactic framings of *sentences* are clear. The material means are spacing, use of graphic devices such as capitals, full stops and so on, which become the modal means of layout and of punctuation. The conceptual, textual and social orientation of the sentence is different to that of the clause. The material means of framing are materially different: sound in temporal sequence, and graphic marks disposed in linear-spatial order.

The move from most speech-like to most writing-like organisation is a gradual and subtle one, involving changes in the material means of framing – the disappearance of voice for instance – although there are recognisable stages on this route. Writers tend to place themselves carefully at a particular point on this path, anywhere between its starting point of a loose, chaining structure of clauses and its endpoint of full syntactic integration. Each point has particular social meanings for that writer around social affiliation, in her or his imagined relation to their addressee(s): from full solidarity to full distance in power. If I imagine myself to have solidarity with a group that constitutes its relations around the open, informal meanings of speech, then that is my reference point. If I imagine myself as having solidarity with a group that constitutes its relations around the less open, formal meanings of writing, then that is my reference point. The move derives its meaning from that starting point, its direction and extent.

At the endpoint of most writing-like forms, we find the resources of written syntax used to produce new words. This is a move that marks the fullest degree of syntactic integration of clauses, the point furthest from the open clausal structures of speech. Here syntactic structures have been fused to become lexical elements, new words. Punctuation in the usual sense appears only for some sections of this route, or maybe it is better to say that it is visible for only a part of the sequence. In other words, if punctuation is the overt marking of conceptual/syntactic/textual ordering, then that ordering takes many different forms, at all points along this route, and uses many semiotic resources, syntactic integration being the one most in evidence at the fully writing-like end.

Here I will show some points on this sequence from speech-like writing to fully writing-like writing. First a short spoken extract (from an interview on a public access radio-station); the speaker was a woman trade-unionist.

> See [. . .] we went through this in '81 [. . .] and I was one of the offi-
> cials [. . .] that were involved [. . .] er once we'd worked out the
> severance side of things [. . .] we were gonna have to deal with the
> people [. . .] who wanted [. . .] to relocate [. . .] and [. . .] they said to
> management [. . .] we had hardship [. . .] management rejected it
> [. . .] then [. . .]
>
> Relatively informal speech (an example of type 1)

This first example has eleven clauses, here separated by '[. . .]'. Only three of these are embedded clauses ('one of the officials *that were involved*', 'deal with the people *who wanted*', 'the people who wanted *to relocate*'). The others are con-joined through a variety of means, for instance intonationally. This is not indicated here, though the dots between 'See' and 'we went' indicate not only a pause but also an intonational linkage, in that the voice has not been lowered fully; this means that the hearer expects a continuation of the same textual seg-ment. The majority of adjoining is done through the use of conjunctions 'and', 'then' and so on. In this text, clauses follow one another, like beads on a chain, one might say, with two or three clauses occasionally twined together.

The second example is the opening and the second sentence of a mock school-leaving examination answer.

> The main pattern of the Australian tax system is a heavy reliance on
> income tax, it has a tendency to cause inflation. It also has relied on
> partly the Keynsian policies, the equity of the system has left something
> to be desired causing uneven income distribution and other problems.
>
> Relatively speech-like sentence-structure (an example of
> type 1; moving towards sentence-structure)

Here the link between the two clauses in the first sentence is made in a speech-like manner, that is, two clauses are simply adjoined '. . . a heavy reliance on income tax, it has a . . .'. With such adjoining, the assumption made by the reader will be that the link is to be made intonationally, that is, as in speech. When this sentence is read as though it were spoken, the voice does not go to a low point at the juncture of the two clauses, but tends to be held at mid-level. The effect is that it is heard as speech, and as speech it sounds fine. When it is read as a written sentence, with the voice − the 'silent voice' of reading writing − lowering at the juncture, there is an uncomfortable lack of closure at 'income tax'. Given the comma-punctuation, the expected relation, with the following clause, is that it should be a relative clause: 'income tax, *which* has a tendency'. The pronoun 'it' can be used as an anaphoric pronoun (a pronoun which refers to specific segments of preceding speech or writing) in writing, if the punctuation indicates completion of the preceding element, in this case, a sentence. That makes it possible to refer to a segment of the preceding unit and import it anaphorically into the next sentence. This is a matter, straightforwardly, of framing. If I have a clearly framed element, then writing – and speech also, if in different ways – makes it possible to refer to (segments of) that element, and bring it into the next one.

If this writer had wanted to have these two clauses as one conceptually unified element, a sentence, rather than as two clauses uneasily together, then a more writing-like solution would have been to use a semicolon instead of the comma, making a sufficiently clear frame. That would have left the clauses as two units of syntactically equal status with the first clause semantically somewhat more weighted. Or he could have used a subordinating conjunction such as 'which' between the two clauses. That would have subordinated one to the other, syntactically and conceptually. Similarly with the second sentence. As they stand, both sentences have two main clauses – and from the perspective of writing that is felt as awkward, or worse. The 'worse' is the judgement which is invited by the syntax of a sentence with two main clauses, namely 'not conceptually ordered'. The conceptual ordering would be achieved by making one clause subordinate. From here it is a very short step, usually elided in teachers' comments, to the judgement 'not capable of complex conceptual ordering'.

A third example is,

> Rejection casts us out to sea on the question of what might that relationship be?
> Relatively weak incorporation of clauses (an example of type 2)

My attention was caught by the manner in which the second clause was handled textually/syntactically within that sentence. This clause, 'what might that relationship be', reports a thought on the author's part, perhaps a thought that was linguistically 'prepared', even if silently, and thus had a real existence: it was ready to be uttered, though in the event it is treated as though it was not actually spoken or written. It is also somewhat awkwardly integrated '. . . on *the question of what* might . . .'. In reading it I felt that I would have written '. . . casts us out to sea on the question "what might that relationship be"'. I might even have used a question mark because this partial utterance actually has a syntactic question-form 'what might that relationship be?' In the author's version there is no punctuation mark other than the question mark; in my version there are punctuation marks, the inverted commas, and the question mark.

Let me trace these steps again. The author formulates a complex point, which includes a question: 'That rejection casts us out to sea on the question of what might that relationship be?' He produces a linguistic formulation for the question, in the syntactic form of an indirectly quoted WH question, even though it is not used as such 'on the question of what might that relationship be?' The form I would have felt more comfortable with is on the question 'what might that relationship be?'

His form has no quotation marks around the embedded clause, so it has lost its status as a real question; it is 'reported' rather than 'quoted'; it is on the road to being syntactically integrated into the rest of the writer's (own) text. He has, however, left the question mark there, to show that there was – and remains? – a real question. (Of course I imagine that this question was his too, but syntactically and textually it is treated as 'from outside'.)

A further option would have been to show that question as 'reported thought' (even if not 'reported speech'), that is, a form which is 'earlier' in the assumed sequence of internal assembly than the actual reported speech. On the question of 'what might that relationship have been' the author has gone one step further in the direction of syntactic integration and processing of this sentence, to integrate the second formerly independent clause more tightly. An increase in structural work has led to a reduced marking of structure: 'the question of what might that relationship be?'

Of course, this utterance could have been processed even further than my suggested form, dropping the question mark, inverting the order of modal auxiliary and subject noun-phrase to move back from the interrogative to the declarative syntax. The fact that there was a question is now no longer signalled by syntax or by punctuation, but by lexis alone, to give something like 'casts us out to sea on the question of what that relationship might be'. This is close to indirect (reported) speech, which is fully realised as 'the question what that relationship might be'.

We could of course change that too, to have a straightforward clause. We would then be closest to transduction, where an utterance and its semiotic material is not *transformed* from its modal realisation in one mode into modal realisation in another, but is *recast* within the potentials of the other mode. Alternatively, we might say – if we knew nothing of the history of this utterance – that the form below is realised in the mode of writing right from the beginning. 'The rejection asks about the relationship . . .'

A fourth example is the opening sentence of another mock school-leaving examination answer.

> The recent call for taxation reform in Australia has been prompted by the fact that Australia's taxation system is becoming less equitable.
> Relatively close integration of clauses (an example of type 3, and type 4, with an example of type 5 embedded in it)

This is a sentence which contains between two and four clauses, something like (not of course in actual utterance): 'recently *someone called* that *taxation should be reformed* in Australia, *which has been prompted* by *the fact* that *Australia's taxation system is becoming less equitable*'. (A more thorough-going parsing might analyse both *taxation* and *taxation system* as nominalisations, that is, as nouns derived from full clausal structures.) Here the point is that in the passage from most speech-like to most writing-like forms, textual/linguistic material has undergone intense ordering and restructuring, the marks of which are invisible in the reordered structure. Here punctuation in the narrower sense does not appear at all. The nominalisation 'the recent call for taxation reform' is an instance of a new noun(-like)/word-element having been formed syntactically from an 'original' form that might have been something like 'someone recently called for a reform'. This new element functions as a subject noun-phrase, and one does not have to work very hard to imagine social-political circumstances in which 'call for taxation' could become a noun; certainly 'taxation call' seems a very plausible candidate for elevation to the dictionary.

If the possibility of judgement of syntactic and then cognitive kinds existed in the case of the first sentence, it exists no less here. This writer's sentences show accomplished syntactic ordering, and from there it is an equally short step to the judgement about conceptual (cognitive) ordering – 'sophisticated' might be the word used. So before I pass from the discussion of these two examples I should mention the issue of gender and its possible role here. Might the first writer have been resisting the move to syntactic/conceptual integration? And if so, why? The first sentence was written by a young man, and the second was written by a young woman. The move to integration is a move to the conventional form, towards the accepted and the valued form. But it is also a move away from the forms of speech through which the young man might be maintaining relations of solidarity with his male peer group. And from that perspective it might be the move towards a group with which he does not wish to show solidarity, either in terms of gender or of class.

The first essay received a grade of 12/20, and the second a grade of 18/20. Several teachers of economics to whom I showed the two essays judged them to be equally competent in terms of the 'knowledge' displayed. Choosing your spot on the line between speech-like and writing-like writing has its rewards and its penalties, though in quite different domains.

In an attempt to understand punctuation, one question is, where does our interest in ordering processes and resources begin and end? Which of the many means of ordering should we treat as punctuation? And which of these are devices for framing? The young woman's sentence shows little punctuation, but very strong framing.

For any written utterance we can construct a quasi-history of its generation. The following list shows one for the sentence we have been looking at in the third example above. It is of course a hypothesis only. The form actually used by the author is shown in bold.

1   [that rejection casts us out to sea] clause 1;
    [through someone asking the question] clause 2;
    ['what might that relationship be?'] clause 3;

2   That rejection casts us out to sea on the question 'What might that rela-
    tionship be?'
3   That rejection casts us out to sea on the question 'what might that relation-
    ship be'.
4   **That rejection casts us out to sea on the question of what might
    that relationship be?**
5   That rejection casts us out to sea on the question of what that relationship
    might be.
6   That rejection casts us out to sea on the question of the possible relation-
    ship.
7   The question of the possible relationship casts us out to sea.
8   Questioning possible relationships casts us out to sea.

The author chose to leave the question in its speech-like form, but moved it one step away from direct reported speech and its punctuation, somewhat towards a more writing-like form. Punctuation is not needed here for two reasons: the speech-like separateness of clauses is no longer present, and the two clauses have been integrated to a degree that goes beyond the need to use punctuation to mark structural dispositions. One might say that syntactic means have taken over from punctuation. In fact, we might say that the more writing-like writing is, the less is there a need to mark features of speech, features which rely on 'sub-vocalisation' of varying degrees. The point on the line that has been chosen by this author declares his affinities with the mode of speech, and I assume with the social organisations that go with that: more open, more equal, more dynamic. It is a consistent feature of his style. This place on the line also speaks of tensions, which lends a certain angularity and masculinity to the writing. Its meaning is precisely the meaning of that position: why not, for instance, go further towards the more integrated, the more writing-like, the more formally academic writing?

The next two examples are also concerned with the connectedness of speech and writing. Consider this sentence, and in particular the listing:

> Our method will be to first consider the implications for theory of the
> four positions articulated in the introduction and then to take up the
> specific issues of (a) empiricism in positivism and beyond (b) post-struc-
> turalist social theory and (c) criticism in the land of the floating signifier.

Why did the writer not place a comma at these three points? Of course we cannot know and asking the author would not provide a definitive answer either, but we can put a comma there and ask about the difference which that makes. Without the comma it is possible to read across the conjunction between these clause-elements quite quickly; with the comma there, a pause seems (is?) indicated, even called for; its duration would depend on the reader's own speech patterns in this case.

Two points emerge from this. On the one hand, the comma is at least a trace of this as a speech-like form, it insists on the prior history of this sentence structure as quite separate clauses; and the comma insists on a silently spoken instantiation of this structure. On the other, it necessitates an intonational performance, so that in my reading with the comma, my voice rises (silently!) to above mid-level on the end of 'introduction', and continues much lower on 'and', a signal in speech that further material is to follow, in a new unit. When I read it without the comma, it is quite difficult for me to recover and hear my silent performance, but in as far as I can, my voice remains level. That is, the intonational level at the end of 'introduction' is at the same height as at the beginning of 'and', a signal in speech that the same unit is continuing.

Any reader will bring habituated practices of reading to a text, in which the more or less residual relations between spoken and written language play a part. The ordering without the comma suggests to me a tighter, denser structure. The punctuation with the comma suggests a less dense, less integrated ordering, one which leans on the forms of speech in a recognisable fashion. My reading shows that 'behind' the system present on the page lies another fully explicit system of spoken ordering, of the spoken speech, which is itself a complex set of systems of intonation, duration, silence, intensity and pace.

We could form a hypothesis about this writer's choice of position on the 'line' – quite close to speech-like forms (but further than I might move). One consequence of this is a relatively tightly integrated conceptual structure (more than I might adopt). In as far as punctuation is an ordering/structuring device oriented towards the reader, the question arises of the effect of this tendency to tighter syntactic integration compared to the effect of a tendency towards more speech-like structures. My hypothesis is that there are contradictory effects: the more speech-like structure is more transparent, may appeal more to readers who are oriented towards speech, may make the material easier of access. However, for readers who are strongly oriented towards writing-like structures, they may seem more appropriate, while the speech-like structures may seem too personal, too informal, not professional.

From a rhetorical point of view, the punctuation which invites or insists on the pause demands a performance – in pacing, intonation, emphasis. Thereby it draws the reader willy-nilly into the act of performing someone else's text in their own preferred or habituated speech-form. In this performance, the other's text is literally made into my own text by me; I internalise the other's text through my performance of it in terms of my habituated practice. It is a highly effective rhetorical device, a highly coercive strategy. In as far as the text which is more distant from speech does not insist on my performance (or does so far less insistently) its coercive effect is less. One would expect demagogues to write in a more speech-like form. On the more positive side, the insistence on the pause gives greater weight to the units, and in this fashion invites analysis of and reflection on each element to a greater degree.

One further example of the speech–writing relation

The resources which we use for representing are always shaped in the cultures and in the social lives in which we act. The example (Figure 8.1) here seems a particularly revealing text from that point of view.

The preceding discussion has I hope provided sufficient analytical/theoretical material to show the issues here clearly, and so I will not go into detailed

---

O-level GCE Art   1958
RSA Arithmetic
But O-level standard was reached in all other subjects except French

Certificate in Management Studies - BTEC 1985

My present occupation is TRAINING INSTRUCTOR with British Gas South East Region.

I had a two week in house training before taking new starters in customer accounts through a two week induction course, training in what I had previously been doing. I then trained Senior Staff in the laws that govern their actions as set out in the GAS ACT. & DATA PROTECTION ACT and the governing bodies of British Gas i.e. the Gas Consumers Council & OFGAS. I had to research and set up teaching aids, plans & organize, time and arrange unassisted and then take the Presentation to all the offices in Kent, Surrey and Sussex. After this I set up and ran ACCOUNTS COLLECTION courses for people familiar with customer accounts but lacking in councelling & advising customers on payment methods etc.

Looking Back

I don't remember anything about the nursery school, I was placed there so that my mother could work, parttime in a factory to supplement my father's wages as a stoker at the Gas works at Vauxhall.

I remember my first day at infant's school, I sat at a desk and waited to be taught, whilst waiting I looked at the A for apple etc pictures all around the walls. I could read them all. The teacher finally said to me would you like to join the other children in the playhouse, I said when will the lessons start. I didn't like joining in their pretend games, the boys wouldn't play properly e.g. weighing on balance scales, they would throw handfuls of counters on instead of noting the numbers & colours. One boy was a laughing stock as his mother brought him to school in a pushchair, but another wet his trousers. I felt sorry for him. Conditions were bad with smelly outside toilets and it was humiliating having to ask the playground attendant for toilet paper. The school was shared by infants and primary pupils but they were kept separate having different start, end & play times.

Figure 8.1 Writing in the private and the public domain: the notion of the sentence once more

analysis. What is striking to me is the clear distinction in forms of writing between the recollection of childhood years and the description of the writer's current professional life. The former, the domain of the personal/private, is in the mode of writing which is close to transcription, particularly in the clause structures of the sentences; the latter, the domain of the institutional/public, is in a mode of writing which is much much further on the line towards writing-like writing; very much closer to transduction. It seems a thin outer layer which this woman writer has acquired as part of her middle-manager training. She has not, however, integrated and fully transformed these quite differently organised resources for herself. The life of the institution, with its written forms, and the life of the private domain, with its much more speech-like forms, are, it seems, held very much apart.

Dynamic interrelations of framing systems

In the discussion below the relation of speech and writing is no longer in the foreground. Here I focus on the clamping together, through punctuations, of parts of a text which stem from quite distinct semiotic domains. In the previous case clauses were drawn together to form more tightly linked structures, in this case, a small fragment from the previous example '. . . to first consider . . .' the two elements drawn together are, in the case of 'first' an element which has a text(-ordering) function, and in the case of 'to consider' an element from the ideational domain. A text-ordering element is integrated into the ideational domain, altering the character of both. The textual becomes ideational, and thereby loses it text-organising function. Both the textual and ideational together move towards becoming a new lexical element. Less punctuation ('to first consider' rather than 'first, to consider') means more syntactic structuring work; the new simpler structure is the result of more syntactic work; and it disguises that work. The split infinitive is the marker of an ordering which, in this case at least, is transgressive. It marks a cross-border trade, from textual to ideational, and from there to the lexical. The prohibition of the split infinitive in prescriptive grammar may well have this as its unacknowledged and unrecognised base, namely a prohibition on transgressive structures, structures which cross and thereby blur boundaries and categories.

Trading between semiotic systems

I have shown two types of framing. One is involved in the move between two different modes, focused on the units of clause and sentence. The other involves the integration of elements from distinct semantic domains, focused here on elements from different functional components of the mode of writing. Many more distinctive instances could be shown, though the principles are the same, and may be relatively clear. The production of text is a complex process of orchestration. In part it is what the writer does to produce the desired order for the text; in part it is done to direct the reader in their reading. In all cases a large number of means are employed to incorporate elements from all sorts of domain into what will or can become a coherent textual/conceptual/rhetorical/ideological entity. Punctuation in the old narrow sense is one of these means. What is clear is that all the ordering systems interact in complex ways.

Framing in multimodal texts: writing and image

The modes of speech and writing are closely linked at three 'points' at least – at the levels of the letter, the word and the clause. This makes one problem of this cross-mode framing less difficult in that some of the crucial elements are quite similar, semiotically: in 'size', in function, in structural potentials. This is not the same in links across modes such as image and writing, to focus on that nearest to hand. This is why I proposed the notion of the 'block', which has a uniform function (and structural meaning) across occasions and sites, irrespective of its content. In discussing this I will make use of two examples, one the homepage of the institution where I work (Figure 8.2), the other from a CD-ROM produced by a member of an MA class in educational design at the Institute of Education.

In asking about the conjunction through framing of elements from the two modes of writing and image, we immediately encounter a problem. How do we read this page (Figure 8.2)? We might take as one possible route the notion of 'entry': there are several ways of entering this page. However, the moment we have chosen 'entry' as a principle of approach, we realise that we have made the decision not to treat this as a (conventional) page at all: with a page there is no question of 'entry'. That matter had been settled by conventions of the traditional printed page, so much so that the question could not arise, it had become naturalised. My approach in fact means that I have chosen to treat this as a new semiotic entity, a 'screen'. 'Screens' have points of entry; traditional pages do not. Or maybe the better way to put this is to say that in screens the point of entry is a problematic issue, whereas for the traditional page it was not. The 'point of entry' for the page is so much a part of conventions that it has ceased to be visible. Here, however, in relation to the IoE 'homepage', there is no principle by which we could treat and read this as a (conventional/traditional) page. By contrast, the page from the science textbook in Chapter 9 (Figure 9.7), does offer the possibility of being treated as a page. It could be 'read', in part at least, even if not very successfully, as a 'traditional page': we could start at the top left corner of one of its columns, and read on across and down. It could also be read as a 'new' page, where we might start the reading by focusing on the images and seeing writing as having an ancillary function.

Here there is no such possibility. The screen is organised on the principles of the logic of the visual: there are graphic blocks, in particular kinds of arrangement. There is, it is true, the functionally derived organisation of the screen, in terms of points of entry, and inevitably the two interact. Reading this as a visual

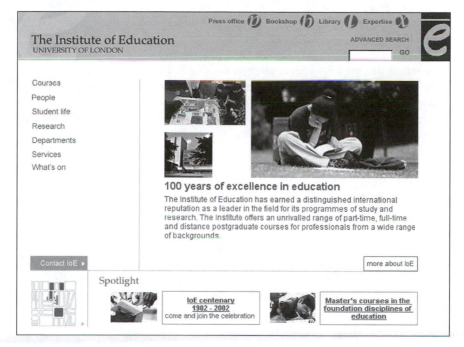

Figure 8.2 Page or screen: Institute of Education website

entity we will need to attend to the visual arrangement, much as we might approach a modernist painting. There are four blocks. Two of these form framing bands horizontally at the top and at the bottom of the screen; each of these has internal structuring, at the next level 'down', so to speak. The two framing bands are separated by 'white space', forming a frame between the bands and the rest of the screen. This produces a rectangular space in the centre. The central space consists of two elements or blocks: the 'menu', so called, on the left, and a block on the right, itself consisting of visual and written blocks – though again, at the next level down.

These two blocks seem 'unbalanced', with the one on the right much larger and more salient. It is at this point that the functional aspects of the entity 'screen' are significant: the 'menu' may be visually less salient, but functionally it is at least equally so. It is in fact *the* significant block on the screen; it is one of the two major paths of access. Readers/viewers/'browsers' (an entirely new term now in relation to literacy!) largely find their own way. The traditionally trained and inclined viewer/reader, such as myself, might choose the large block of image and writing perhaps not so much as a point of entry – though it is that too – than as a spot to rest for a moment. I know that much younger users of the site would go immediately to one of the 'entry-points'; indeed the technology is able to track the routes of entry taken, itself a useful insight into forms of 'reading' or use. It may be then that the central square area is balanced, with the functional significance of the menu 'heavy' enough to counterbalance the 'weight' of the larger and visually more salient block to the right of it.

In fact there are eleven 'entry-points', which themselves respond to or perhaps reflect the interests of potential 'visitors' (another new term in relation to literacy). The significant point – and one which I stress in Chapter 9 – is that 'reading' is now a distinctly different activity to what it was in the era of the traditional page. Reading is the imposing of the reader's order on this entity, an order which, while of course responding to what is here, derives from criteria of the reader's interest, disposition and desire. This is reading as ordering. Even when I have decided to enter via a category on the menu, it is my choice which category I choose to enter.

At this point I do not wish to analyse the individual elements further – just as I did not do so in the case of clauses. But the principles and criteria of framing are worth reflecting on, as is the effect of this framing/punctuation. Taking the central large 'band' as an example, it brings together two distinct elements: the spatially/visually large element of image and writing, and the smaller, though functionally large element, the list of categories making up the menu. The latter opens the path to specific information, responding to the visitor's needs and wishes. It is on the left, the space of the given: that which we take for granted. Information readily classified, and ease of access to information, is here the taken-for-granted starting point of website communication. It has a specific purpose – whether that is booking my plane ticket or, as here, entering on a career in higher education – and that is the (very large) 'new', that which is to be achieved. The framing brings together 'means' – the information, and 'ends' – the desired goal, in one single new semiotic entity. Just as with some of the framings in the written instances, the fact that what is brought together is categorically unequal disappears; the new semiotic entity makes its own new semiotic-social sense.

It may be worth pointing out that all this is very much part of a transitional era: when I click on 'contact IoE' I am more or less back to a traditional page, with its organisation, as indeed I am, even more so, when I click on 'more about IoE'.

The instance from the CD-ROM that I discuss here (Figure 8.3) presents a screen of a different kind. It looks entirely conventional: two blocks, an image-block and a writing-block themselves framed, in the original, in a background of blue.

The unusual – and less conventional – feature here is that the image is on the left, and the writing on the right. We start with the image as given – it is *the* taken-for-granted mode of communication – and writing has an ancillary function, namely of glossing what the image does. The framing produces that as the unit: a merged element of image-writing, with image as the taken-for-granted mode, and writing as the subsidiary mode which glosses the meaning of image.

In this case it is useful to move to the next level down. It is here that we get a further insight into what is being framed. The image is 'typical' of a particular

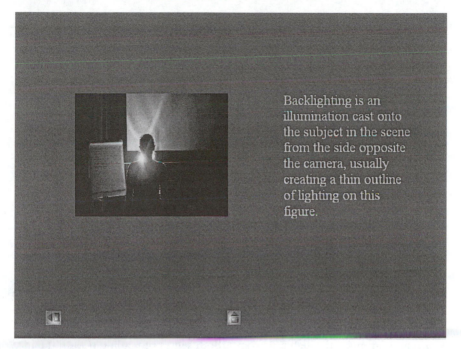

Backlighting is an illumination cast onto the subject in the scene from the side opposite the camera, usually creating a thin outline of lighting on this figure.

Figure 8.3 Multimodal compositions: CD-ROM

aspect of filmic practice – backlighting in this case. The written text is conventionally academic in its form. It seems that the new medium is being used partially to achieve something new – this conjunction (though that could be done on the page also) – and something conventional, keeping the text as a whole safely within what can be treated as seriously academic. However, the typeface is interesting in that context. The serif font, Times New Roman, is used as an additional means to ensure the safety of tradition. The question raised at that point is this: is 'font' also mode?

This is not all that needs to be said here: I have not mentioned the elements and processes that establish coherence and cohesion across multimodal ensembles. These are, again, similar in semiotic principle, and distinct in the material and cultural form of the means of doing this. The task of establishing the principles here as in many areas is at the very beginning.

9

READING AS SEMIOSIS

Interpreting the world and ordering the world

From telling the world to showing the world

The current landscape of communication can be characterised by the metaphor of the move from *telling the world* to *showing the world*. The metaphor points to a profound change in the act of reading, which can be characterised by the phrases 'reading as interpreting' and 'reading as ordering'. The metaphor and the two phrases allow us to explore the questions that reading poses – narrowly as 'getting meaning from a written text', and widely as 'making sense of the world around me' – through a new lens. Both senses of reading rest on the idea of *reading as sign-making*. The signs that are made by readers in their reading draw on *what there is to be read*. They draw on the shape of the cultural world of representation, and on the reader's prior training in how and what to read. New forms of reading, when texts *show the world* rather than *tell the world* have consequences for the relations between makers and remakers of meaning (writers and readers, image-makers and viewers). In this it is important to focus on materiality, on the materiality of the bodily senses that are engaged in reading – hearing (as in speech), sight (as in reading and viewing), touch (as in the feel of Braille) – and on the materiality of the means for making the representations that are to be 'read' – graphic stuff such as letters or ideograms, sound as in speech, movement as in gesture.

Some things are common to 'reading' across time, across cultures, across space, namely those which derive from the way in which our bodies place us in the world, ranging from the physiology of vision to the structure of the organs which we use for speech and hearing, to the organisation of the brain and its inherent capacities for memory, for instance. At the same time, many things are not common across cultures, times, places. Some things which seem part of our 'nature' are shaped by culture in important ways, such as the training of memory for instance. Forms of learning may have as much to do with human culture as with human nature. Above all, *the shape of what there is to read* has its effects on 'reading'. Reading practices, and the understanding of what reading is, develop in the constant interaction between the shape of what there is to read and the socially located reader and their human nature.

Immediately, there are the differences between alphabetic writing and logo-graphic or pictographic writing: the one orienting readers towards sound, the other towards meaning. Script systems range from those which attempt to represent sounds graphically as letters, as the alphabet does, to those which attempt to represent meaning as images, as do, in various forms, logographic and pictographic scripts. Even within alphabetic writing there are deep differences in the use of 'lettered representation' over different periods and in different cultures. As it happens, we are in a period where vast changes are taking place in this respect. In the Western, alphabetically oriented world, the change is one where image is ever more insistently appearing with or even instead of writing.

No one theory can deal with everything necessary for a full understanding of 'reading'. In my approach, a semiotic one, I focus on the 'how', the 'what with' and the 'why' of representation and communication: how, in what way, with what material and cultural resources, do we make the *signs* that represent our interests? That focus is one slice of the pie, so to speak. Ethnographers of writing and reading want to know where and when and for what purposes reading happens; what the environments are and look like in which reading happens. Researchers coming from media sociology want to know the shape of the whole media-field in which reading and the book have their contemporary uses and functions, a place in which 'reading' vies with all other media for the user's time, energy and attention. Closely related are the interests of those who ask about power, about exclusions and inclusions, and about domination through texts. Others ask about reading from the point of view of leisure and pleasure: given that there is such a vast range of media, what uses are being made of reading for entertainment, for fun, for relaxation, but also for ostensibly more serious purposes? Yet others ask questions which come from phonetics and phonology; yet others focus on more strictly psychological issues such as memory, recognition, retention and so on.

My own starting point is this: the increasingly and insistently more multi-modal forms of contemporary texts make it essential to rethink our notions of what reading is. As I have been demonstrating so far, many contemporary texts make use of image and of writing at the same time, using both to carry meaning in specific ways. In that context, a theory of reading which relates to the graphic material of 'letters' alone is no longer able to explain how we derive meaning from texts. At that point we are faced with a choice: either we treat 'reading' as a process which extends beyond (alphabetic) writing, and includes images for instance; or we restrict 'reading' to the mode of alphabetic writing quite strictly, and attend separately to how meaning is derived from images. Even then we would still need a theory which tells us how to combine meaning derived from writing and from image into a single coherent entity. And that would leave the question which I have raised earlier, of whether ideas of 'reading' derived from alphabetic writing fit easily or at all with non-alphabetic writing systems.

141

In fact in the contemporary situation the problem is sharper still. As the screen becomes the dominant site of communication – even if (still) only in its social and mythic impact rather than actually in quantitative terms – 'reading', as the process of getting meaning from a textual entity, will need to deal with more than just writing and image. A CD, or a web-page, may make use of music, of speech, of moving image, of 'soundtrack', as well as of (still) image and of writing. All these need to be 'read' together and made into one coherent text in 'inner' representation (as indeed they have to be when we watch a film).

In other words, the two meanings of 'reading' are always much more closely aligned than we allow ourselves to think. 'Reading the world' through different senses – sight, touch, hearing and even taste and smell – is always present in 'reading', even when we ostensibly focus on script alone. Why should it worry us – for those of us who are worried – to include image in the scope of reading? One answer might be that in Western alphabetic cultures, writing is seen quintessentially as the transliteration of speech into storable, durable form through the means of letters. Speech is seen as underlying writing. Of course, in these cultures, an opposite view holds sway at the same time, namely that writing is the 'real' form of language, the valued form, and the form which guarantees meaning. At any rate, both views see a strong connection between speech and writing, in which letters are the means of transliterating speech – 'capturing sound' is a metaphor frequently used. 'Reading' is then the process of unlocking both sound and meaning from letters: only letters (and the words and sentences formed from them in complex ways) give access to meaning. Image, in this view, does not contain meaning; or if it does it is not 'read' in the same way as writing.

The view that writing is tied to sound is at best a partial truth. Members of the communities of the speech-impaired can learn to read, even though they have never heard the sound of language. In some alphabetic languages (Hebrew, Arabic) only consonants are represented in writing; vowels are absent, or are indicated by superscripts or subscripts only. And in pictographic forms of writing it is in any case not sound which is (predominantly) represented in the symbols of the script. Nevertheless, it is a view which is deep-seated and potent in Western views of reading, and at times it forms the bedrock of common sense on the issue – as much in approaches to the teaching of reading as in high theory philosophy à la Derrida.

There is also the quite paradoxical fact that many of the claims and practices which emanate from this position, as in rules for 'spelling' – that is, writing words correctly – take writing as the starting point and reduce 'reading' to a set of instructions for telling readers how to get from the letter to the sound. They are rules for 'sounding out writing', and not for turning speech-sound into letter sequences. That is, they provide rules for turning letter-sequences into sound-sequences. An example I think of might be rules such as 'the k in knight is silent', or 'the letter a is pronounced as ai when there is an e on the end of the word, as in lame'.

'Reading' needs either to be discussed overtly as the general human urge and capacity for deriving meanings from (culturally) shaped materials which are thought to be the bearers of meaning; or to be treated as a culturally and historically specific instance of that general capacity. In other words, I do not think it is possible to deal with 'reading-as-such' in any useful fashion. It is possible to talk about the general human capacities that are involved, both physiological and semiotic, and it is possible to attempt to describe how these capacities are shaped at a particular point in the history of a society in relation to the shape of what there is to be read. In this chapter I will make some comments about both: I will attempt to say something about the general semiotic principles involved, and about the shape of 'what is to be read' in my society at this point, and how that makes us think about 'reading', now. I will deal with the former by focusing on 'reading as sign-making', and with the latter by asking, 'what is characteristic about writing using the roman alphabet?' Because this moment in time is different, in the ways I have already indicated several times, I will also focus on new forms of reading of new forms of text.

Reading as sign-making

Let me begin with a very simple example. I have discussed it before (Kress, 1997a), but it will help here to develop a sufficiently rich account of 'sign', and of reading.

The context in which the sign was produced was, roughly, this. I was sitting in my study, working, and our then 3-year-old daughter was sitting on the floor, 'doing her work', in this case attempting to write a thank-you card to a friend. She came over to my desk and asked me to write 'thank you' for her, on the bit of paper which was going to be the 'card'. My quickly written 'thank you' is reproduced in Figure 9.1 (overleaf). After about a minute or so she returned, saying, 'Look, I've done it', showing me the mark/sign which is here at the bottom of the paper.

The question that this raised for me, and I am not fully certain that I have yet answered it for myself, is this: what was it that she *had* done? And what principles were at issue for her, in her reading?

Clearly she had 'read' my quickly written sign, the 'thank you'; equally clearly she had not *copied* it. Notions of 'copying' or of 'imitating' are ready to hand to describe what children do, but they ensure that we ourselves misread what is at issue. On the one hand, whatever else the child's sign might have been, it was not a copy, not even an imperfect one. On the other hand, the notion of 'imitation' already implies a decision on our part to treat the 'inner' sign that results from her reading as not fully a sign, not based on principles of interpretation and, equally, the outwardly visible sign that she made from that 'inner sign' – which she made on the sheet of paper – as simply being a doodle.

Here is not the point to elaborate a theory of the sign, but it may be useful simply to state my position on this (fuller accounts may be found in Kress,

Figure 9.1 'Early' child writing: 'look, I've done it'

1993b, 1997a; Kress and Van Leeuwen, 1996). In the social semiotic approach which I adopt (Hodge and Kress, 1988) signs are motivated combinations of form and meaning (in the Saussurian parlance, of *signifier* and *signified*) in which the form is already the best, the most apt, representation of the meaning which the maker of the sign wishes to represent. That means that form and meaning do not stand in an arbitrary relation to each other, but that the relation is motivated: 'this form best expresses the meaning that I wish to represent'.

However, 'the meaning that I wish to represent' is only ever a partial representation of the object or the phenomenon that I wish to represent. It is a common misunderstanding or misapprehension that a representation is full, that it fully represents some thing in the physical or semiotic world. But quite to the contrary, representation is always partial. If I draw a car, I cannot draw all the features that make up that car; if I tell you about my new car – however enthusiastically I might do this – it will be a partial account only. However, the partiality of my representation is not an accident: I represent that which encapsulates or represents my 'interest' in the phenomenon that I wish to represent *at this moment*. I might wish to represent the sleekness of my car, or its size, or its white-walled tyres. The sign is therefore always both a representation of what it was that the sign-maker wished to represent, and it is an indication of her or his interest in the phenomenon represented *at that moment*. It is never more than that, never a full representation of the object in the world.

Signs are made both in outward production (in writing, in drawing, in gesture and so on), and are then visible, audible and communicable, and they are also made in inward production (in reading, in viewing, as much as through all forms of culturally shaped perception – taste, smell, touch). In (semiotic) principle there is no difference between inward and outward production; both result in the making of a sign. In (social) practice there is a vast difference between being able to make outward representations – and having the means for communicating them – and not being able to do so, for whatever reason. Outward production results in signs which are visible, audible and communicable; inward production results in signs which become visible, audible and so on only when they become the basis of new signs outwardly produced. These new outwardly produced signs allow us to make inferences about the shape and the characteristics of the inwardly produced signs that preceded them.

There are three significant points in this brief excursion into a theory of sign. The first point is that as the analyst of signs made, whether by a child as in the example above or by anyone else, I have to treat them as motivated conjunctions of meaning and form, that is, the form of the sign is the best available indicator of the meaning which the children wanted to represent. It entails that from the form of the sign I can make strong inferences about the meaning of the sign. That is not possible if I regard the sign as an arbitrary relation of form and meaning. The second point is this: the sign made outwardly (whether by the child or by the adult) is based on the sign made before, inwardly, as the result of the 'reading' made. This sign is therefore the best available evidence and data for a hypothesis about the shape of the sign made as a result of the reading. It is the best data we can have for understanding the processes and the effects of reading, and the same applies to 'learning'. The third point concerns *interest*: the shape of the sign gives me a strong indication of the *interest* of the maker of the sign, at the moment of the making of the sign. That of course is invaluable evidence for the processes of learning, of whatever kind.

With this quick sketch of 'sign' in mind, I will now look again at the tiny example, and ask again what it was that the child *had* done. Clearly she does not know the letters of the English alphabet, although I happen to know from many other instances – some appear below – that she was at that time 'working' in some way with the issue of 'what is a letter' – whether through attempts to write her own name, or to 'write' more generally. In order to understand my written model she has to engage in a task of visual analysis. To do that she needs principles of analysis, and one of the principles which she adopts, seemingly, is that things which are joined together physically must belong together as a unit of meaning. On the basis of this principle she can then produce her sign: it is neither merely or simply a copy, nor is it an imitation. The sign that she has produced is a *transformation* of the original. It is not the original, but it is the result of the application of principles of analysis to the original to produce a transformation which is performed on the elements and the structure of the original, carried out in line with the interests of the reader.

In this instance the sign that was produced outwardly had followed quickly on the reading of the initial sign. I make the assumption that the 'inner' sign produced by the child had strong similarities to this outwardly produced sign, and from that I feel able to deduce some ideas about how she has read. These

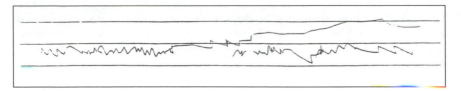

Figure 9.2 'Early' child writing in an alphabetic writing culture

would include the assumption that she paid very close attention to the charac-teristics of the structure that she had read, that she read these in terms of principles which she already held, or 'had', so that the transformed sign was the product of the original sign transformed in line with the interested action of the child. Such an approach promises an insight into the child's actions and, beyond that, an insight into the processes of reading much more generally.

My second example (Figure 9.2) is much like the first, and I give it here as support of this approach. It concerns what is sometimes called 'emergent writ-ing', produced by the same child, growing up in an alphabetic writing culture, in England.

There is a temptation to treat this as 'scribble', as the (3-year-old) child's (unprincipled) attempt at imitating the *appearance* of writing, and of course, to some extent that is right. But the contrast with Figure 9.3 shows that there is much more to this than the dismissive term 'scribble' would lead us to imagine: Figure 9.3 is the 'emergent writing' of another 3-year-old child growing up in a ideographic writing culture, in Taiwan.

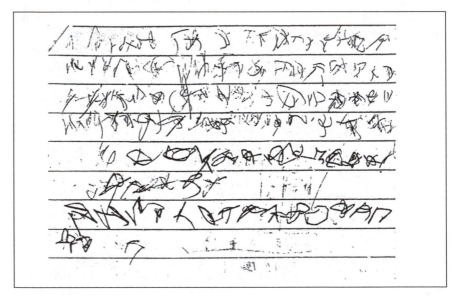

Figure 9.3 'Early' child writing in a pictographic writing culture

The comparison of the two examples shows that each of the two children has applied principles to their rendering of the script system of their respective cultures. We can attempt to read off – using the notion of the motivated sign – what each of the two regards as the underlying *logic* of each script. The first child's 'sign' suggests that she sees writing as consisting of linking of simple elements, which do not differ much from each other; which are repeated, in sequence, conjoined; and which are arranged in lines. The second child's 'sign' suggests that she sees writing as consisting of complex elements, not linked; each element distinct in shape from the others, not repeated; in a sequence, each discrete, and arranged in lines.

When we see each example by itself, in isolation, it is difficult to see the transformative work done by the children, to see the meaningful signs made by them in their reading. The contrast and the comparison reveal what is otherwise not so clearly apparent, namely the semiotic work that is done here. Each of the two children have 'read', in the full sense of the word, the script systems of their culture. They have made their meaning of each script-system, a meaning which appears in their outwardly made signs.

My next example, Figure 9.4 (overleaf), shows the process of reading as sign-making, some three to four years later. The examples come from two different primary schools; both the children were seven at the time they produced these small texts.

The reading which preceded these two texts is of more diverse materials; it was reading of a range of more complex text-materials as well as the 'reading' of much talk by the teacher and of looking at illustrations. Indeed this is a 'reading' of a diversity of texts, spoken by the teacher, and shown in a book, or drawn on a whiteboard, and so the complex signs that appear here are based on a multiplicity of 'readings' at many levels, brought together – re-presented – here as a complex new sign. I will not talk about the children's acute hearing-as-'reading' of the speech of their communities, as it is revealed in their phonetically precise spellings. Instead I wish to explore the issue of the necessary prior resources – which includes 'principles' – without which reading is not possible. My focus is on the two children's 'reading' of *frog-spawn*. The resources applied differ in the two cases. The boy who wrote 'frogs born' focused on semantic resources, broadly speaking, while the girl who wrote 'frogs sporn' relied more on syntactic resources. I assume that in each case the children had met this word in speech, and for both it was a word they had not encountered before. Neither of them has a difficulty in constructing some phonological/morphological entity, and to transliterate that from a spoken and heard form to a graphological/written form.

At that level there is no problem. The problem arises at the level of meaning, and it is solved by each of them in distinctly different ways. James ('frogs born') draws on the semantic resources in the materials provided for him by the teacher (teacher's talk, images, talk with his neighbour). 'This is about reproduction', he seems to say to himself, 'so obviously this unknown word must be "born"'. The resultant reading, the linguistic entity 'frogs born' has no syntactic

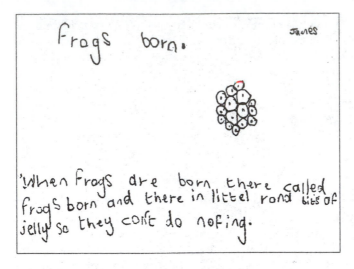

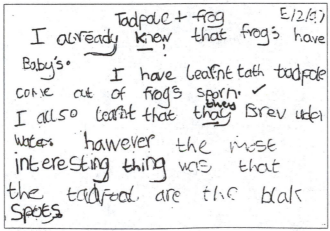

Figure 9.4 Drawing and writing: 'frogs born'

status. A reader of his reading will need to do work to make it grammatical: supplying an assumed elided 'are', to give 'frogs are born', for instance. Emily, by contrast, draws on syntactic resources available to her. These do not (necessarily) come from the classroom. They are the resources drawn from her experience of language more widely: 'ah', she seems to say to herself, 'I have come across forms like this before, "mum's bag", for instance, or "my brother's Playstation". This must be another one like it. I don't know what a "sporn" is, but that's not unusual; so many new words, every day'.

With this last example I have moved to the border between reading of script and reading considered much more widely. I have also moved into the discussion of reading as a process that relates to multimodally constituted texts. James had drawn an image of 'frogs born' – and the image shows clearly that he knows 'what he is talking about'. We need to see the overall meaning of his text as a composite of the written and the drawn elements. In meaning, they have a partially overlapping and a partially complementary function in relation to each other.

However, to get a full sense of what is involved in the process of reading I will take another example, which embeds 'reading' much more widely in the lifeworld of the reader – and of course of the writer too. My example, Figure 9.5 (overleaf), is familiar to everyone. Here it is the horoscope from a giveaway newspaper, for 19 January 2002. The text, as I say, is commonplace, innocuous; and 'readable', in a full sense, only in the contexts of the life-worlds of the readers who attend to this type of text. (Of course we know that many readers of the paper 'look at' the horoscope, or make fun of this kind of text – and many more do not even do that – but they are, by definition, not really readers of the text.)

Of course, there is no particular problem here in terms of linguistic complexity – always provided that the reader has a relatively full competence in English. There are 'culturally specific' issues such as the idioms – in the sign of Capricorn – 'giving the girl a good send-off', 'if you get my drift' or – in the sign of Pisces – 'the heat is . . . off', 'sit back and take it easy', 'come back to earth'. And there are some more specifically cultural matters such as – in Capricorn – 'all things Venusian' or – in Pisces – 'Mars leaves'; though now 'cultural' has changed to mean 'those in that group which knows about the attributes of the gods Venus and Mars in classical mythology'.

However, the real work of 'reading' lies somewhere else. For a start, it rests on the assumption that readers take the whole enterprise seriously, that they see this practice as a perfectly usual part of their life-world. But specifically it rests on the readers' willingness and ability to select aspects of their lives as being relevantly attachable to each of the brief accounts or predictions. So a reader whose sun-sign is Capricorn will need to interpret larger or smaller aspects of her life as being relevantly addressed by the description. What is it in her life that will make sense of 'indulging yourself in all things Venusian', and what is 'the drift' that she needs to get? How, and with whom, can she give 'the girl a good send-off'? And similarly with Pisces, what was the 'heat' which is now 'being turned off', and in what ways does this Piscean know that he cannot 'sit back and take it easy'? How can he 'come back to earth' to 'finish what he started'?

What may seem the quirky problems raised by reading a horoscope – though readers of such texts see nothing quirky in that – turns out to be the entirely normal act of reading that all readers need to engage in constantly. If the meanings of the horoscope text seem particularly vacuous – what heat was turned off? What was started that needs to be finished off? – vacuous, in that each question can have as many different answers as there are readers, then that is only because we allow ourselves to be persuaded that reading is not usually like that. Of course the degree of vacuity varies, and even with the horoscope there are days when the reader is struck by the aptness of the brief

successes. But once the party is over, the hard work really starts.
Gemini 0906 4710782

CANCER
(Jun 22–Jul 23)
For too long, it appears you have waited in the shadows as far as your working life is concerned. Well, now it is time to claim what is rightfully yours.
Cancer 0906 4710783

LEO
(Jul 24–Aug 23)
Being brave is something that comes very naturally to you, but only when you feel like it. This is a day for feeling like it and not lazing around sleeping.
Leo 0906 4710784

VIRGO
(Aug 24–Sep 23)
Arguments of a personal nature are coming to a close, but what is the outcome? You may not believe this but it is better to think status quo than change.
Virgo 0906 4710785

LIBRA
(Sep 24–Oct 23)
As if there isn't enough in the heavens pointing to a successful sex life in your chart, here comes more help. Now I really am getting fed up with all of it.
Libra 0906 4710786

SCORPIO
(Oct 24–Nov 22)
I know that you are not going to be in the best frame of mind today but, if it helps, I can tell you that you are about to get something off your chest that helps.
Scorpio 0906 4710787

SAGITTARIUS
(Nov 23–Dec 21)
As money pressures are lifted a little over the weekend, you can get ready to concentrate on spending that extra income you will have. How about a bar of chocolate?
Sagittarius 0906 4710788

CAPRICORN
(Dec 22–Jan 20)
Over the weekend, Venus leaves your sign so give the girl a good send off by indulging yourself in all things Venusian. Eat, drink and be merry, if you get my drift...
Capricorn 0906 4710789

AQUARIUS
(Jan 21–Feb 19)
Now a more dynamic period begins, you are likely to feel motivated, but where are you going to put all that energy? You could do worse than tackle finances.
Aquarius 0906 4710790

PISCES
(Feb 20–Mar 20)
The heat is being turned off as Mars leaves your sign, but that doesn't mean you can sit back and take it easy. Come back to earth and finish what you started.
Pisces 0906 4710791

ARIES
(Mar 21–Apr 20)
Whatever you have been holding back on, you should not do so any longer. Whoever it is who needs to hear what you have to say, now is the time to do it.
Aries 0906 4710780

TAURUS
(Apr 21–May 21)
No more wallowing in a pit of 'might have been' and 'should have done'. You are being given a second chance at something and this time there will be no errors.
Taurus 0906 4710781

GEMINI
(May 22–Jun 21)
The party season is far from over as you celebrate some

Calls cost 60p per minute at all times. Phone forecasts are changed weekly

Figure 9.5 Horoscope

prediction and others when there is no 'reading' available to her or to him. But the processes and the principles are the same.

The world as told: reading as interpretation

I want to turn now to an examination of contemporary forms of *what there is to read*. If what reading in the narrower sense is depends on what – in any society

– the usual forms of 'graphic' communication are, it becomes essential to engage in that kind of analysis. In addition, and as my framing metaphor of *from telling the world to showing the world* suggests, *what there is to read* has been undergoing fundamental changes. We are moving into a world in which image will be much more dominant as a public mode of communication.

The strongly felt relation between sound and letter in Western alphabetic societies is at times so strong that letter and sound are confused and are seen as the same, and not only in popular common sense. Statements such as 'English has five vowels: a, e, i, o and u' can be found in manuals produced for teacher education even now. English has *five letters* for representing, depending on how we analyse them, about *twelve vowel sounds* (not counting diphthongs and triphthongs). There is a reality to the letter–sound relation, but it is more tenuous than is usually assumed. Nevertheless, it does make writing relate closely to speech, particularly for people who are not deeply embedded in a literate culture. *Sub-vocalisation* is one sign of this: people sound out the writing that they are reading, more or less fully. (We know that in western Europe reading used to be 'reading aloud' until some five hundred years ago.)

For readers who sub-vocalise, reading is a process – I call it transduction – which moves writing back from its visual/graphic form into a spoken form, from letters to sounds. Speech has many linguistic features which writing does not have – intonation, duration and rhythm for instance – and even though these are not marked in written texts (with truly rare exceptions) they are restored to speech by most of us even in our silent reading. That reveals an otherwise hidden feature of writing (sometimes marked in practices of punctuation), namely that for many – even highly literate people – the syntax of writing remains to some extent organised on the principles of the syntax (and texture) of speech. This becomes apparent whenever we have read into a sentence, or into a text, and find that we have given it an intonational shape which becomes unsustainable, in the sense that it leads to *no sense* semantically (and syntactically).

Transducing writing back into speech, in the process of reading, takes the reader back to the semiotic logic of speech, which itself derives from the materiality of sound. Human speech-sounds have to be uttered one at a time, so that the logic of temporality and temporal sequence provide the deep ordering principle for speech. One sound has to be uttered after another, one lexical element after another, one clause after another, and so on. Of course, even in speech, simple succession can be modified, both lexically (with conjunctions of various kinds – *because, so that, therefore, nevertheless*) and textually/syntactically (with various forms of syntactic subordination). But even without the transduction of writing back to speech, the logic of speech – of temporality – remains in writing, even if it is made less immediately apparent, especially in 'formal' writing, by the syntactic means available. This means that whereas *in speech sequence (as parataxis) is dominant, in writing hierarchy (as hypotaxis) dominates*, whether we are looking at the (size) levels of phonology/graphology, of morphology, of syntax or of text.

Not all alphabetic script systems insist on the same close relation to sound as do the cultures using the 'Western' (roman, cyrillic) versions: in Arabic and Hebrew versions of the alphabet only consonants are represented, and vowels, if marked at all, are present as super- or subscripts attached to consonants. In other words, not all sounds are transliterated. Nevertheless, for alphabetic systems it seems to be true to say that language is at the first step represented as being about sound (and only at a second step as being about meaning), by contrast with ideographic script systems, where language seems to be represented at the first step as being about meaning, and at a second step as being about sound. It is worth pointing out that the sound–letter relation does not exist for the communities of the speech-impaired, who are nevertheless able to 'read' script or writing even though they have never heard the sound of speech. In a different way, the letter-as-image relation is broken for the blind, for whom reading means 'feeling writing'.

The world as shown: reading as design

It is when we turn to texts produced with letter and image that further distinctive features of writing with letters appear. This may be best shown by focusing on the logic of image, to contrast with the logic of (writing and) speech. As I have suggested, the logic of speech – and by extension of writing – is that of time and sequence, and the logic of image is that of space, and of simultaneity. Figure 9.6 shows the contrasting characteristics of the two logics.

This example comes from a class of 6-year-olds who visited the British Museum in London. On the day after the visit, the teacher asked the class *to draw a picture* and *write a story* of the visit. Figure 9.6 shows a picture drawn by one boy and his story below (the two were produced by him on separate pieces of paper). The logic of the story is clear: sequence of actions/events in time is the organising order. The logic of the image is equally clear: this is about the use of space to *display* the elements and their relation to each other – 'me and the mummy' – which are most significant to this young person in his recollection of the day.

In my reading of the story and of the image I am positioned very differently: the one *tells* me about the world of events in sequence, the other *shows* me the world of relations between objects. The one *tells* me about the significance of events and of their sequential order; the other *shows* me the salience of the elements regarded by the boy as the most significant in his recollection, and their relation to each other. I might ask further about the manner in which I as a reader am positioned: the story has a *reading path*, both literally, along the lines of writing, from top to bottom, from left to right, as well as in its simple sequential unfolding. It is clear and given; if I wish to go against it, I have to work hard to do so. The syntax which gives order to the elements of the text, the sentences, is also clear, and strictly given: I cannot read elements 'out of order', in the sentences or parts of sentences (for the concept of 'reading path' see Kress and Van Leeuwen, 1996).

Our visit to the museum

We went to Clapham Junction and we went on the train to take us to Waterloo.
We went underground and then we took a tube and we all went to Goodge
Street. We walked to Russell Square where the museum was. After, we went on
a tube, after we went on a train we walked to school.

Figure 9.6 'Our visit to the British Museum' (with thanks to Eve Bearn)

The image by contrast does not have such a clearly set reading path: I might start with the figure of the boy, and move to the mummy which he is showing me. Or I might start with the central figure of the mummy, taking spatial centrality to indicate centrality of meaning, and move from there to the figure of the boy who stands to the side as 'my guide'. With more complex images, the question of the reading path becomes, if anything, more free. This is not to say that images do not display (and adhere to) 'regularities', to a 'grammar'. Images are not beyond convention, and viewers of images do not simply act 'individually'. It is to say that at this moment in history the force of convention does not press as heavily on makers of image or on viewers, perhaps in part because images have remained outside the very close control of social and cultural power which has been applied to writing in particular. Individual readers do act in accordance with socially established practices of viewing. More complex narratives, by contrast, need not give me greater freedom or openness in the reading path. It may also be the case that – as in languages with relatively free word-order – it is not that they do not have grammar, but that the grammar as resource offers other potentials than a language with a strict word-order. Work in the psychology of image recognition may offer useful insight at this point.

I might go further and ask about the 'lexis', that is the 'words' of speech or writing, and the 'shown or depicted elements' in images. In another example from this class, a boy writes as a part of his story (again largely about events in sequence): 'I liked the mummies and all that stuff'. The word 'mummies' is known to me; but that knowledge does not allow me to attempt to reproduce in a drawing what that mummy actually looked like. The mummies that he drew (two, lying down), as much as the mummy represented here, are however quite specific: they *show* me what they were like in the child's recollection. I want to say that at the level of lexis there is a paradoxical difference, given common-sense views about language and image which see language and word as precise and explicit, and image as imprecise and inexplicit. While the lexis of a language, in speech or writing, consists of (relatively speaking) a fixed number of available elements, each element is relatively open in meaning. In visual lexis, however, there is no fixed number of available elements, but each element, which is each time newly produced, is fixed, in terms of being specific about what it represents.

In my last example, Figure 9.7, I want to show how image and writing go together in multimodal texts, and how they might be read together as a text which is internally coherent. The example comes from a science textbook for 13- to 14-year-olds; it was first published in 1988.

Several points need to be made. The comments about the logics of writing and of image apply here pretty much as they did in the example drawn from the writing and drawings of the 6-year-olds in my discussion of the British Museum examples. I said that there is a deep difference in the engagement and representation of the world through image and through writing. Two quite distinct versions of the day are offered to the 'reader' in image and in writing, along the lines that I have suggested: the world represented as a sequence of action or event versus the world represented as objects and their relations.

This is no less the case here. Here the issue is not what happened on a particular day, an account of events, but an account of an issue, a topic in the science curriculum. Writing and image broadly share the page, with somewhat more space given over to image than to writing. The significant point, however, is

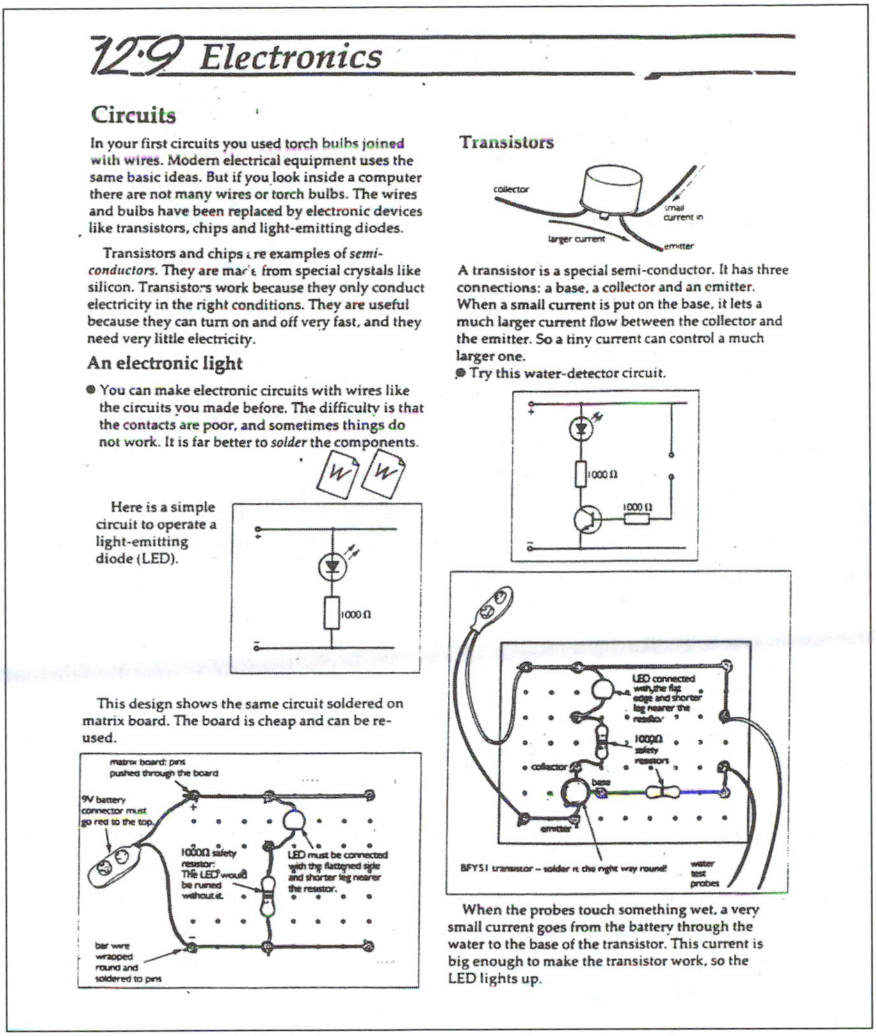

12·9 Electronics

Circuits

In your first circuits you used torch bulbs joined with wires. Modern electrical equipment uses the same basic ideas. But if you look inside a computer there are not many wires or torch bulbs. The wires and bulbs have been replaced by electronic devices like transistors, chips and light-emitting diodes.

Transistors and chips are examples of *semi-conductors*. They are made from special crystals like silicon. Transistors work because they only conduct electricity in the right conditions. They are useful because they can turn on and off very fast, and they need very little electricity.

An electronic light

● You can make electronic circuits with wires like the circuits you made before. The difficulty is that the contacts are poor, and sometimes things do not work. It is far better to *solder* the components.

Here is a simple circuit to operate a light-emitting diode (LED).

This design shows the same circuit soldered on matrix board. The board is cheap and can be re-used.

Transistors

A transistor is a special semi-conductor. It has three connections: a base, a collector and an emitter. When a small current is put on the base, it lets a much larger current flow between the collector and the emitter. So a tiny current can control a much larger one.

● Try this water-detector circuit.

When the probes touch something wet, a very small current goes from the battery through the water to the base of the transistor. This current is big enough to make the transistor work, so the LED lights up.

Figure 9.7 Page from a science textbook

that there is a specialisation of functions between writing and image. Writing is used to provide the pedagogic framing for this part of the curriculum – what we did last time, what we will do now, how well it worked or did not work, what it would be best to do, and so on. Image is used to represent that which is the issue, the core of the curricular issue here: what a circuit is, what the elements of a circuit are, how we think about circuits theoretically, and what circuits are like in practice. That content does not appear in any part of the written text. Writing is used for that which writing does best – to provide, in fact, an account of events, and image is used for that which image does best, to depict the world

that is at issue, in terms of the significant elements and their (spatially represented) relations to each other. Writing is, by and large, about the action and
events involving the significant participants – both the 'you' and 'we' of the students, and the objects and elements of the curricular world, of the circuits.

This difference in the use of modes here is motivated in two ways. One is the
motivation of 'best fit': that which is best represented as spatial display is shown
as image, and that which is best represented as event and action in sequence is
told in writing. In other words, the use of the mode rests on the inherent affordances of each mode. Of course, the inherent affordance of the mode has large
aspects of past social and cultural work to it; it is possible because of cultural
work with the affordance of the material aspects of the mode. This cultural
aspect I call *functional specialisation*. That this is culturally and historically specific
is shown by the fact that thirty or forty years earlier, textbooks for the same
age-group used writing for the curricular content. That which had to be represented about the curriculum was represented through the mode of writing. Of
course, in order to be able to do that, writing had to be, and was, very different.
Its syntax was hugely more complex, in order to deal with the complexities of
the matter that had to be represented.

The second motivation is both curricular and pedagogic: curricular because
it may be felt that an entity which has spatial existence 'in reality' is best represented in the spatial mode of image; and pedagogic, because it may be felt that
this generation, and this group of students, is best addressed through image, for
a variety of reasons. Image figures hugely in the lives of young people; image
may be seen as more immediately accessible; image may therefore be seen to be
the better communicational route to the mass-audience of science now – as
against the elite audience of science thirty, forty, fifty years ago. Past uses of
writing and image are instructive in this respect: textbooks of that other era
used writing as the dominant mode, not conscious that there was a choice of
mode – which in a sense there was not then: image was not culturally and
above all socially 'available' for full representation – but certainly conscious that
the audience was an elite audience, and gender-specific.

This represents a sharp, a near total, difference to textbooks from even thirty
years ago in which the curricular content was communicated in writing and
images served as 'illustration': that is, they repeated something that had been
'said' in the written text in some form. It is instructive to realise that textbooks
then could be read, that is, they could be realised in the sounds of speech, no
matter how awkwardly unspeech-like the writing actually was.

Choosing how to read: reading paths

The page in Figure 9.7 cannot be read aloud; it is not meant to be read that
way. The conception of text underlying this page, and how it is to be used and
handled is simply different to older pages and texts. The written text here is not
the full representation; it has a function which is complementary to the visually

represented text. That complementarity is not straightforward. At times the written parts of the text are labels of image, or instructions in relation to image; at times they are relatively independently coherent textual elements – even though they have a specific function in relation to the text overall. If we insisted that reading aloud what is written here were to be seen as a full reading, we would get sound strings which do not form a coherently organised text, and the reading would miss out those aspects of meaning, the curricular content, which, after all, is the central aspect of this text-page, and which are realised visually.

There is then a question about how to read this page as an integrated, coherent text. At this point the question of the reading path arises, because in some ways there has to be a reading 'across' the two modes, a reading that brings together the meaning realised via the two modes. In older forms of page this may seem not to be an issue: we start at the top-left corner, read across to the right, return to the left one line down, and continue. There is seemingly no choice. And indeed, if we are interested in 'getting the meaning' of the text as it was intended – allowing for the transformative action of the reader in any reading – we need to adhere to that reading path. But just because an action has become totally habituated does not mean that the choice is not there. There are forms of pathology in which this habituation has not happened, and those in which it has unravelled. However, even in quite usual forms of reading, such as 'skimming', we tend to depart quite significantly from such paths. Children learning to read find this seemingly obvious issue not at all straightforward, and it is instructive to look closely at their careful analysis of this question – disentangling directionality from linearity (see Figure 9.8, overleaf), and directionality of individual elements such as letters and letter-sequences in words from the directionality of lines.

In these examples here, the child reader/writer has puzzled about this issue in the way I described above; successively, over time, and with more knowledge of this system, she comes closer and closer to the regularities which her culture has adopted.

As we know this matter of the reading path is a cultural decision. Different cultures have made different decisions about reading paths in their writing systems, whether from right to left or from left to right, in lines or in columns, circular or linear. Multimodal texts open this question again, in two ways: once in terms of directionality, and then also in terms – more problematically perhaps – of what the elements are which are to form the 'points' along which we trace the reading path.

If we take the 'circuits' text (Figure 9.7) as our example, we can show that there is a choice to be made. It can be read as a new text, not only in being multimodal, but new also in standing uneasily between being a text to be *read* in the mode of traditional written text, though with images included, or a text to be *viewed* as a kind of image, with writing included. If we take it as an older form of text, a text that conforms to the rules, conventions and logic of the older page (and of writing), then the older, linear form of reading path applies

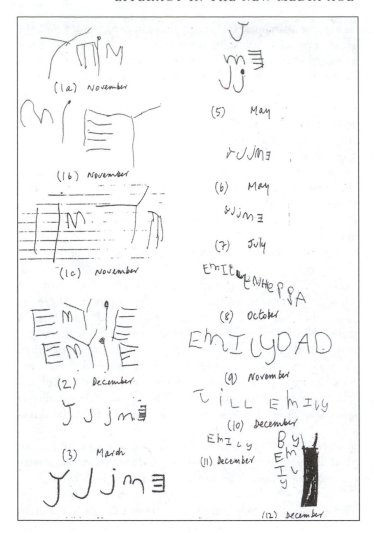

Figure 9.8 'Early' child writing: linearity and directionality

to it. We would start at the top of the left column, read across, then down, across, and so on. We would, however, encounter the problem of what the elements of this text to be read are when we came to the first image, and its 'caption', on the left.

At this point we have to make a decision about the 'elements' that are to be read together. In the written text, we read – I will make this assumption here without justifying it – sentence by sentence, as the relevant meaning-units of the text. That is, we read at one level 'down' from the overall unit. Do we, when we come to it, move to the image and read it immediately at the same level, at the level equivalent to 'sentence'? Of course, to do so would require that we know as much about the constitution of the image as we do about the constitution of the written part of the text. But that is not the only issue.

My assumption is that in reading such texts we proceed differently. When we encounter pages or texts of this kind, obviously constituted of distinct modes, we do a kind of modal 'scanning' of the page. In real time this would be next to instantaneous, but it would tell us that the text is composed of elements of distinct modes, and this provides us with a strategy for a reading of the page or text. The scanning would tell us that there are elements – blocks, of writing and of image – on this page. As a second step we would decide which of these, if either, is the dominant mode. We would then know to integrate the non-dominant mode into the dominant, or treat both as equal and read them conjointly. A further component in the strategy might be to assess what the *function* of each of the two modes in the text is, both at a structural level – are they complementary to each other or is one supplementary to the other? – as well as in terms of their specialised meaning-role – does writing, as in the example here, have the function of 'pedagogic framing', and image that of representing curricular content? This double assessment would provide a strategy for reading the page or text.

Just as in the scanning of a sentence, say, where we have a preliminary sense of the major components which shapes our initial approach to its reading – of course the actual reading may need to be revised along the way – so this assessment gives us a sense of how to read the page: there are 'chunks', elements, units of meaning, of differing function, structurally in their relation to each other and in their meaning-relation. The first scanning might give sufficient sense to the experienced 'reader' of such a page for her or him to proceed with a reading 'below' the level of these elements. 'Experience' here would indicate both prior encounter of such pages or texts, and membership of the relevant social/textual community, that is, someone who both understands what is at issue socially and culturally, and understands usual modal forms of realisation of these issues. At the points of transition from one modal 'block' to another, there is then an expectation for the reader of two kinds: for instance 'now I will get information which complements that which I have just had' and 'I will now get information of this kind (curricular, let's say) rather than that kind (pedagogic, let's say)'. The reading would then proceed at that next level 'down', in terms of the elements which exist in that block, at that level, in that modal realisation.

This would not tell us what reading path to adopt. That decision would be another result from the first scanning, and it would depend on two things: on the one hand, the look, the organisation, of the page – how are the blocks organised, spatially, in relation to each other? And, on the other hand, the reader's already existing disposition as a reader. A reader who had been socialised into traditional forms of reading may wish to persist with that as a possibility, even when that is really difficult in terms of what the page is like. Other readers, socialised into newer forms of organisation through the significance in their lives of the screen, might wish to read even a (relatively) traditional page in terms of a non-linear reading path. So a reading path is nearly as much a matter of the social as it is of the semiotic. Given that readers socialised in the traditional forms of the page and of the mode of writing are those who have social power now, whether as parents, educators, politicians or media-pundits, it is not surprising that there is such outrage at the newer semiotic forms. They are felt as challenges to social power, which they are.

The semiotic and the social power of the screen is now such that its influence reaches all sites of representation. It may be that the designers of the science page believed, if they thought about it at all in those terms, that they were constructing a traditional page, though made attractive for the readership of school-science now. The fact that that readership is one of all children and young people who go to school, which now encompasses very nearly all young people up to late teenage, of both genders, would very likely have influenced their design decisions. The question of 'appeal' would have been strongly felt, and indeed the understanding that the young look at the screen, rather than read the book, would have been present. So in a sense, the rules, conventions and logic of the image-space, which are nowadays predominantly the arrangements of the screen, would apply to their design even if in this roundabout way.

Reading as establishing and imposing criteria of relevance

To conclude this part of my discussion I wish to look very briefly at a page which is influenced by the screen in every way: it reports, so to speak, the screen, and its layout, its organisation is very much that of the screen (Figure 9.9).

The screens of computer (or video) games are multimodal – there is music, soundtrack, writing at times – yet overwhelmingly these screens are dominated by the mode of image. As the graphics become ever more sophisticated, the forms of reading necessary to play at least some of the games successfully become more subtle and demanding. (I am not here talking of the many other conceptual/cognitive demands to do with plot, for instance, or sense of character, or strategies of various kinds.) Here I wish to focus on that aspect of 'reading' alone which has to do with making sense of the organisation of the visual space – visual analysis which rests both on visual acuity and on a highly developed sense of the visual organisation of specific kinds of screen. Linearity is certainly not a useful approach to the reading of these screens – it is visual clues such as salience, colour, texturings, spatial configurations of various kinds, the meanings of specific kinds of element either natural or human-made, which allow the player to construct a reading path, which tracks the path of the narrative. The strategies for successful reading are every bit as complex as those of the written page – one might be tempted to say, more complex, given the pre-established reading path of the page – but in any case, and certainly, different. It is not that there isn't a reading path, though many games of the 'role-play' variety

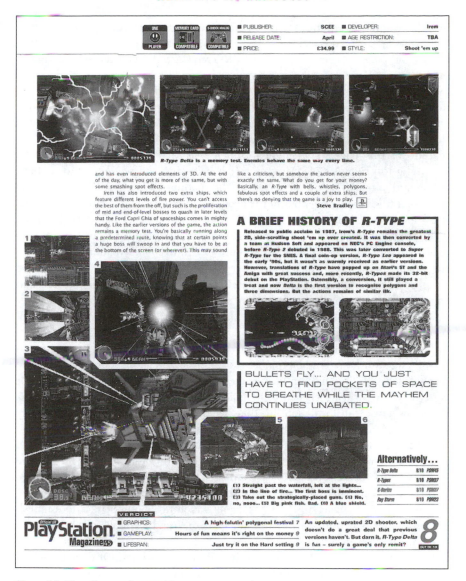

Figure 9.9 New forms of text: video-game magazine

(say, a game such as *Final Fantasy*), or even action adventure games such as the famous Lara Croft, offer alternative reading paths, something not encountered on traditional pages. Readers of such screens are used to a different strategy. To call it a freedom might be mistaken in that these games do have their rules, their conventions, and at the moment at any rate, the reader's real ability to be genuinely 'active' in constructing reading paths that are actually new is not existent.

The point, however, is that readers who come from such screens to pages are

used to reading differently. Many pages now are constructed to meet the different strategies and expectations of these readers, and this example is one. It is
the second page of a review of a game, *R-Type Delta*. As with the school science
textbook page, here too there is a functional specialisation of writing and image.
Writing provides the description of *how the game works*, and what it does; the
image shows *what it is*, especially the all-important aspect of the graphics of the
game. When one watches a reader of these pages reading, one is struck by the
similarity between the reading of the screens which are here discussed, and the
reading of this page. The guiding principle is that of 'following relevance',
according to principles of relevance which belong to the reader – and perhaps
are shared (already) by his community. The reading path is not 'regular', in the
sense of a traditional page, but nor is it regular in an easily described other way.
It is established by the criteria of relevance which the reader brings to the page.
The elements which are read – images are certainly attended to first or in preference to word – are each very carefully examined. The reading path is not
regular in spatial or linear terms – there is no clear sequence which might be
circular or linear or have some other form. The reading path is established
according to the principles of relevance of the reader. Of course, as I mentioned, the page is already designed with this kind of reader and these kinds of
reading principle in mind.

But here lies an absolute and I think profound difference between the traditional page and its reading path, and the new page – derived from the
principles of the organisation of the screen – and its reading path. The former
coded a clear path, which had to be followed. The task of reading lay in interpretation and transformation of that which was clearly there and clearly
organised. The new task is that of applying principles of relevance to a page
which is (relatively) open in its organisation, and consequently offers a range of
possible reading paths, perhaps infinitely many. The task of the reader in the
first case is to observe and follow a given order, and within that order to engage
in interpretation (where that too was more or less tightly policed) the task of the
reader of the new page, and of the screens which are its models, is to establish
the order through principles of relevance of the reader's making, and to construct meaning from that.

It is clear to me that these are utterly different principles. Of course each of
these belongs to vaster social forms of organisation. They do not exist simply as
inexplicably different forms: the one fits into the social forms and orders of the
preceding era; the other exhibits some of the social forms and orders, requirements and tasks and demands, of the present and the future era. It is, I believe,
simply impossible now to expect young people to read in the older manner,
other than as a specialised form of learning, where clear reasons will need to be
given about the constitution of that difference and the purposes of maintaining
it. Where that is not done, the tasks of that learning are made difficult for many
and impossible for some. The screen trains its readers in certain ways, just as
the page trained its readers in its ways: the latter had its uses and functions and

purposes, which were the uses and functions and purposes of the society in which it existed. The new form has its uses and functions and purposes in relation to new social, cultural, political and economic demands. It is not the task of the young to puzzle about and discover that, and it is not surprising if they treat with incomprehension and disdain that which makes no sense and cannot be made sense of for them by their parents, teachers and others, who can offer only their annoyance and outrage.

Maybe in passing we might note two things, however. One is that these new arrangements have spread from the screen well beyond the pages of Playstation magazines – as of other magazines – and of school science (as of other) textbook pages. Newspapers, pamphlets, reports of various kinds are all being reconfigured by this move. The reader of the tabloid newspaper who may have none or only the most minimal amount of writing on the front page of the paper that they buy may not give much time to reflect on the trend that they are part of, and may even be entirely willing to go along with the populist rant of a columnist in that paper against the trend. And in that, he or she may only be different in degree from the reader of the 'quality' paper which is affected by the same move, even if to a lesser extent.

The other is to note the manner of reading of writing by those who are entirely inward with the reading of the new pages and of the screens. As I said, many of these games do have writing, whether in tabular form as instructions, specifications of qualities of weapons, and so on, or as bits of verbal interaction as part of the visually and verbally realised narrative. When I have watched expert players at play I have been amazed at the fact that I am unable to take in the written text and its information in the time during which it appears on the screen. I am aware that I am not a particularly fast reader, but I am not particularly slow either. I have checked on numerous occasions whether the players were able to read and had read the written bits of texts, to find both astonishment on their part at my question, and confirmation that they had indeed read what had appeared. They were always willing to tell me their principles: 'you read the letters as they come up' (sometimes with a condescending 'Dad!'). And it is true that I had waited, and still have to do so, until what I consider a sufficient amount of text to be there on the screen. My orientation it seems really is different: I am oriented to notions of 'completed text'; they are oriented to notions of 'information as it is supplied'. I have no doubt that both are useful; and equally I have no doubt as to which will be most essential in their future lives.

Reading paths and access to knowledge

Writing and image have coexisted for a long time, and in different ways. In the period of the dominance of the page (and the book) and writing, the page was organised according to the logic of writing. Image, where it occurred on the page, was subordinated to that logic. In the new period of the dominance of the screen, and of image, the screen (as the currently most prominent form of image-space) is organised according to the logic of the image; writing, where it occurs on the screen, is subordinated to the logic of the screen and the image. That has fundamentally significant consequences for reading. For instance, in the case of the page from the science textbook above (Figure 9.7), if we treat the page as an 'old' page, then it is read according to the logic of writing: from top-left-hand corner to the right, and all the way down. In that reading path, the reader encounters the highly abstract image of the circuit first, and moves from there to the realist representation of the circuit. The move, in other words, is from the highly generalised (the theoretical abstraction) to the empirical/specific. If, however, we treat this page as a new image-site, the reading becomes a different one. Now the logic of the image-space obtains, and we look for the meanings of the spatially organised display. Now the semiotics of a framed space, in which left and right, bottom and top, centre and margin, have been used and developed in Western cultures in particular ways, lends significance to the elements which appear in those spaces. In this ordering, this logic, the realist image at the bottom occupies a space which in the Western visual semiotic has the meaning of (the empirically) 'real', the 'grounded', and the highly abstract image above it has the meaning of 'ideal'. This reading, which reads from bottom – 'the real' – to top – 'the ideal' – corresponds to a different epistemological position than the earlier one: the one is broadly inductive, the other broadly deductive. One of the fundamentally distinctive principles of modes of scientific – and other theoretical – approaches is coded in this feature.

Shifts in power: (re)producers of multimodal texts

This raises again the question of the reading path, though in a different way. In a sense an initial assessment made by the reader at the start of their reading as to how the text is to be read – whether as a page of the older kind or as screen (or page) of the newer kind – is not due to an idiosyncratic, individual response. It has much or everything to do with the reader's socialisation into a particular media environment, and the valuations of media (book or PC, for instance) and modes (writing or image, for instance) in that media landscape (see Boeck and Kress (2002) for a discussion of that issue). Dependent on that assessment, different logics then apply, and different strategies of reading. For me, socialised in the high era of the page, of the book, and of writing, my naturalised strategy leads me to see the page as the domain of writing, and to treat the screen similarly. In other words, such dispositions have much to do with social characteristics, among which age (as *social generational* difference) for instance, gender possibly (note the public alarm in many Western countries about the differential patterns of achievement of boys and girls in 'literacy'), and no doubt others play their part. Those who have been socialised into the contemporary media world may be disposed to see the screen as their point of reference for strategies of reading; those who were socialised into the former media world may see the page as their point of reference. For members of the two (or more) groups, what appears to be the same text calls forth different strategies of reading, and gives rise to different readings of what are in reality different texts.

This is a power that, at the moment, lies more with the reader than with the text or its maker. It is a new power in the sense that in the former era there was no such choice: a written text was to be read as a written text, and a page as a page. Reading paths in many new pages are relatively open; I am thinking here of the pages of contemporary magazines with many images, and 'blocks' of text, often quite small blocks of text arranged around the page, not in a linear order (left to right, top to bottom) but in an order either deliberately left (relatively) open for the reader, or open because settled conventions do not yet exist in the same way as they existed for the 'densely printed page' (Kress and Van Leeuwen, 1996) of the former era. The relative openness of the reading path applies to most images also, and for similar reasons (which is not to say that visual representation does not 'have' a grammar; it is to say that the grammar is open to different use). Here as elsewhere we need to bear in mind the contexts of reading, and the distributions of power which obtain. As I suggest below, the school, as an institution founded on the mode of writing and on the medium of the book, has its valuations, deriving from a former era.

The shifts in power are not all in one direction. In the case of the reading path it seems to be the case that conventions have not yet reached as far or in the same detail as they had in the case of the densely printed page. No doubt that will change, and I am aware that work such as that here and in relation to images much more generally – establishing 'grammars' of the image – will make its own contribution to that development. But I mentioned above that 'lexis' works very differently in speech and writing than it does in image. Images demand an epistemological commitment, a precision of representation, which words do not. To repeat my earlier example, if I say, in a science lesson 'every cell has a nucleus', I have made no 'commitment' about where in the cell the nucleus is located. As an answer to an exam question, 'Mention the most important constituents of . . .', this would constitute (part of) a correct answer. If I am asked to draw a cell, I am forced, whether I wish it or not, to make a 'commitment' precisely on this issue: I have to place the nucleus somewhere. It is a consequence of what I have called the logics of the visual mode of representation. The effect for the reader, however, is that something which is open in language (the meaning of 'has') is not open in image. A possibility of supplying meaning which in the case of speech or writing rested with the hearer or reader is taken from her or him. To cite again the well-known experience of the disappointment in seeing the film of the novel: the written text calls forth the work of 'filling' relatively vague lexis with the meanings of the reader or hearer. The 'lexis' of the visual is in that respect precise, not open, and does not call forth that work. There is a paradox here in that the traditional view had been that image needed the precision of the word, to give it, in the terms of Roland Barthes, 'anchorage'. This has consequences for the work of the imagination:

the world of the word demands and permits work of the imagination which is not facilitated by, and is perhaps even closed off in relation to, the world of image. At the same time the image permits kinds of imagination not facilitated by the word. In relation to reading paths, for instance, the image (or the new page) offers possibilities to the viewer for the establishing of relations between elements in the representation, which in the syntax of speech or writing are fully pre-given.

It will be essential to look with great care at the 'semiotic affordances' of image, of writing and of speech, and of multimodal texts, to see how the relative powers of makers and receivers of texts are reconfigured in this new dispensation. The power of the reader to remake the text in its reading – something recognised since the work of Roland Barthes in the late 1960s (Barthes, 1977) and now part of a common sense around reading – depended precisely on the affordances of writing. The syntax of writing is stable, and there is a considerable fixedness of the reading path in written texts. The lexical elements in writing are pre-given, so that it is possible to write dictionaries of the language (even if lexis is also constantly expanding). However, this stability in syntax, and of (aspects of) textual organisation, is complemented by a relative semantic openness of the lexical elements themselves, which need the reader to fill them with meaning.

The viewer is, as I have suggested, positioned very differently. The image is semantically precise and closed: or at least many types of image are – it will be important to study this carefully. But the syntax of images, and the reading paths to be followed by the viewer, are much more open to the ordering, designing work of the viewer. I do not wish to make an assessment here, other than to say that there will be shifts in kinds of work, forms of imagination, possibilities for the transformative work of reading as sign-making, and therefore shifts in the relative powers of readers/viewers and makers of texts. In a multimodal text the picture is correspondingly complex.

The work of reading, and the demands made of readers, will, in this new landscape, be different and greater. The anxieties of cultural pessimists about the 'decline in cultures of reading' (sometimes expressed more recently in that questionable phrase 'dumbing down') are premature. The opposite will very much be the case.

The future of reading in the multimodal landscape of the 'West'

The screen is now the dominant site of texts; it is the site which shapes the imagination of the current generation around communication. The screen is the site of the visual, of the image. This does not mean that writing cannot appear on the screen, but when it does, it will be appearing there subordinated to the logic of the visual. This will have many consequences: reading will increasingly proceed in terms of the application of the logic of the image to writing. But a further development, which is already apparent and which will intensify, is that the always present visuality of writing will become intensified. At the moment this appears in a number of seemingly disparate ways, for instance the attempt to make the meaning units of writing correspond more closely to an iconic/mimetic visual shape, through indenting, bullet points, boxings of various kinds, use of frames. Or, in a different way, the use of fonts, of size points in the same direction. Increasingly, written elements are used as visual elements in compositions of a visual kind in the first instance. The affordances of fonts as images are being used more and more. The latent visuality of the graphic medium of writing will become more foregrounded. The relation of writing to sound will become correspondingly weaker, although the potential of voice to machine interaction constitutes a force moving in the direction of sound.

The use of image as a fully representational mode is having its effects on the very syntax of language. As part of the 'communicational load' of a message goes to the image, the need for syntactic/conceptual complexity of the written part of the message/text diminishes. Reading of written text is becoming simpler, for instance in the decreasing clausal complexity of sentences, and it is becoming specialised. At the same time, reading of the multimodal message/text is becoming more complex. In the new landscapes of communication, with the dominance of the new media, and with the 'old' media (the book for instance) being reshaped by the forms of the new media, the demands on readers, and the demands of reading, will if anything be greater, and they will certainly be different. That constitutes the new agenda for thinking about reading.

10

SOME ITEMS FOR AN AGENDA
OF FURTHER THINKING

Requisite theories of meaning

The changes in representation and communication which are affecting alphabetic writing have not run their course by any manner of means. The technological changes, as much as the new economic and social conditions which are affecting forms of representation, are still ongoing, at a pace and in directions which will lead to further profound changes. In this respect the convergence of media is a major factor. Multimedia messaging is already available. An article in a daily newspaper – cut out for me by a colleague – mentions a Californian company which is developing 'multimodality' in the form of programs that convert gesture to writing, for instance. As a lesser instance, the possibility of direct voice-to-machine interaction has existed for some time now, even though with limitations. These are major forms of transduction which already exist – in the latter case from a mode based on sound to a mode based on graphic substance. All we can do at the moment is to look at what there already is, and extrapolate a little; what appears looks very different from that which has been.

The major task is to imagine the characteristics of a theory which can account for the processes of making meaning in the environments of multimodal representation in multimediated communication, of cultural plurality and of social and economic instability. Such a theory will represent a decisive move away from the assumptions of mainstream theories of the last century about meaning, language and learning. The major shifts concern a whole range of hitherto taken-for-granted understandings, for instance about stable systems of representation, about the stability (guaranteed by the force of convention) of rule-systems, about the arbitrariness of the constitution of signs. In all these, a major feature was the assumed centrality of language and, deriving from that, the assumed foundation of 'rationality' in language. In these theories, language 'users' were marginal to the 'system' of language in the sense that their actions had no significant effect on the system; users used the resources of the system, they did not change it.

A fully requisite theory will rest on the understanding that the resources of representation are always in a process of change. While there is – necessarily – convention, the stability of the resources for representation is always contingent. The assumption that there are rule-systems will be replaced by an understanding that systematicness is socially produced, and is a sometimes more and a sometimes less useful fiction. The signs of all representational resources are recognised as 'motivated' conjunctions of form and meaning, produced out of the interest of the sign-maker, whose 'use' of representational resources is agentive and transformative. Sign-makers act out of their interest but with an awareness, more or less explicitly held, of the history of the resources, expressed as the force of convention.

The assumption of the centrality of language will be replaced with an understanding that modes of representation are used in relation to a multiplicity of factors, such as the sign-maker's sense of what are the apt modes for representing, given a certain audience and therefore specific relations between sign-maker and audience. Out of this awareness of the always rhetorical task of communication arises the arrangement of modes which are in play in a message/text. This is reflected in the foregrounding or backgrounding of modes, determines their communicational load in a specific instance of communication, and indicates their centrality or otherwise in instances of communication. Of course the message-maker's action does not guarantee the reception of the sign-complexes in the way they might have been intended. Here too, the theory which sees reading as transformative overcomes a long-standing problem in debates on communication. 'Rationality' is lodged equally in the use of all modes. At the same time there is a serious challenge both to the assumption of a single kind of rationality with a single set of features, and to the separation of rationality and affect. There will be much more open notions, which bring materiality, bodyliness, sensuality and affect into the centre of attention together with rationality and cognition – or challenge the distinctions between such categories.

The notion of competence in use will give way to that of interested design. Competence in use starts with that which exists, shaped in the social history of the group in which the user acts. Hence competence in use is oriented to the past. It is also oriented to allegiance to the conventions of the group. Design, by contrast, starts from the interest and the intent of the designer to act in a specific way in a specific environment, to act with a set of available resources and to act with an understanding of what the task at hand is, in relation to a specific audience. Design is prospective, future-oriented: in this environment, with these (multiple) resources, and out of my interests *now* to act newly I will shape a message. In design, resources are transformed in any number of ways – whether in new combinations of modes or in the constant transformative action by sign-makers in producing newly made signs.

Creativity is an automatic consequence of such action – both in the new combinations of resources and in the inevitable transformations of existing resources in the design and production of the message. Creativity becomes normal and unremarkable in every instance of sign-making. Innovativeness, in the sense of producing 'the new', is, equally, an automatic consequence of sign-making: all signs are new, all combinations of resources in the making of a specific message are likely to be new.

Imagination

This leaves a question about 'imagination', the process of 'supplementing' a message with meaning, of 'adding meaning' to a message. Throughout the book I have insisted both that signs are always newly made, and that meaning is realised differently in different modes. In the new making of signs the sign-maker 'supplies meaning' so to speak, whether in the outward production of the sign – in articulation – or in the inward production of the sign – in interpreta-tion. When I start 'dreaming', 'taking off', so to speak, from one interpretation, one inwardly made sign, to the next and to the next and to the next in my 'imagination', then this process is no different to the usual processes of semiosis which take place all the time.

The question is therefore not 'is there imagination?' because there always is; rather the question is 'does imagination have different form or shape or charac-teristics with different modes?' In Chapter 9 I began to answer that question around the emerging differences in reading that are characteristic of the new period. I suggested that in speech or writing the work of 'imagination' – at the simplest level – consists in filling the relatively 'empty' elements along the strictly prescribed reading paths with the reader's meaning. Of course, these ele-ments are then configured, at other levels, into more complex elements, whether larger narrative structures or other generic/textual entities, themselves interacting with each other in complex designs both of the writer's and reader's making. I suggested that in image(-like) messages, by contrast, the reading paths tended to be much more open, or not readily apparent, or not even discernible or present, while the entities themselves were plain full of meaning. Here the supplementing of meaning consists much more in the imposition of an order onto a set of elements, and the ordering of a world seemingly or actually left unordered. 'Imagination' now becomes a different activity, one which focuses on the possibilities of the ordering of full elements rather than on the supplying of meaning to ordered elements.

In multimodal ensembles, of writing and image, or of writing, speech, image, music and so on, the possibilities of supplementing messages with meaning mul-tiply, and incorporate the demands and the potentials of imagination of all the modes involved. To this we must add the never absent process of synaesthesia, the transduction inwardly, in interpretation, between modes – from spoken to visual, from sound to colour, from image to smell, and so on.

The new theory of meaning and semiosis – and deriving from these, of learn-ing – which I believe is called for will need to concern itself with such issues. In the move from the cultural and social dominance of the modes of speech and writing to others, this is a crucial question. Are there forms of imagination which will be less prominent, less usual, less habituated? And if so, what should our response be to this possibility? This is, however, quite a different approach to one that bemoans the withering away of imagination as an already decided, a foregone, event.

If we take seriously the goal of facility in design as the new essential pedagogic aim in communication, then the work and the place of imagination will in any case be entirely different to what it has been so far. It will extend to semiotic work involving the entirely ordinary, the everyday, and the banal. Competent performance in relation to one mode as hitherto envisaged, with imagination reserved for interpretation involving specially valued texts or, more rare still, the making of such texts, will be replaced by the much more demanding tasks precisely of selection, arrangement and transformation, involving many modes, in always new environments, with their always changing demands.

Modes, bodies and dispositions

In all this, the questions around gains and losses are entirely in the foreground. Forms of imagination are inseparable from the material characteristics of modes, from their shaping in a society's history, and from their consequent interaction with the sensoriness, the sensuousness, of our bodies. Introducing a concern with materiality and the senses into representation brings the long-standing separation in Western thinking of mind and body into severe question, and therefore challenges the reification and consequent separation of cognition, affect and emotion. It becomes untenable to assume that cognition is separable from affect; all representation is always affective, while it is also always cognitive. In fact, the existence of these two terms is shown to be a problem. Even now, in writing this, I am tempted and really forced to say – because the lexical and syntactic resources of written English are organised in this way – that *representation is always both cognitive and affective*, and I am forced into using both terms, as distinct, discrete, as seemingly real. There is a need not just for rethinking, but for re-lexicalising, the language.

Once this has been achieved – it has not, so far – we can begin to look in a fuller sense at the interrelations of modes and human social dispositions. What is the effect on dispositions of the dominant use of the visual rather than of the oral, of the visual-written rather than the oral-spoken? Not just in terms of effects on memory, but in terms of deeper bodily dispositions? What would human dispositions be like if we were to rely much more on actional modes? Or on the visual? These questions have complex and multiple answers. As I suggested in earlier chapters, the language modes dispose us towards seeing the world in terms of temporality and sequence, and in doing so they tend to make us see the world in causal relations. This is more so in languages such as English because it is combined with lexicalisations of actions on the one hand and, on the other, with the (more or less) residual case-systems of Indo-European languages, which tend to imply – even if weakly – that the subject-noun of a clause has agentive force. This produces a potent disposition – never overtly expressed and yet insistently conveyed with nearly every message. All this is then further entrenched by narrative as the dominant genre of European (as of other) cultures.

If this produces dispositions through words and grammar, there are equally strong dispositions produced through the very materiality of the voice. The tonal and rhythmic features of the voice constitute a message-system of vast complexity, attuning us in myriad ways to all kinds of aspects of our social, cultural and affective interpersonal worlds. Culture shapes here as much as it does in other ways – shaping dispositions towards pace, energy, modulation, variability or stability.

There are yet further aspects: traditional forms of reading require the reader to follow the set reading path and to fill the entities which are encountered with the reader's meaning. It is an activity which is inwardly directed, 'inner-directed'. The form of imaginative activity which it fosters is withdrawing, directed to inner activity, contemplative. It is not action on the world, but action by the individual on the individual in line with materials taken from the world. The new forms of reading by contrast require action on the world: to impose the order of a reading path on that which is to be read, arising out of my interests. Ordering a message entity in the world in this manner is a different form of action – not contemplative but actional, not inner-directed but directed outwardly. In the traditional forms of reading, knowledge was set out by the writer in a sequentially ordered fashion, and interpreted in that order by the individual for her/himself in the act of reading. In the new forms of reading, knowledge is not necessarily set out in such an ordered, sequential manner, but is frequently shaped by the reader in the act of determining/constructing/imposing such order by the new reader. This is a very different manner of engaging with the world. It has many affinities with other aspects of the contemporary world, with its demands for obtaining information and linking pieces of information horizontally, with its turning away from 'bodies of knowledge' and towards currently relevant information, and so on.

At this point the question arises yet again: is this problematic, and how is it problematic? Can we envisage a world which is so reduced intellectually, spiritually, emotionally, culturally, socially, politically, that all we can be focused on is the instrumental, the pragmatic, the gathering of information, unreflectingly? Will there be no need for reflective action, for introspection, for reassessment and critique? Will understanding in its profounder sense not be needed?

This is a question about imagined worlds, and about imagined human dispositions. In any case it is already clear that the human social subjectivities formed in such environments will differ from those formed in the stable world of the former communicational givens.

Authorship, authority and knowledge

When everyone can have the status of author, authority wanes or disappears. In Foucault's theorising authorship is rare, a sufficient criterion for marking off not only an '*oeuvre*', but also a set of discourses. The affordances of the new technologies of representation and communication enable those who have access to them to be 'authors', even if authors of a new kind – that is, to produce texts, to alter texts, to write and to 'write back'. Where before the author was a publicly legitimated and endorsed figure, now there is no such gate-keeping. In the former era knowledge was assessed case by case, and that which passed muster was admitted to the status of canonical knowledge. Whether in the form of school curricula, or of the books on the shelves of libraries, or the 'knowledge' disseminated by the organs of the media, or knowledge emanating from anyone of a multitude of public institutions, it was clear what was and what was not knowledge.

Of course, this was based on a relation of knowledge to power, not on one of knowledge to truth. But in that era, power determined truth, so no difficulty arose. There was also a regulated relation between knowledge and canonical modes of representation; in most cases, the canonical mode was that of writing, and within that mode there were canonical genres in which the texts were articulated. Indeed, it is probably better to say that the question of canonicity did not in fact arise: the relation was naturalised to such an extent that the relation of knowledge to realisational mode, and that of knowledge, mode and genre, were, by and large, invisible. Of course, this has to be qualified by making mention of the 'linguistic turn' in the humanities and the social sciences, which did question, precisely, the obviousness and naturalness of the relation of representational mode to knowledge and truth.

In the era of multimodality, however, the relation of mode and knowledge has become newly problematic. Mode, it is clear, has a profound effect on the shaping of knowledge. However, this time the problem cannot be settled by recourse to power, because there is no longer an unquestioned acceptance of such power, not even in schools. Given this absence of power and of authority, the answer is to insist on the teaching of *principles* of assessment, analysis and comparison. As it has become impossible either to teach or to assess what is true or authoritative, it has become essential to provide principled means for assessing claims around truth and authority. In this, the processes and environments of representation are crucial.

The awareness of design in production/articulation as much as in interpretation, and an awareness of the always present rhetorical aspects of design, will be essential in this.

'Standards' and their decline

At times I watch our son and his friends – and it *is* boys usually – playing around and with their Playstation. The skills which they demonstrate – skills of visual analysis, of manual dexterity, of strategic and tactical decision-making at meta-levels – leave me entirely perplexed. It is not clear to me that these children are victims of a general decline in mental abilities. All the games make use of the visual, but they always make use of much more: there is a musical score, there is rudimentary dialogue, and there is writing – usually as in comic strips, in a box above the rest of the visually saturated screen. The speed at which the written text comes and goes can be adjusted. The pace at which it is set by the players is always too fast for me to read: I can never follow the text fully. Occasionally I have attempted to test whether the players have read and followed the written text, and have found each time that while they have, I have lagged behind. But in lagging behind in reading, I have not, at the same time, been paying attention to the other features of the screen and of the game, all moving at great speed, nor have I been physically manipulating the controls.

It is in this context that I wonder what is meant by a 'decline in standards' as far as reading ability is concerned. While I am not a fast reader, I do not count myself as someone who has problems with reading either. Yet my reading speed is not sufficient to take in the information from the written mode alone, never mind the far greater amount of information that comes from the visual mode, or of demands other than visual analysis, such as strategic decision-making, and the use of the controls most of all. There are astonishing ranges of skill and ability at issue here, which those who make assertions about standards seem not to have taken cognisance of in any way. Clearly, the skills of reading which are at issue here are not the skills of reading which the school still focuses on. However, they strike me as much more aligned with what the young may need later in their lives.

Again the question arises for me about what is demanded and produced here. Certainly, the skills of near instant response are essential; though I am not clear whether there is ever time for reflection, for assessment, for the quiet moment of consideration and review. It is not programmed into the game. What dispositions are imagined here, and prepared for the future, and where can an educational agenda that would wish to encourage other aspects of human being-in-the-world be developed?

These are the skills of the multimodal world of communication. They entail differentiated attention to information that comes via different modes, an assessment constantly of what is foregrounded now, assessment about where the communicational load is falling, and where to attend to now. It is not the form of reading which I was taught – sustained, concentrated attention over an extended period, reading where the only attention went to the text which was being read. By contrast, this is reading for specific purposes, for the information that I need now at this moment. As I mentioned earlier, we may wish the young to learn my form of reading also; I am certain that it has benefits and rewards, and that it is and will remain essential at times. But such a form of reading now needs to be taught as a specialised task, not as *the* form of reading that defines what reading is. In my view, the objection of young (and especially male) readers to the school's agenda stems from there.

So there is a large and very difficult agenda, to begin to unpick what reading has been, what it has been for, what it can and must be, and what of the past practices of reading ought to be brought forward into the future. This is not, in my view, a project governed by nostalgias, but a project which is entirely hard-headed and clear-sighted. It asks about the human dispositions which we may wish and need to foster in order to remain able to act fully in response to all the demands that humans will continue to meet. As curricular agenda it demands that we engage with the young on the grounds of their experience, and at the same time show them with greater confidence than is usually the case now why in such an agenda reflection is essential for them. What is its utility for them, in their lives even now?

I have spoken of different demands, different forms of imagination. It seems clear to me that the demands made of the new generation are greater in all respects, but above all they will be and already are different. And what appear as playful diversions rapidly become central demands. The young are teaching themselves because the old cannot or will not. Take 'texting' as an example. The keyboard of the mobile phone is configured entirely unlike the keyboard of the old typewriter which persists to this moment as the keyboard on my laptop computer. This keyboard is based on the use of the alphabet in a specific language, English – in German it is configured slightly differently to take account of its frequency of letter use and the salience of certain letters. But in each language so far the alphabet as a transcriptional system dominates. In text-messaging the alphabet is reconfigured in line with different demands: not as a transcriptional system, but as a system of *information*: pressing five times on the key marked 6, in the mode 'write messages', produces the letter ö. Letters co-occur in groups of three or four, so that in one sense the alphabet has been reduced to eight 'letters' – eight information entities, among which of course differentiations can be and are made. These arrangements can be adjusted, and they are in a moment of transition, both in individual use and in the facilities provided. Those with older forms of socialisation would want to keep the alphabetic arrangement. The younger generations are adapting the affordances to a new and complex kind of iconic writing.

It is not hard to see how puns or abbreviations – playfulness again – will transform the potentials of sign-making: no longer ruled by the alphabet's relation to the sound-system of the language, but by a new relation in which the currently developing affordances of this new mode make possible new signs and sign-combinations – new possibilities of meaning. This will become even more the case as images make their way into this developing mode.

It may be worth making a small diversion at this point, on the issue of spelling in English. We all know that English is the possession of many people around the world, and not just of the English or their near cousins. In as far as spelling attempts to stay close to the sound-system of the language which is being 'spelled', the problems of spelling in a globalising communicational world will become impossible to manage. Text-messaging is moving, in some discernible ways, in the direction of solving this problem at one level, both in its likely increasing use of visual entities, and in its tendencies towards consonantal spelling – a preference in abbreviations of consonants over vowels. Here the problems of the relation of sound-shapes and letter-shapes are less immediate and acute.

And maybe it is best to leave the discussion precisely at this point: at a point where we can get a glimpse of one tiny yet telling aspect of the likely futures of literacy, and also at the point where I began the discussion, more or less - with the profound changes in the social, economic and technological world which in the end will shape the futures of literacy. However, we are the makers of meaning, and we can move into that period with a theory that puts us and our sign-making at the centre – not free to do as we would wish, but not as the victims of forces beyond our control either. That is the point and the task of theory. That will need to be the guide of our practices.

BIBLIOGRAPHY

Barthes, R. (1977) 'The death of the author' in R. Barthes (1977) *Image – Music – Text*, London: Fontana

Barthes, R. (1997) *Mythologies*, Harmondsworth: Penguin

Barton, D. and Hamilton, M. (1998) *Local Literacies*, London: Routledge

Barton, D., Hamilton, M. and Ivanic, R. (eds) (1999) *Situated Literacies: Reading and Writing in Context*, London: Routledge

Bazerman, C. (1981) 'What written knowledge does: three examples of academic discourse', *Philosophy of the Social Sciences*, vol. 11, 361–87

Bell, A. and Garrett, P. (eds) (1998) *Approaches to Media Discourse*, Oxford: Blackwell

Bernstein, B. (1996) *Pedagogy, Symbolic Control and Identity: Theory, Research, Critique*, London: Taylor and Francis

Bhatia, V. K. (1993) *Analysing Genre: Language in Professional Settings*, London: Longman

Boeck, M. (2000) *Das Lesen in der neuen Medienlandschaft (Reading in the New Media Landscape)*, Innsbruck: Oesterreichischer Studienverlag

Boeck, M. and Kress, G. R. (2002) 'Unequal expectations: child readers and adult tastes' in A. Sanchez (ed.) (2002) *Windows on the World: Media Discourse in English*, Valencia: Federico Domenech

Bryant, P. and Bradley, L. (1985) *Children's Reading Problems*, Oxford: Blackwell

Bull, G. and Anstey, M. (1996) *The Literacy Lexicon*, Sydney: Prentice Hall

Christie, F. and Misson, R. (eds) (1998) *Literacy and Schooling*, London: Routledge

Clark, R. and Ivanic, R. (1998) *The Politics of Writing*, London: Routledge

Cope, B. and Kalantzis, M. (eds) (1993) *The Power of Literacy: A Genre Approach to Writing*, London: Falmer Press

Cope, B. and Kalantzis, M. (1997) *Productive Diversity*, Sydney: Pluto Press

Cope, B. and Kalantzis, M. (eds) (2000) *Multiliteracies*, London: Routledge

Eco, U. (1996) 'Afterword' in G. Nunberg (ed.) (1996) *The Future of the Book*, Turnhout, Belgium: Brepols

Faigley, L. (1998) 'Literacy after the Revolution: 1996 CCCC chair's address' in T. Taylor and I. Ward (eds) (1998) *Literacy Theory in the Age of the Internet*, New York: Columbia University Press

Fairclough, N. (1992) *Critical Language Awareness*, London: Longman

Foucault, M. (1959) 'Orders of Discourse' in R. Young (ed.) (1981) *Untying the Text*, London: Routledge and Kegan Paul

Gee, J. P. (1990) *Social Linguistics and Literacies: Ideology in Discourses*, Lewes: Falmer Press

Gee, J. P. (1999) 'The new literacy studies: from "socially situated" to "the work of the social"' in D. Barton, M. Hamilton and R. Ivanic (eds) (1999) *Situated Literacies: Reading and Writing in Context*, London: Routledge

Gee, J. P., Hull, G. and Lankshear, C. (1996) *The New Work Order: Behind the Language of the New Capitalism*, Boulder, CO: Westview

Goodman, S. and Graddol, D. (eds) (1996) *Redesigning English: New Texts, New Identities*, London: Routledge

Goswami, U. and Bryant, P. (1990) *Phonological Skills and Learning to Read*, Hillsdale NJ: Erlbaum

Halliday, M. A. K. (1979) *Language as a Social Semiotic*, London: Edward Arnold

Halliday, M. A. K. (1989) *Spoken and Written English*, Oxford: Oxford University Press

Hamilton, M., Barton, D. and Ivanic, R. (eds) (1994) *Worlds of Literacy*, Clevedon: Multilingual Matters

Harris, R. (1991) *The Origins of Writing*, London: Duckworth

Hasan, R. and Williams, G. (eds) (1995) *Literacy in Society*, London: Longman

Heath, S. B. (1983) *Ways with Words: Language, Life and Work in Communities and Classrooms*, Cambridge: Cambridge University Press

Hodge, R. I. V. and Kress, G. R. (1988) *Social Semiotics*, Cambridge: Polity Press

Hyland, K. (2000) *Disciplinary Discourses: Social Interactions in Academic Writing*, London: Longman

Ivanic, R. (1997) *Writing and Identity*, Amsterdam: John Benjamins

Jewitt, C. (2002) 'The move from page to screen: the multimodal reshaping of school English' in *Journal of Visual Communication*, vol. 1, no. 2, pp. 171–96.

Jewitt, C. (in press) 'Multimodality and new communication technologies' in P. LeVine and R. Scollon, *Discourse and Technology: Multimodal Discourse Analysis*, The Georgetown University Round Table on Languages and Linguistics 2002, Washington, DC: Georgetown University Press

Kress, G. R. (1989) *Linguistic Processes in Sociocultural Practice*, Oxford: Oxford University Press

Kress, G. R. (1993a) 'Genre as social process' in B. Cope and M. Kalantzis (eds) (1993) *The Power of Literacy: A Genre Approach to Writing*, London: Falmer Press

Kress, G. R. (1993b) *Learning to Write*, London: Routledge

Kress, G. R. (1994) 'Against arbitrariness: the social production of the sign as a foundational issue in critical discourse analysis', *Discourse and Society*, vol. 4, no. 2, pp. 169–91

Kress, G. R. (1995) *Writing the Future: English and the Making of a Culture of Innovation*, Sheffield: National Association of Teachers of English

Kress, G. R. (1997a) *Before Writing: Rethinking the Paths to Literacy*, London: Routledge

Kress, G. R. (1997b) 'Visual and verbal modes of representation in electronically mediated communication: the potentials of new forms of text' in I. Snyder (ed.) (1997) *Page to Screen*, London: Routledge

Kress, G. R. (1999a) 'Genre and the changing contexts for English language arts', *Language Arts*, vol. 32, no. 2, pp. 185–96

Kress, G. R. (1999b) 'Issues for a working agenda in literacy' in T. O'Brien (ed.) *Language and Literacies*, Clevedon: Multilingual Matters

Kress, G. R. (2000a) 'Design and transformation' in B. Cope and M. Kalantzis (eds) (2000) *Multiliteracies*, London: Routledge

Kress, G. R. (2000b) *Early Spelling: Between Convention and Creativity*, London: Routledge

Kress, G. R., Jewitt, C., Ogborn, J. and Tsatsarelis, C. (2001) *Multimodal Teaching and Learning: The Rhetorics of the Science Classroom*, London and New York: Continuum

Kress, G. R. and Van Leeuwen, T. (1996) *Reading Images: The Grammar of Graphic Design*, London: Routledge

Kress, G. R. and Van Leeuwen, T. (1998) '(The critical) analysis of newspaper layout' in Allan Bell and Peter Garrett (eds) *Approaches to Media Discourse*, Oxford: Blackwell

Kress, G. R. and Van Leeuwen, T. (2001) *Multimodal Discourse: The Modes and Media of Contemporary Communication*, London: Edward Arnold

Lankshear, C., Gee, J. P., Knobel, M. and Searle, C. (1997) *Changing Literacies*, Buckingham: Open University Press

Lemke, J. (1998) 'Multiplying meaning: visual and verbal semiotics in scientific text' in J. Martin and R. Veel (eds) (1998) *Reading Science*, London: Routledge

Leu, D. J. Jr (2000) 'Our childrens's future: changing the focus of literacy and literacy instruction', *Reading Online*, www.readingonline.org/electronic/RT/focus/index.html

Luke, A. (1995) 'Genres of power' in R. Hasan and G. Williams (eds) (1995) *Literacy in Society*, London: Longman

Luke, A., Comber, B. and O'Brien, J. (1996) 'Critical literacies and cultural studies' in G. Bull and M. Anstey (eds) *The Literacy Lexicon*, Sydney: Prentice Hall

Macken-Horarik, M. (1998) 'Exploring the requirements of critical school literacy' in F. Christie and R. Misson (eds) (1998) *Literacy and Schooling*, London: Routledge

Martin, J. (1993) 'A contextual theory of language' in B. Cope and M. Kalantzis (eds) (1993) *The Power of Literacy: A Genre Approach to Writing*, London: Falmer Press

Martin, J. and Veel, R. (eds) (1998) *Reading Science*, London: Routledge

New London Group (1996) 'A pedagogy of multiliteracies: designing social futures', *Harvard Educational Review*, vol. 66, pp. 60–92

Nunberg, G. (ed.) (1996) *The Future of the Book*, Turnhout, Belgium: Brepols

O'Brien, T. (ed.) (1999) *Language and Literacies*, Clevedon: Multilingual Matters

Olson, D. (1994) *The World on Paper*, Cambridge: Cambridge University Press

Ong, W. (1982) *Orality and Literacy*, London: Fontana

Radway, J. (1987) *Reading the Romance*, London: Verso.

Sanchez, A. (ed.) (2002) *Windows on the World: Media Discourse in English*, Valencia: Federico Domenech

Snyder, I. (ed.) (1997) *Page to Screen*, London: Routledge

Street, B. (1984) *Literacy in Theory and Practice*, Cambridge: Cambridge University Press

Street, B. (1995) *Social Literacies*, London: Longman

Street, B. (1998) 'New literacies in theory and practice: what are the implications for language in education', *Linguistics and Education*, vol. 10, no. 1, pp. 1–24

Swales, J. M. (1990) *Genre Analysis: English in Academic and Research Settings*, Cambridge: Cambridge University Press

Taylor, T. and Ward, I. (eds) (1998) *Literacy Theory in the Age of the Internet*, New York: Columbia University Press

Unsworth, L. (2001) *Teaching Multiliteracies across the Curriculum: Changing Contexts of Text and Image in Classroom Practice*, Buckingham: Open University Press

Van Leeuwen, T. (1996) 'Moving English: the visual language of film' in S. Goodman and D. Graddol (eds) *Redesigning English: New Texts, New Identities*, London: Routledge

Van Leeuwen, T. (1999) *Speech, Music, Sound*, London: Macmillan

Van Leeuwen, T. and Jewitt, C. (eds) (2001) *Handbook of Visual Analysis*, London: Sage

Young, R. (ed.) (1981) *Untying the Text*, London: Routledge and Kegan Paul

INDEX